SPIRIT OF THE CENTURY

SPIRIT OF THE CENTURY

OUR OWN STORY

THE
BLIND BOYS OF ALABAMA
WITH PRESTON LAUTERBACH

hachette
BOOKS

NEW YORK

Hachette Books
Hachette Book Group
1290 Avenue of the Americas
New York, NY 10104
HachetteBooks.com
Twitter.com/HachetteBooks
Instagram.com/HachetteBooks

First Edition: March 2024

Published by Hachette Books, a subsidiary of Hachette Book Group, Inc. The Hachette Books name and logo is a trademark of the Hachette Book Group.

The Hachette Speakers Bureau provides a wide range of authors for speaking events. To find out more, go to hachettespeakersbureau.com or email HachetteSpeakers@hbgusa.com.

Books by Hachette Books may be purchased in bulk for business, educational, or promotional use. For information, please contact your local bookseller or Hachette Book Group Special Markets Department at: special.markets@hbgusa.com.

The publisher is not responsible for websites (or their content) that are not owned by the publisher.

Print book interior design by Bart Dawson

Library of Congress Control Number: 2023948296

ISBNs: 9780306828218 (hardcover); 9780306828232 (ebook)

Printed in the United States of America

LSC-C

Printing 1, 2024

To all the singers with the Blind Boys of Alabama
who preceded us, including Clarence Fountain, George Scott,
Johnny Fields, Olice Thomas, Billy Bowers, Paul Beasley,
Ben Moore—and for Velma Traylor

CONTENTS

A PREACHER IN SONG

THE ROOTS OF GOSPEL quartet music run deepest in Birmingham. The Alabama city is to quartets what Florence is to Renaissance art: if not a precise beginning point, certainly the place where the genre flourished.

Driving out of downtown, past the 16th Street Baptist Church where four little girls died in a 1963 bombing, beneath the towering statue of Vulcan, Roman god of forge and fire, the street leads over railroad tracks as the car slows into the neighborhood of Elyton, once the Jefferson County seat, past a junkyard heaping with scrap metal nearly as high as Vulcan's eye, past a swampy cemetery where city fathers molder in stagnant water, at last stopping outside a white duplex tucked back off the pavement. Here lives a master of a true American art form: Jimmy Lee Carter, leader of the Blind Boys of Alabama.

Jimmy was at the helm, initially as Clarence Fountain's copilot, as the Blind Boys became American pop culture icons. Between 2002 and 2005 alone, with the core members all in their seventies, they won four Grammy awards, toured the six inhabited continents, and collaborated with a who's who of pop music, singing a Tom Waits song as the theme for the TV show *The Wire*, recording an Edgar Allan Poe tribute with Lou Reed, and appearing in a film with Beyoncé. They appeared on every morning and late-night network TV show with every host from Katie Couric to Jay Leno. In February 2005, the Blind Boys performed at the Grammy Awards show, their highest-profile gig. No other gospel quartet has come close to their visibility or approached their number of miles traveled.

Carter walks unassisted down the hallway of his home into the living room. He shakes hands with his guest and sits in a coffee-brown leather recliner. He wears a tame Hawaiian shirt and sharp-creased dark-gray slacks. He has a gold wristwatch on his left arm. Without his sunglasses, you can see the left eye looking straight ahead, but the right eye is nearly closed, a sliver of white peering through the lid. Carter asks his partner to pass his Ray-Bans, and he puts them on. There isn't a Grammy in sight, but a cap hanging on the wall bears his nickname: Jimster.

Carter's life parallels the history of quartet gospel. Born in Birmingham in 1932, he grew up in an era of jubilee singers and gospel quartets battling for supremacy in huge programs in front of thousands of fans. Local groups like the Dunham Jazz Jubilee Singers and the Birmingham Jubilee Singers, singing sweet and skillful harmonies, laid a foundation for quartet music in the 1920s and 1930s. Their complex interplay sounds like the vocal version of the intricately designed quilts woven in Gee's Bend, two hours south.

The hard gospel quartet leader—Jimmy's role now—added raw, sanctified fire to the jubilee's rhythmic, melodious backdrop. Though the true innovator of this style is hard to pinpoint, one of the earliest hard leads came up through Birmingham's scene, his name with a ring of legend to it, Silas Steele. Masters of this local phenomenon, like Steele and his onetime partner Charles Bridges, moved to New Orleans, Houston, Dallas, and Chicago, and trained groups in those cities, weaving the Birmingham sound into the very fabric of the gospel quartet style of the 1940s.

The Carters lived in Ishkooda, a community southwest of the city, toward Bessemer, the cradle of the local quartet scene. "When my mama would take me to church, we had an old preacher there," Carter said. "He was all right. He could make me feel something. I didn't know what the Holy Spirit was at that time. I guess I do now."

Carter's father mined iron ore in Red Mountain. He worked underground, with thousands of men, some going miles deep, around the clock for three shifts. Others who were there said that the music grew in those dark mines, keeping the men together, spirits intact, giving them a reason to show up every day. When Jimmy was thirteen years old, his father died down in that mine. The songs that lifted the spirits of men underground also soothed Jimmy's sorrows as they laid his father below the red clay.

The uniqueness of steel work to Birmingham sprang from that soil. No other location in the world contains such large natural deposits of coal, iron ore, and limestone in such close proximity. While the Mississippi Delta soil tied its Black population to farms, Birmingham's Black laborers toiled in mines, mills, and factories. The music that developed among these people emphasized collaboration, each man doing his job for the collective good. Though the Blind Boys were never totally of the Birmingham scene, the city's unique history and culture run through the veins of the group's longtime leader. Now there is a sense of loss and decay around Birmingham steel as the industry shut down and jobs disappeared. Yet the vitality of Jimmy Carter on stage remains.

To see mild, gentle Jimster relaxing at home, one could hardly think he's the same one on stage growling, chanting, and charging into the audience to share his energy with the people. Every entertainer has to figure out how they can will themselves to get back up on stage night after night and smile their way through a song they've done five thousand times with freshness, enthusiasm, and spontaneity. The Blind Boys lead singer has his own way to power up.

"When I step on stage, I'm not Jimmy Carter," he explains. "I'm the Spirit of God."

From where I've sat, the most impressive aspect of the Blind Boys' phenomenal success is how little it fazes them. They are as unpretentious as a bag of McDonald's at the White House—which happened, by the way.

This authenticity is the core of their success. Longtime leader Clarence Fountain, who died in 2018, once said that Lou Reed could not sing his way out of a paper bag. Clarence meant no harm. Lou and the Blind Boys collaborated on a number of projects over the years. Clarence personally liked Lou and complimented Lou's guitar playing. Lou Reed sang with style. His fans are not wrong to admire him. When you appreciate where Clarence came from, however, his paper bag statement seems fair.

Clarence had shared the bill with Mahalia Jackson when Lou was in kindergarten. He'd toured with Sam Cooke while Lou was sneaking his first smoke. The average big gospel quartet program during the genre's heyday featured maybe forty vocalists more gifted than Reed. A half dozen of Fountain's co-leads in the Blind Boys—men unknown to history—sang with more spiritual ferocity, more sublime talent, greater technique, and greater emotional subtlety than any member of the Rock 'n' Roll Hall of Fame or the current Top 40. Clarence Fountain earned the right to be alpha supreme. He wasn't about to play nice for PR purposes. I go so far as to say you wouldn't have wanted him to play nice for PR purposes. The Blind Boys deliver unvarnished truth on record, on stage, and in conversation.

This isn't to say that the Blind Boys don't value their collaborators. They just don't feel starstruck after what they've been through—what you're about to go through while reading their story. On the other side, when we return to the pop culture icon phase after the rest of the journey, you'll understand. The humility and realness that they've developed on their path is exactly why the Blind Boys are beloved; it's exactly why people want to collaborate with them. You can hear it in their voices.

Blindness figures heavily into their unique perspective as it does their music. According to one former member from long ago, since the Blind Boys don't see their audience, they have to feel them. He said that their sound comes from the heart and not from anything external. As Jimmy Carter says to fire up the audience, "I can't see you; I need to hear you." Blindness has been the group's superpower. As all founding members were born into sharecropping families (other than Carter, from Birmingham) across the state of Alabama and raised during the Depression, blindness provided the boys a way out, as their so-called handicap broke the narrative that hundreds of thousands of people born into the same circumstances have lived.

The Blind Boys' success has also led to spiritual tension, a theme of their entire story. They chose the Lord's path as children together in school and vowed to never stray. They resisted offers to sing rock 'n' roll as many of their quartet-world colleagues, from Sam Cooke to Lou Rawls, crossed over to sing secular music, while artists with audible church roots, like Aretha Franklin, hit it big in pop. The Blind Boys became known in more recent years of glory for their rendition of "Amazing Grace," sung to the tune of "House of the Rising Sun." Success has come with a sense of compromise.

"These songs that have made us famous," said Carter. "I sang those songs but just can't feel justified. I've been trying to. There were some of these things I'm still not satisfied with. The Blind Boys of Alabama are a gospel group. Not anything other than that. We do it, we have to change with the times, but that still don't make me like it. My message is to tell the world about Jesus—that we need to be born again. I'm a preacher in song."

But the world of sin holds redemption for the Blind Boys. "We have gone and sang in nightclubs and in bars, and we have touched people in there," Carter said. "I feel all right about that. If they don't come to church, we bring church to them. Like Clarence Fountain said, 'We didn't come here looking for Jesus—we brought Him along with us.'"

───◆───

The Blind Boys are a product of a uniquely American musical institution known as the gospel highway. Though never designed to revolutionize entertainment—or really designed at all, for that matter—the gospel highway was a collective Black enterprise that stretched nationwide at its strongest, much like the fabled Chitlin' Circuit. Made up of hard-traveling spiritual singers, concert-promoting preachers, AM radio deejays, and, of course, hundreds of thousands of fans, the gospel highway ran from massive urban centers of worship like Washington Temple in Brooklyn, to big-time mainstream venues like the Apollo Theater in Harlem all the way down to little back-road country churches and school auditoriums in the Deep South.

For virtually every person who worked it, in one capacity or another, the gospel highway was a labor of love, staffed not only with name groups but also with local and regional weekend warrior musicians who worked straight jobs all week and loaded up their old vans on Friday afternoon to run the roads and get back Monday morning to do it again. Local freelance musicians picked up band gigs with the bigger groups passing through. Church ladies took out ads in local newspapers for the next big program, leaving their phone numbers for ticket reservations. Families housed and fed traveling performers along the way, and the Blind Boys might be under their roof one weekend and the Staple Singers the next, making the circuit one big family. Without any overarching organization and despite the grind, the blowouts, and the paydays that never happened, the system worked: the music flourished. The gospel highway made history, with artists like Mahalia Jackson, Sister Rosetta Tharpe, the Soul Stirrers, the Dixie Hummingbirds, and, of course, the last survivors of those roads, the Blind Boys of Alabama, all making an indelible impact on American music, influencing the very mainstream that rejected gospel.

The gospel highway did not, however, record much of its own history. Typically, a group's last record and next show were heard and advertised on AM radio, but artists received little if any other mass media notice. Promoters advertised some concerts in local newspapers, but virtually no information concerning the artists and their lives came out in real time.

This book reflects Blind Boys history in that it is a chorus of many voices. Without much of a paper trail, I've needed help from a variety of people to tell what went down. For me compiling the story and for you reading it, we have to be grateful to those who made this history and this book happen. You hold a testament to the power of community and to the Blind Boys' ability to connect with a vast range of people across time, place, and race. Interviews with Black nonagenarians in the Deep South and dudes in Southern California made this possible. This book does not solely tell the Blind Boys' story; it also explores the musical worlds they've traveled. Long interviews with firsthand participants—not only the Blind Boys but their former bandmates, rivals in the quartet world, ex-girlfriends, and children—have provided the closest contact with this history.

After the Blind Boys' humility and authenticity, my favorite aspect of this story is the regular occurrence of wild and unpredictable events, things that you wouldn't ever suspect a group of visually impaired, highly religious men to have to deal with. One member of the Blind Boys rivaled Ray Charles as a visually impaired ladies' man. They've worked with lowdown conmen and brilliant businesswomen, sung for handouts in back-road churches and for Broadway audiences. They've gotten dragged into a number of nefarious schemes, through no fault of their own, and always landed on their feet. An LSD-induced musical vision changed their lives and helped bring them to where they are today. A surprise awaits you at virtually every stop along the gospel highway. I was blown away until the last day of writing at the sheer number, high quality, and great diversity of celebrity cameos in the Blind Boys' story: Prince, President Barack Obama, Lee Ann Womack, Don Imus, Morgan Freeman, John Legend. They toured with Robert Plant, performing in Tasmania—according to Plant, practically the last place on earth he hadn't played. They sang the gospel classic "Didn't It Rain" with Tom Jones in Australia. They headlined the Fillmore in San Francisco, the Royal Albert Hall in London, and Lincoln Center in New York. They played the Playboy Jazz Festival at the Hollywood Bowl, with Hugh Hefner and a group of playmates seated up front at a table. After the show, the group's manager told them, "It's a good thing you guys can't see, you could have gotten really distracted," and they all had a laugh.

It's a good thing that we're getting the Blind Boys' history at last. Having researched blues, R&B, and soul, I can tell you that the Lord's music leads to greater longevity than that of the devil— there are far more ninety-year-old veterans of the gospel highway than there are of the Chitlin' Circuit. Still, nothing lasts forever. Too many stories of the Blind Boys have already gone beneath the ground. Now we have only one man who can tell about the first songs they sang together back in the 1930s, who can bring back to life for a moment the other founding members at their beginning.

"When the Blind Boys started out, we wasn't thinking about accolades or money," Carter said. "We just wanted to get out there and sing gospel. I'm not all about accolades—they're good to have— but I love just being ol' Jimster."

In all its humility, authenticity, and triumphant glory, this is the story of a group of blind singers who are planted at the very roots of American music. Yet they did not stay there. However you want to measure their journey—through time, distance, technological developments, or cultural trends—no American band has ever come so far.

PART I.

GENESIS AND REVELATIONS

CHAPTER 1

HAPPY LAND

SEVEN-YEAR-OLD JIMMY LEE CARTER stood outside the Alabama School for the Negro Deaf and Blind in Talladega. He thought the world had come to an end. Blind from birth, he related to the world through sound. At this moment he heard the heart-crushing one of a car driving away on gravel, carrying his mother back home to Birmingham. It was suppertime on a Wednesday in September 1939.

Standing on the curb outside the school, he felt a hand grasp his. A teacher had come to meet him. He followed her inside to the cafeteria. Hearing voices of children growing loud around him, Jimmy sat down to a meal of grits and gravy.

Jimmy had lived with his parents and five older brothers in a house on the grounds of Ishkooda ore-mining camp, where his dad, Major Carter, worked for the Tennessee Coal, Iron, and Railroad Company. The decision to send Jimmy to Talladega had not been easy. His father wanted no part of it, and Jimmy tended to agree. His mother, Cassie, thought it best, though it pained her to let Jimmy go. She never forgot how it felt to leave him in Talladega, the only question being who had cried more, her or Jimmy.

The school, according to a 1931 news article, addressed the "problem of making useful citizens of negro boys and girls handicapped by blindness or deafness." The deaf learned to be farmers, cobblers, and carpenters, "while the blind boys [went] in for commercial broom and mop manufacturing and music." The visually impaired youngsters were called "blind boys" long before the brand became iconic. The census taken in 1940, the year after Jimmy's arrival, lists him and just under seventy other blind boys and girls in residence at the school, with a nearly equal number of deaf children.

His first morning alone, Jimmy brushed his teeth, got himself dressed, and heard a group of boys approach. He felt a punch crash into him. He reached and grabbed ahold of his attacker and, as Jimmy would recall, "beat the dickens out of him." Much to Jimmy's surprise, he had made his first friend. He and Paul Lewis would remain close for years to come.

They managed to get themselves down to breakfast, and the routine of the next several years unfolded. They learned to read braille and do math. They received vocational training in broom and mop making. They took music with Miss Elsie McBride, who taught piano and voice and offered choral training.

Though the Negro deaf students farmed the land surrounding the school, and the local newspaper reported a production of six thousand cans of food on campus, the blind students ate meagerly and suspected that the best of the food went to the White deaf and blind, schooled in another facility. At night, students were locked into the Black school building, which the otherwise friendly local paper would describe as a "potential death-trap for children."

Jimmy learned quickly that a blood feud between the blind and the deaf simmered inside the school walls. As soon as the locks clicked after dark and the teachers left, the Negro blind readied for battle. The deaf attacked, first throwing hot water on the blind. The blind countered by negating the one advantage of the deaf—they turned out the lights. All things being closer to equal, the two sides brawled to exhaustion and crawled back to their bunks.

Fights with the deaf weren't the only cause of physical pain for the blind. In later years, former students would report that school staff had abused them.

Jimmy found solace in music. He felt like he'd been born singing. He joined the male chorus at school and sang hymns with fifty or so other boys. When dignitaries visited the school, the chorus greeted them with songs. A 1943 news story notes the boys' rendition of "Rock of Ages" for a school board inspection.

One member of the boys' choir raised his voice about the rough treatment and bad food given them. The outspoken boy's name was Velma Traylor. Jimmy heard Velma and the school's principal have it out. Velma's nerve impressed Jimmy. Velma was eight years older than Jimmy, and with his age and courage, other students gravitated to him. He could also sing the best of any of them and so became a leader among the young blind boys.

Music wasn't their only method of escape. Somehow Velma had learned how to get out of the school building and leave campus after classes ended, and he had made friends with a general store owner in the McCannville neighborhood less than a mile from school.

Velma had partial but limited eyesight. Another older boy named J. T. Hutton also had partial eyesight. Jimmy could only perceive bright light. Little as he was, he still wanted to get away as badly as the older boys did. So he walked out with them, Hutton or Traylor in the lead, others behind in single file with their hands placed on the shoulder of the boy in front of them. "We held on to each other as we went," Jimmy would recall.

As soon as that 3:30 bell rang, they'd be off. Sometimes there would be as many as six going down the road like train cars. Jimmy felt sure they'd been seen, but no one ever chased them down. They had no time to waste. At 4 p.m. *Echoes of the South* broadcast over Birmingham station WSGN, regularly featuring the most thrilling artists the boys had heard: the Golden Gate Quartet. At the Killough family's store, the boys could spend their pocket change on peanut butter and crackers and glue themselves to the radio for as long as they liked.

Out of Norfolk, Virginia, the Golden Gates were an all-vocal group singing in the jubilee style with intricate harmonies and bright, shining leads. The Gates conjured magic not so much from the material as from their arrangements. Jubilee singing emphasized expertly executed harmonics, bouncy rhythm, and clean, sharp delivery. Their repertoire jumped the sacred-secular boundary, with ancient spirituals like "Wade in the Water" alongside hot pop hits like Nat King Cole's "Straighten Up and Fly Right" and the Andrews Sisters' "Shoo Shoo Baby." As quartet scholar Jerry Zolten has pointed out, by the 1940s, the Gates were singing novelty secular numbers, performing with instrumental backing, and collaborating with Bing Crosby.

Back at school, Velma Traylor and his gang of followers formed a singing group patterned after the Golden Gates. The core membership included J. T. Hutton, Olice Thomas, George Scott, Clarence Fountain, and Johnny Fields. Little Jimmy Carter joined, with Fields's encouragement, though he had to stand on a chair to measure up to the older boys. Jimmy's status as an original member of the Blind Boys of Alabama comes from his participation in these early sessions.

The boys worked out quartet arrangements for as many voices as they had singers. To this day, many quartets have more than four members, but the arrangement style of four-part harmony—lead, second tenor, baritone, and bass—defines a quartet regardless of how many members it contains.

Like the Golden Gates, the youngsters emphasized harmony. Unlike the Gates, they stuck to spirituals like "Didn't It Rain," leaving pop music alone. They worked out their parts as they went, singing until they found who could hit the right note in a given place. They had learned from Miss McBride how to tune up their voices with the piano. She had them sing scales in choir. They had fun on their own, discussing arrangements, teaching each other the parts, and putting the pieces together to build a song. Johnny Fields sang bass even if he wasn't exactly Ol' Man River. Velma had a high range and a powerful voice. He could deliver sweet or rough sounds and sing any part, but in keeping with his seniority and personality, he mostly took the lead. Clarence Fountain sang baritone. To Jimmy's ear, George Scott sang the swooping jubilee-style tenor as well as anyone in the Golden Gates. Olice Thomas and J. T. Hutton rounded out the group's backing vocals.

All were from different corners of Alabama, all but Jimmy hailing from rural areas and tenant-farming families, growing cash crops on rented land. They bonded around a shared sense of spirituality. When they sang, they felt the presence of God within them.

The Spirit strengthened as they brought their voices together. All of the young singers came from strong church backgrounds. Even without sight they could still see the differences between spiritual and worldly. Jimmy would recall, "When the group started out we pledged to the Lord to do gospel and not deviate."

Not only did they harmonize vocally and spiritually, but the boys shared the same perspective on where they were going and how the Alabama School for the Negro Deaf and Blind figured into their future. None of them had the least bit of interest in broom and mop making. They hated the abuse, and they hated the food. The quartet became a family, protecting and nourishing those in it.

As his early years at the school wore on, Jimmy got to know Clarence Fountain well. Clarence came from Tyler, southeast of Selma in Dallas County, where Jimmy's grandparents lived. When Jimmy visited his grandparents in the summer, he'd get together with Clarence too. Like Jimmy, Clarence was the baby of the family, with five older siblings. Clarence's parents, Will and Ida Fountain, had been born in the 1890s. The family lived on rented soil in the Oldtown community. Clarence had been born a twin in 1929, but the other was a stillbirth. A deaf child who lived nearby had told them about the school in Talladega, and Clarence went there in 1936 or 1937.

At school, Jimmy grew fond of Johnny Fields. Born in Lowndes County near Montgomery in 1927, Johnny was the protector and organizer of the group. Jimmy still recalls how Johnny took care of him during fights with the deaf boys and saved him from abuse at the hands of school staff. Johnny gathered the troops for quartet rehearsals and as bass singer became the backbone of the boys' sound. When a teacher at the school picked up on the quartet's activity, he told the boys he'd give $5 to the one who came up with the best name for the group. Johnny Fields almost immediately blurted out, "The Happy Land Jubilee Singers!"

Their true destiny still lay ahead.

The process of coming together in chorus, meeting in spare time to sing quartet for fun, assembling a lineup, developing a sound, and making a first name for themselves took the Happy Land Singers several years. Sometime, somehow, word about the quartet spread outside campus. Jimmy recalls that during the World War II years a local man named Ves Lawson got the school's permission to take the group out on Sundays after church. They'd sing "house-to-house" as Jimmy put it, entertaining on the fly for whoever wanted to listen for whatever money they wanted to give.

Lawson took the boys to perform at a military installation that group members recalled only as a "soldier camp," possibly Anniston Air Force Base ten miles from Talladega. Here they entertained the troops and learned the first hard lesson of showbiz. As Clarence Fountain reflected, "We didn't know nothing from nothing. The guy took us over there and beat us out of our money." Estimates run from $3 to $4 earned and lost through these first hardscrabble performances.

Nevertheless, the soldiers loved the boys, and with their applause grew confidence and ambition. With this taste of the world outside school, the boys grew more dissatisfied with life at the institute. Velma Traylor's arguments with the principal soon boiled over, and the school expelled Traylor. He relocated up the road from Talladega to Gadsden, where he stayed with an aunt and remained in touch with his friends at school. He booked little jobs for them on weekends.

They continued to sing and slip away as much as possible. Listening to Birmingham quartets on the radio in the afternoon, the boys thought they could sing just as well. When the spring 1944 term ended, they left campus for the summer holiday, hoping they'd never come back.

So far the plucky, resilient inmates starving in a cruel, abusive institution seem like Charles Dickens characters. Unlike the heroes of *Great Expectations* and *Oliver Twist*, though, the blind boys had no secret noble heritage to spare them from the grinding jaws of obscurity. Greatness would have to be of their own making.

CHAPTER 2

BIRMINGHAM

"THEY ASKED ME TO come along, but my mama wouldn't let me go," said Jimmy Carter.

Five years after Jimmy's mother left him on the curb outside the school in Talladega, he had found friends and figured out his purpose in life. But in late spring 1944, he headed home to Birmingham, while the Happy Land Singers lived out his dream.

Jimmy's mother thought that at the age of twelve, Jimmy could not survive independently. The boys were young; Clarence Fountain was still several months shy of his fifteenth birthday. Velma Traylor, though, was twenty and had made plans for the group since his expulsion from school.

Jimmy spent that summer in Birmingham by the radio, where he heard the city's finest vocal groups: the White Rose Singers, the Ensley Jubilee Singers, and the Blue Jay Singers with local celebrity Silas Steele. At his home church Jimmy even got to hear a professional in person, Queen C. Anderson from Memphis. Her power and vocal glory overwhelmed him. And, of course, Jimmy seldom if ever missed his 4 p.m. appointment with *Echoes of the South*.

Jimmy had to make the most of his life without sight. He heard his brothers having fun, running in and out of the house. One of them would come and scrap with him a little and let him win. But he mostly lived his life in his own world. He was a healthy, energetic boy who had to take things slower than he would have liked. He questioned God about why he'd been blinded while his brothers all could see, but Jimmy never lost faith.

Meanwhile, the Happy Land Singers congregated with Velma Traylor in Gadsden, forty-five miles north of Talladega, and booked their earliest gigs on the fly. Traylor rehearsed and disciplined the group with a stick in his hand to whack anyone who lost the harmony. They sang at a little church for an offering and caught the attention of someone in the audience who invited the group to perform at another little church. Fame could not have been more remote as the source of each day's food was a total mystery. In these circumstances, the ultimate longevity and glory of this journey was beyond their wildest hopes. And the journey would become so painful, horrifying, and uncertain that its outcome in history would have seemed absurdly impossible at its outset.

After working the Gadsden area to the ground, the boys were drawn into the center of the state and the soul of the gospel quartet world. The Birmingham quartet scene in 1944 was enough to devour a group of visually impaired teenagers. Though the lasting impact of Birmingham quartets doesn't match the legacy of the Mississippi

Delta blues scene of the 1920s and 1930s, the depth of musical talent and baseline excellence of the Birmingham quartets rival the achievements of other great American music cities. The quartets' names flash poetic flare and neighborhood pride: Five Silver Kings, Big Four of Bessemer, Voices of Heaven, Golden Bell Quartet, Four Mourning Doves of Ensley, Moments of Meditation, and the Faithful Few, among many. Though the groups featured mostly all-male lineups, the mixed family group called the Ravizee Singers featured female lead vocals, and the almost all-girl Southland Memories won the big Birmingham quartet contest in 1943, taking with it a $100 prize.

Just as you can hear the isolation of the Delta in its blues and the multicultural worldliness of New Orleans in its jazz, the teamwork and cumulative achievement of a great quartet has its grounding in the mines of the Birmingham steel industry, where the lives and livelihoods of all men required the full effort of each, and the cooperation of the labor movement united individuals for the betterment of many.

Scholar Doug Seroff traced the genealogy of Birmingham quartet music to a singer named R. C. Foster. Foster had learned the academic jubilee style favored by the choral groups at Fisk University, Hampton Institute, and Tuskegee Institute. Foster organized his own much smaller outfit among his coworkers in a mine. Another early Birmingham quartet went by the name Rolling Mill Four in honor of their work in a factory that produced steel plate. As Seroff has reported, an early group of renown known as the Dolomite Jubilee Singers disbanded when one member died in a mine explosion.

Bob Friedman, founder of the Birmingham Black Radio Museum, interviewed many local quartet singers, including Norman Wooding, a singer and broadcaster who had worked for Tennessee Coal and Iron at Red Mountain, like Jimmy Carter's father.

Wooding told Friedman that the MacMillan Jubilee Singers, another of the city's oldest groups, organized among coworkers in the mine. Wooding's father, meanwhile, trained with quartet leader and steelworker Charles Bridges and later joined the MacMillans. Wooding heard groups of guys harmonizing in the bathhouse as they got cleaned up after a shift. He said, "I sung in the mine for all my lunch period. I worked on a song there, when I got out I brought it to the group...We didn't have nothing else to look forward to but that."

The beauty of Birmingham quartet music, captured in a collection of recordings Seroff produced as the *Birmingham Quartet Anthology*, springs from a nurturing embrace of sound. The lyrics are fine. The complexity of rhythm and harmony, however, are as experimental as in any American genre south of bebop. Singers found room to improvise not in the wide-open spaces of a song but in technique. The best of them, like Dunham's Jubilee Singers, who had recorded long before the Golden Gates became popular, stayed in smooth harmony, four or five voices singing as one, until one or more peeled off from the rest, breaking time or shifting texture only to return beautifully to the fold like the feathers of a wing.

In the book *To Do This You Must Know How*, Seroff and Lynn Abbott have shown that, like New Orleans jazz or Mississippi blues, the Birmingham quartet style disseminated as singers and groups moved to other locales and trained singers in the style, making the city hallowed ground for one of America's foundational sounds.

Birmingham's excellent local quartet tradition fed off of a rich national culture of Black vocal groups. The rising tide that lifted all boats in this sea was the Fisk Jubilee Singers. Organized out of a historically Black university in Nashville, the Fisks had traveled the world, performing for European royalty the so-called Negro spiritual repertoire that had evolved largely in the religious practices of enslaved people. The name *jubilee*, however, harkens to the biblical celebration of God's gift of freedom to the Israelites, expressed musically in a note blown from a ram's horn trumpet. In America, *jubilee* came to refer to Black liberation from slavery. The Fisks celebrated freedom and preserved a history that had not otherwise flourished in print. And so, vocal music evoked and honored the memory of unknown, long-silent singers. The more recent popularity of groups like the Mills Brothers and the Ink Spots certainly had a hand in underwriting the 1930s and 1940s Birmingham quartet renaissance as well.

Unlike jazz and blues in other parts of the South, quartets operated not at the cheap, gaudy fringe of the community but in the mainstream of Black Birmingham, enjoying grassroots support from churches and local radio, with venues of all sizes hosting events seemingly every weekend for decades. The music received a massive boost from big business in the titanic figure of A. G. Gaston. Born in 1892, Gaston had built an empire beginning with a burial insurance firm that branched into funeral homes before diversifying into a Black business school. Gaston would later create a financial institution and open the famous A. G. Gaston Motel in downtown Birmingham, a focal point of the city's civil rights movement during the 1950s and 1960s.

In 1942, Gaston sponsored the first of many massive Birmingham quartet contests at Legion Field, where the University of Alabama played its home football games. A reported twenty-five thousand fans attended. Photographs in the *Weekly Register*, Birmingham's Black paper, showed packed bleachers and fans huddled on the sidelines wearing crisp Sunday attire. One fan remembered paying a quarter to get in, though you'd get in free if you could show that your account with Gaston's Booker T. Washington Insurance Company was up to date.

Clarence Fountain recalled that he and other members of the Happy Land Singers regularly attended huge programs featuring numerous quartets and hosting thousands of fans, either at the stadium or indoors at the city auditorium. Having listened to gospel sponsored by the Smith and Gaston funeral home over radio station WSGN, the boys knew of the establishment's influence on quartet music. Velma Traylor must have hustled them up a meeting there because a man named J. U. Goodman left his job at the mortuary to take over the group's management. Clarence Fountain recalled that Goodman smoothed out the difficulties of life on the road, while Johnny Fields said that Goodman and his wife, Christine, looked after the blind boys like parents and kept the group at their three-bedroom bungalow, still standing in Birmingham's South Woodlawn neighborhood.

"We got lucky," said Fountain. "Brother Goodman showed us the way of life. Showed us how to survive. He kept us clean. I was worried about eating, nothing else. If I got my stomach full, I was alright."

Goodman booked them into churches and schools, and he drove the singers from gig to gig in his 1939 Buick. Fountain felt that the boys' blindness shielded them from some of the pain of segregation on the road. "We were kind of lucky," he said. "Usually people would come out and see a carload of blind guys and bring us our food and we'd eat in the car and head on to the next town."

Goodman had worked closely with a wide range of churches while with Smith and Gaston, and to book the Happy Lands he tapped into networks of ministers within all of the prevalent denominations. All of the Baptist preachers associated, as did all of the African Methodist Episcopal preachers and the Pentecostal-Holiness churches. Each denomination functioned like its own circuit, with branches in the communities around Birmingham and small Alabama towns farther afield. Win one, you might win them all as word of mouth darted from church to church. "Preachers liked him," Fountain said of Brother Goodman. "He had an easy time."

Goodman served a purpose for the group for years to come: he was their eyes. Young musicians are always ripe to be taken advantage of, and in those days visually impaired ones were even more easily deceived as they could not take a head count of an audience to estimate ticket sales or accurately gauge a payout beyond doubt. The group typically kept the lion's share of a sixty/forty split of the ticket sales or offering with the sponsoring minister. On the road, the boys stayed in people's homes, usually sleeping like sardines on a living room floor. Goodman took care of their money. Clarence kept a pretty full stomach. Nothing really troubled them. Their voices started getting out there.

One day in June 1944, Jimmy Carter tuned in his radio as he religiously did to catch *Echoes of the South*. This time, he didn't hear the Golden Gate Quartet. To his surprise and delight, the Happy Land Jubilee Singers filled the airwaves with their youthful arrangements of classic spirituals like "Blind Barnabas." Jimmy wanted more than ever to be with the group and prayed he'd join them. In a mere four decades, the prayer would be affirmatively answered.

Being newcomers in an established, competitive market, the Happy Lands found both opportunity and frustration in Birmingham. Clarence Fountain remembered battling at one of the big quartet contests and losing in the finals to the Ensley Jubilee Singers. One of Birmingham's semipro groups, the Ensleys performed for fifty years on radio, at live programs, and later on local TV. Fountain attributed the loss to the Ensleys' superior popularity rather than any real difference in talent. The Happy Lands, despite making headway in the capital of quartet gospel, felt restless and began ranging out of town.

With Goodman's management, the group got some bookings with a far-reaching Birmingham promoter named William Pope. A brief notice for an early out-of-town appearance indicates a growing popularity for the young group. "The Happy Land Jubilee Singers will appear at the Mt. Calvary auditorium this afternoon at 3 o'clock," the *Anniston Star* reported. "The public is invited and a large attendance is anticipated."

Likely through Pope's powers, the Happy Lands landed a big program out of state in Atlanta in the summer of 1945, supporting the best gospel quartet of them all, the Blue Jay Singers.

Innovative in sound and pioneering in business, the Blue Jays had started in Birmingham, and by 1930 they were singing over radio station WBRC every weekend in the 8:30 Saturday night slot. Rev. W. D. Hargrove, the city's first radio preacher, promoted the Jays in and out of town on the same line of country churches in Prattville and Tuscaloosa that the Happy Lands would trace. The Blue Jays featured two lead singers, Charles Bridges and Silas Steele, both of whom had worked in the mines or furnaces of Birmingham.

Bridges, born in 1901, had led the Birmingham Jubilee Singers, who recorded dozens of songs between 1927 and 1930. Steele, born in 1911, had joined the Blue Jays in his teens. Bridges's Birmingham Jubilees competed with Steele's Blue Jays, per a 1930 news story that gives a rare, brief glimpse of the musical fertility and creative energy of this underappreciated, scarcely documented renaissance: "Don't forget the state championship quartet contest, Sunday evening, April 27...The winner will be given a championship belt and arm bands, along with a five night's engagement, two in Georgia, three in Tennessee. The Bessemer Harmony Four, Red Rose, White Rose, Blue Jay, L. and N., [and] Birmingham Jubilee quartets are expected to participate."

Though the winner seems lost to time, the Blue Jays were reported within the next year to have played to diverse enthused audiences. "The Blue Jay Singers sang at Jones Chapel Sunday night. The church was unable to hold the crowd," read one report, while an ad in the *Birmingham News* had the Blue Jays on the Easter service at a large, new, and relatively progressive White church, the Birmingham Gospel Tabernacle, pastored by Rev. Glenn Tingley.

Bridges joined forces with Steele in the Blue Jays around 1940. By the time their paths crossed with the Happy Lands in August 1945, the Blue Jays had recorded, broadcast on radio, and relocated from Birmingham to Dallas to Chicago, spreading their unique style of quartet singing.

As the Happy Lands were developing their own style, they happened to encounter an influential artist of what would be called *hard gospel*, the defining sound of the next several decades of quartet singing, a style of attack that would influence mainstream pop and endures to this day.

The Blue Jays' Silas Steele brought the intensity of fire-and-brimstone preaching to the rhythmic, harmonious backdrop of jubilee quartet style. Rev. Isaac Ravizee, member of a brilliant family quartet, described Steele on stage to Doug Seroff, saying, "Silas was a small man and thin, about 5'10"... And when Silas would sing he'd lick out his tongue... Silas would walk from one end of the stand to the other and brother, whew, people'd be there shoutin' all on top of one another." So it was that the cool, sweet, slick jubilee harmonies of the Golden Gate Quartet began giving way to the raw emotion of a preacher possessed by the power of God.

This meeting of the up-and-coming Happy Lands with the trendsetting Jays was more than another night on the road. This was the biggest show the Happy Lands had played, facing a crowd of thousands at the Atlanta City Auditorium. This type of big-ticket program with multiple groups would be the way of the gospel business during its burgeoning golden age.

This night in Atlanta held even greater musical importance. The Jays had yet to record their two masterpieces—"Standing on the Highway" and "I'm Bound for Canaan Land"—but already featured both songs in their set.

Current music fans who aren't particularly drawn to overtly Christian lyrics should understand that one of the more prevalent and beautifully explored themes in gospel is the afterlife. If pop music exists in some part to help avoid such meditation, gospel revels in it, as did ancient Egypt. The fears with which we anticipate our journey beyond are allayed, and our arrival, in "I'm Bound for Canaan Land" and songs like it, delivers joy like nothing this world can hold. Gospel music performs this human duty as seemingly every other facet of pop culture ignores it.

"Standing on the Highway" is allegorical, evoking life, in deep American cultural code, as "that lonesome highway." The recording features tour de force backing vocals with stunning textures and heart-skipping rhythmic shifts so brilliant that the support overshadows the dual lead shared among maybe the two best leads ever combined. The delicacy and perfection of the accompaniment on this and other Blue Jays recordings are fine enough to make one fantasize about being a backup singer.

"I'm Bound for Canaan Land" is as good as humans can sound. Even the dependably flawless intricacy of the backing vocals in their excellence doesn't surpass a breathtaking Bridges-Steele dual lead, the two best at their best. Bridges and Steele harken back to the past and foreshadow the future of quartet style. Bridges delivers the opening verses, his clean, sharp, strong sustain carrying the tune in jubilee fashion until he relays the lead to Steele halfway through, as if passing the torch to a new era.

Even in a culture that treats its treasure like trash, the obscurity of the Blue Jays, in particular these two transcendent recordings, is a grave injustice, as heartbreaking as a thunderous Silas Steele lead. Blessed with supernatural talent and massive spiritual power, the Blue Jays poured more magic into three minutes of shellac than virtually anyone else in the long history of American music. For the Happy Lands, working with the best at this crucial moment of their development hit them like something heaven-sent.

The shift in gospel from sweet to hard came through artists needing to bring more to live audiences in a competitive environment. "You had to listen to whatever trend was going that day," Clarence Fountain said. "You better be able to follow it up. In the gospel field, we heard what everybody else was doing, and tried to do better." Fountain described the key to emulating the innovative Steele: "We tried to holler louder than everybody else. We learned how to put jubilee singing and gospel singing together. You better learn how to do that. In order to stay out there, you better know how to do what other groups can't do."

The boys were becoming more than singers. They realized that they had to perform. Jubilee singing depended on tight harmonies, which required specific physical location: members of a group had to each stand on a dime around the microphone in order to get their sound right. That style didn't lend itself to the most dynamic stage routines. As competition between quartets increased in big-package programs that featured numerous groups, the quartet style evolved, with choreography as well as fiery leads as singers moved with a mixture of rhythm and Holy Spirit, swinging hips and shaking legs like latter-day rock stars.

That night in Atlanta in 1945 proved momentous for yet another reason. A preview of the Blue Jays–Happy Lands doubleheader published in the *Atlanta World* contains the earliest use of the Happy Lands' future name, or something like it: "The Jays will be assisted by . . . Four Blind Boys and a Guitar of Birmingham."

This not only indicates an early use of the Blind Boys name but highlights how the group had begun to distinguish its sound: the guitar. That belonged to founding member George Scott. Clarence Fountain would recall, "All the other groups were singing a cappella. That guitar gave us a different sound."

On the guitar, there was only one inspiration: Sister Rosetta Tharpe. Like other sacred stars, she had a hard time staying completely committed to the Lord. Nevertheless, her guitar had a profound effect on listeners. Jojo Wallace, guitarist of the Sensational Nightingales quartet, a professional since 1946, said, "I've never seen anyone play guitar like her in my life. And sing. Never seen no one before her or after her could play like that. She was some guitar player. Tremendous."

Of quartets at the time, George Scott and the Happy Lands were among the first to feature guitar. At this point, Scott likely fretted an acoustic to open a song and quietly chorded behind the singers. He would, however, continue to develop his style, plugging in the electric by the early 1950s.

——◆——

The Black gospel world as a whole was a relatively new thing compared to the ancient inspiration of its soundtrack. Hymns and spirituals had been the earliest truly African American forms of music. But the big business of gospel had taken off in the early 1930s, largely thanks to a reformed bluesman. Thomas Dorsey had straddled the fence, attempting to balance his love of spiritual music with the necessity of eating. As a secular performer, he achieved success nearly unmatched in pre–World War II blues, recording the massive hit "Tight like That" with Tampa Red and touring with the "Mother of the Blues," the great Ma Rainey. Personal catastrophe soon outstripped his professional achievement—Dorsey's wife and baby died in childbirth around the time "Tight like That" was released. The trauma inspired Dorsey's composition of perhaps the most recorded and performed sacred song in American history, "Precious Lord, Take My Hand." A near rival in ubiquity would be another Dorsey number, "Peace in the Valley." Dorsey proved important to the careers of other artists and influential to the business as a whole. He helped to organize a national body dedicated to training and performing gospel, and he more or less pioneered the gospel highway, uniting country churches and big-city congregations on a circuit he traveled, selling his music and training singers in its performance.

Though gospel draws on classic spiritual energy and tradition, modern lyrics, as Dorsey most successfully wrote, differed from their biblical forebears. Unlike in so-called Negro spirituals, you'll hear few if any references to Moses, Noah, Samson, or Delilah in modern gospel, because the perspective derives from the Evangelical Christian personal relationship with Jesus.

The first gospel stars, including Mahalia Jackson and Sallie Martin, came out of Dorsey's lead and chorus style. By the time the Happy Lands hit the road, Mahalia had risen above the genre on her way to American phenomenon status. She would play a few programs with quartets, but Jackson had her own show and presentation style, and as an attraction, she didn't need the quartets to fill the hall in the way that quartets needed each other. Nevertheless, her existence lent credibility and importance to the Black gospel scene at large. Her appearance as a single act in Macon, Georgia, on November 30, 1946, garnered a photo and full headline above the fold in the local paper, while a concert featuring the Pilgrim Travelers, among the favorite male quartets of all time, was advertised like a want ad under the heading "Notice" further down the same page.

Considering that the group had no record and only spotty local radio support, the Happy Land Singers expanded their territory almost unbelievably between 1945 and 1947, as far south as St. Petersburg, Florida, and north to Dayton, Ohio, and Chicago. "They have had a great success on the present tour which included many of the larger cities in the East," read a preview for a Pittsburgh show in that city's nationally read *Courier*, while the *Tampa Bay Times* offhandedly referred to them as "nationally known."

During this time, the group had its first big lineup change. They would survive many. Donald Ray Hutton, son of charter member J. T. Hutton, said, "My daddy stuck with them until June 9, 1946. That's when him and my mama got married. My dad was supposed to go to Chicago with them after that. My mama all of a sudden laid a strict law down to my dad and just put it before him. 'You got to make up in your mind who you want, me or the group,' she said. He didn't get to go to Chicago. My mama didn't want no man just staying gone all the time."

J. T. Hutton made a home in Birmingham, where he became a minister, raised a big family, and hosted his old colleagues when they passed through.

After Hutton retired to Birmingham, the Happy Lands kept a high profile there. The local African American *Weekly Review* published congratulations for the Happy Land Jubilee Singers in May 1947, though for reasons too obvious at the time to specify.

They performed at a large White church, the Gospel Tabernacle, in August 1947 as part of an integrated program that featured Rev. Glenn Tingley, who had showcased the Blue Jay Singers at the same venue fifteen years before. Tingley's sermon that day with the Happy Lands was titled "Science Just Discovers That the Bible Is Absolute Truth!"

Integrated gospel music programming like this has been, is, and likely always will be a rarity. Though there were Black and White mirror worlds—vocal quartets, Holiness churches, and charismatic preachers praising the same Jesus on each side—Sunday church has been referred to as "the most segregated hour of the week" with ample reason.

Birmingham had integrated airwaves thanks to the many pioneer broadcasters and entrepreneurs who embraced the medium. The growth of Black radio in Birmingham seems to have branched off of the city's vital gospel scene. WSGN and WJLD were early supporters, where A. G. Gaston and Bill Blevins spotlighted spiritual music. A White radio announcer named Trumon Puckett began the popular and long-running *Old Ship of Zion* show in 1944. A dry cleaner and moonlighting Birmingham gospel quartet manager named Leroy Garrett hand-built a radio station in Talladega, one of the first Black-owned broadcasting ventures in the state. It's little wonder that numerous high-profile gospel artists, including Alex Bradford and Dorothy Love Coates, were coming of age in Birmingham in those days.

But the Happy Lands hoped to gain broader exposure and left Birmingham. Clarence Fountain said that they needed more radio support, and judging by the quartet-crowded radio logs published at that time in the Birmingham papers, the decision made sense. "If you didn't get heard on radio, you didn't get heard at all," he said. "Everywhere you went, you had to broadcast that you were in town and say that if [people] wanted to hear some good singing, they had to come to the show."

After three years of improvement and development in the bastion of quartet gospel, the Happy Lands relocated to Chattanooga, Tennessee. "You keep inching up," Fountain recalled. "You go here, you go there. You find something good that you're able to stand on to let people know that you're trying to make it. You're scuffling, and people will help you along the way. That's the way it was back in those days."

The move nearly destroyed them.

Meanwhile, back in Birmingham, Jimmy Lee Carter and his family had suffered a horrible tragedy.

"The day of my daddy's funeral, they closed the mines down," Carter recalled. "He was killed on the job, in the mine. It was an ore mine. Great big rocks crashed down on him. I was thirteen years old, home for the summer in 1945. He died on a Friday. Some of the people came to the house from the mine. They said to me, 'Your daddy's been hurt in the mine.' I said, 'Is he hurt bad?' They said, 'He's dead.'"

Carter continued, "I didn't know whether my mother could take it or not. Daddy was a likable guy who helped people out that had difficulty. A lot of people were devastated. I never did know for sure, but I think the mining company gave my mama a little pension after he had gone. We didn't have to leave even though we lived on the camp."

CHAPTER 3

(FIVE BLIND BOYS)

IN THE FALL OF 1947, the Happy Land Jubilee Singers gave their first big program in Chattanooga at Alleyne Memorial AME Zion Church on the busy corner of 16th and Williams streets. Though they had left manager J. U. Goodman behind in Birmingham, they felt that Velma Traylor could handle the job. They bought a car and hired a driver, and the early returns looked promising.

They had found a home with a man in Blowing Spring, Georgia, five miles south of downtown Chattanooga. The group got its first exclusive radio spot, validating the move from Birmingham. Johnny Fields recalled that the group sang every weekday morning on WDOD from 6:15 to 6:30. Their gospel business connections broadened with the exposure.

New Orleans booking agent James Payne picked up a few dates for the Happy Lands to work with his group, the Soproco Singers, that November. From a temporary base in the mining town of Lynch, Kentucky, the two quartets performed somewhere different every night for two weeks in coal country on into West Virginia. Payne had the two groups routed back through Chattanooga and on to New Orleans for a big program with the Pilgrim Travelers and the Kings of Harmony.

The Soproco Singers and the Happy Lands left Chattanooga for New Orleans together in separate cars, but the blind singers realized that they had left their suits behind and headed back to Blowing Spring. Shortly after the Soprocos arrived in New Orleans, Payne expected the Happy Lands to get in at any moment. Instead, he got a call from Johnny Fields.

"I got some bad news for you," Fields told Payne. "We can't get to New Orleans."

Payne asked, "Why not?"

Fields replied, "Traylor just got killed."

The story Payne heard and the stories that came out later don't follow the same details. The bottom line, however, is that the Happy Land Jubilees' lead singer, twenty-three-year-old Velma Traylor, had died of a gunshot wound. And how could the explanations for this tragedy all agree? When five blind boys play with a gun, pure chaos is the only outcome.

As Payne told scholar Lynn Abbott years later, "The way he got killed, they went back to the place they were staying. The guy they were staying with went back to holler at them. He had his bag with his tools in it. He had a .38. They were feeling around in the bag and got that gun out. He had unloaded it but left one bullet in the barrel. Johnny said Traylor picked up the gun and snapped it one time, snapped it twice, snapped it the third time, and the fourth time it went off, and they heard Traylor hit the floor."

Of course Payne's story came secondhand. Clarence Fountain was there. His explanation is more troubling and less exact. "All of us were standing around in a circle," Fountain recalled. "All of the blind boys had their hands on the gun. We didn't know it had a bullet in the magazine. It went off. We'd all had our hands on it. Traylor got the bullet, and it killed him instantly."

Traylor's death certificate gives the only official ruling available, that his death had been the result of an accidental gunshot wound. None of the survivors faced any legal trouble, and that's as far as the incident went.

The *Chattanooga Daily Times* of November 16, 1947, published an obituary.

TRAYLOR—MR. VELMA, manager of the Happy Land Jubilee Singers (five blind boys) widely known singers from Alabama, was accidentally killed Friday evening at Blowing Springs, Ga.

The last word on Traylor foreshadows a new direction for the group, giving another early public mention of its future name. More immediately, though, uncertainty hung over the blind boys.

"That was the lead singer. He was good too," Payne said. "He was a nice singer and a nice guy."

Fountain added, "That's the worst thing that could ever happen to us. We cried for days."

Back at school in Talladega, Jimmy Lee Carter and other students had followed the Happy Lands' progress with great interest. When former Happy Land singer J. T. Hutton phoned the news of Traylor's death in to the school, Carter couldn't believe it. Others were shocked, and all wondered how such a tragedy could have happened.

The group needed serious help if they were going to continue, a possibility Fountain doubted at that time. He figured they'd give up and go back home. Booking agent James Payne felt for them: blind, leaderless, and stranded, with a dark cloud hanging over them. He thought he could at least get them to New Orleans and furnish a decent substitute for the time being. A former member of Payne's Soproco Singers, Rev. Paul Exkano, had returned home to New Orleans from the road in previous months and taken the pulpit at King Solomon Baptist Church.

"Payne called me up and said he had a group of fellas he wanted me to meet," Exkano told Lynn Abbott. "He brought them to my house."

Exkano resigned from his church. He bought the boys a set of matching suits from the tailor shop where he had his nine-to-five. The lineup, down to four blind boys, consisted of Fountain, guitarist and tenor singer George Scott, Olice Thomas, and Johnny Fields, plus Reverend Exkano, whom the boys took to calling "Doc."

Exkano had the perfect skill set to continue modernizing the blind boys' sound. As a minister, he understood performance preaching, and as a quartet veteran he knew the business—the Soprocos had sung on New Orleans radio and performed around the Deep South for at least as long as the Happy Lands had been out. Though a New Orleanian, Exkano connected powerfully to the very roots of Birmingham quartet style. He had learned quartet singing under trainer Gilbert Porterfield from Bessemer, the Birmingham neighborhood where quartet greats Silas Steele and Charles Bridges had lived.

Exkano's role in the group's history has been diminished. Truthfully, though, it's no exaggeration to say that in the short term he saved the group and in the long term was as important as any other individual in creating the sound and image at the heart of the Blind Boys of Alabama. Exkano's most significant achievement would happen rapidly and right away, of great immediate necessity. He helped a shy young baritone singer become one of the singular voices of quartet gospel's golden age. Two weeks shy of his eighteenth birthday, Clarence Fountain became second lead of the Happy Land Jubilee Singers.

They picked up almost where they had left off at Traylor's death, battling the Soproco Singers in early December at the Eureka School in Hattiesburg, Mississippi. But there, the connection to booker James Payne went cold.

As their most trying year ended, the group remained headquartered in Chattanooga, though Reverend Exkano found them new, if not upgraded, digs to get them away from the site of Traylor's death. "Lady's house we stayed in, she was a poor lady," Exkano said. "She had an apple tree in the backyard. She cooked us apples for breakfast, apples for lunch, apples for dinner. I went and got some red beans and rice, I did the cooking."

Gospel quartets did what they called wildcattin' after the wildcat drilling strategy in the oil business of trying to strike it big in a place with no known production. They set up camp and hoped. Gospel wildcattin' required a local radio spot to put the drill in the ground. Rather than making money on their fifteen minutes of local fame, a group would have to raise money or a sponsorship to cover their airtime. They used radio as a means of advertising their presence in a community, to drum up a gig, advertise the show, and make some money at the door until the well ran dry. "You know when your time's up," Fountain said.

After Chattanooga, they returned to Birmingham and an equally unglamorous situation. "We stayed in a little old place next to a man's house called the Switch," Exkano recalled. "We were in and out of there for two or three months."

And, unbeknownst to themselves, they were on the verge of the biggest breakthrough of their lives. After the tragedy of 1947, 1948 would turn out to be their year.

Exkano reconnected the group with Birmingham gospel booker William Pope. Exkano talked Pope into putting the boys on a big program at the auditorium. As with many mythical, musical break-throughs, the Happy Lands' began in a shower of money. The crowd spoiled them with bills and coins tossed on stage at the climax of their show. Pope's eyes opened. The next thing Exkano knew, he heard from one of the top gospel promoters of the Northeast.

"I got this call from Ronnie Williams," Exkano said. "He said he could pay four or five hundred dollars to get [us] there and then he'd raise an offering. He said he had the other blind group coming and he wanted both of them. He said, 'You'll do all right.'"

CHAPTER 4

"ACCLAIMED THE WORLD CHAMPIONS!"

IN 1948, A LIVE, in-person gospel program featuring Sister Rosetta Tharpe or Mahalia Jackson with a quartet like the Dixie Hummingbirds, the Soul Stirrers, or the Golden Gates could pack a few thousand fans into a big-city venue. Sister Tharpe, the Gates, and the Birds had held prestige bookings at Café Society in Greenwich Village. But the genre as a whole had no collective national presence, no major record company commitment beyond a few artists, no national booking agency support, no *Billboard* chart. Even premium Black-owned media, like the glossy feature magazine *Ebony* and the tabloid-style *Jet*, mostly ignored gospel while focusing on blues and jazz. The gospel world of the Happy Land Jubilee Singers thrived at the grassroots, through scuffling artists, hustling preachers, indie record companies, and the wide-openness of AM radio. The support of the genre came not from mainstream mass media or the topflight entertainment industry but from passionate individuals operating with more good faith than good sense.

One totally unique entity within this world had come up through its ranks and seized an opportunity to create opportunities for others in the field: the Coleman Brothers. They grew up in the Tidewater region of Virginia, like Birmingham, a hotbed of jubilee quartet activity back into the 1920s. The family moved to Newark, New Jersey, and assembled a vocal group after the fashion of fellow Tidewater Virginians the Golden Gate Quartet. Lander Coleman emerged as lead vocalist, and Melvin Coleman became the business front man. The family group made good, touring with the cast of the 1932 motion picture *I Am a Fugitive from a Chain Gang* on the Warner Brothers circuit of theaters. They joined the Golden Gates as some of the few Black vocalists with network radio support, with programs on NBC and CBS. When President Franklin Delano Roosevelt died in 1945, the Coleman Brothers quartet sang on the coast-to-coast broadcast of his funeral, and a group of blind quartet singers down south happened to catch them.

On the road the Colemans noted the scarcity of accommodations for African Americans. Lander tired of staying at the YMCA or being outnumbered by roaches in so-called hotels. They pooled their salaries from CBS radio and, as Russell Coleman recalled, "sold our cars and put together every dollar" to purchase a five-story building at 59 Court Street in downtown Newark for $20,000.

The Coleman Hotel had seventy-two guest rooms, a spacious lobby, a cocktail lounge, and, in the basement, the studio of

Coleman Records. Just as they had found clean, comfortable lodging in short supply for the gospel traveler, they had also noted the hard luck facing artists capable of recording their music. Coleman Records became one of the first companies to record the burgeoning national gospel quartet scene.

Now, this time period has become known as the golden age of gospel, but that's according to a few critics after the fact who have assessed in perfect hindsight the breakthrough freshness and outstanding quality of the spiritual music produced during the 1940s and 1950s. Thanks to the success of Mahalia Jackson as a recording artist and performer, this golden age would also prove to be a breakout time for the Black gospel business, with bigger audiences and more recording opportunities available than at any time previous. Had you told these quartet artists in 1948 that they were in a golden age, though, most would have asked where the gold was and wondered if they could have some. So the phrase *golden age* holds true for the art of gospel performers if not their reality. Competition figured into this golden age as a key factor: a critical mass of talented groups devising to outdo one another brought the creative energy out of all. This competition and sparking creative energy took place live, in person, on stage.

Aside from the Colemans, Newark had some of the strongest support for gospel in the country, with multiple event promoters, ample radio time devoted to the genre, and plenty of large venues to showcase the music. Proximity to New York and Philadelphia, two of the largest gospel markets in the United States, didn't hurt either.

One of the more ambitious and resourceful gospel promoters in the country, Ronnie Williams, staged a battle in early 1948. With Barnumesque flair, he pitted not one but two visually impaired gospel groups in vocal combat. He billed the pair, the Jackson Harmoneers and the Happy Land Jubilee Singers, much more effectively, as the Blind Boys of Mississippi and the Blind Boys of Alabama. A friendly rivalry and two iconic American music brands were born. Gospel scholar Opal Nations reported that the first blind boys battle took place, appropriately enough, at the Laurel Garden boxing arena in Newark.

Williams promised the Happy Lands a $400 or $500 payday and put them up in Newark's finest colored accommodation, the Coleman Hotel. Rev. Paul Exkano, the Happy Lands' eyes, chauffeur, and vocal trainer, recalled that the boys rehearsed their set down in the Coleman Records studio. Melvin Coleman listened in. "Y'all got a good group," he told Exkano. "You should be making records."

Exkano couldn't help but agree, though he had more pressing matters at hand. "We practiced for the program...and they listened to us," Exkano recalled. "That Sunday evening, the two blind groups met."

The Jackson Harmoneers, newly rechristened the Blind Boys of Mississippi, had organized at the Piney Woods School, first working to raise funds for the academy before going pro on their own. They had a head start on their Alabama counterparts, having recorded out west and lived in Chicago, absorbing the influence of the Soul Stirrers. Like the Happy Lands, the Mississippi group had its own set of eyes, Rev. Purcell Perkins. Exkano and Perkins knew each other, and the Soproco Singers, Exkano's old group, had sung over New Orleans radio station WWL during the same period that the Jackson Harmoneers had a time slot at the same station. As of early 1948, the Harmoneers had more experience than the Happy Lands and a more established lead. Archie Brownlee of the Harmoneers is remembered as a most passionate, dynamic quartet front man. Reverend Exkano knew what he and the Happy Lands were up against.

The audience was the decisive factor in a quartet battle and maybe the key ingredient, besides talent, in the golden age of gospel. There had been formally judged quartet contests in Birmingham, in which harmony and diction were considered, but the big-city battles were of a different breed. The audience decided the winner, maybe not so much directly in terms of applause but in how passionately people responded to a quartet. Shows were, after all, religious experiences. People acted out in the theater the same way they acted out in a church or at a revival. The Spirit moved them. So, naturally, whichever group brought the Spirit to the people had more purely channeled the Holy Ghost. Through the music, they had all become closer to God. For the crowd, this meant a raucous experience of ecstasy, of shouting, leaping onto seats, dancing in the aisles, physically pulsating, eyes rolling, and sometimes collapsing, fainting, and falling out. The group that brought this spiritual power to the people removed any sense of dignity and decorum from the respectable, neatly attired fans in attendance. Or, in their words, the winning quartet "wrecked the house."

Archie Brownlee was a calculated house wrecker. His pleading voice contained vulnerability, but his falsetto shrieks chilled the blood and raised the gooseflesh. Brownlee destroyed an audience with passion that bordered on the operatic. His screams seemingly awakened a generation of soul singers from Ray Charles to James Brown. Reverend Exkano recalled getting an early taste at this first battle of what would be the Blind Boys of Mississippi's best-selling record, a funky version of the Lord's Prayer called "Our Father."

"Archie got up there and said, 'Oh-oh-oh-oh-oh, our father,' and that was the end of the journey," Exkano said. But despite taking the brunt of Brownlee's showstopper, the Blind Boys of Alabama had something for the house. Exkano and Clarence Fountain had worked up an arrangement of the Coleman Brothers song that had been performed over the airwaves for FDR's funeral, a title that dramatically played on Fountain's blindness: "I Can See Everybody's Mother but Mine."

Many years later, Fountain said that the Blind Boys of Alabama had taken the house that Sunday in March 1948. Exkano remembered a victory for the bottom line. "People was throwing money on the stage and I had people stuffing it in paper bags. We made two or three thousand dollars," he said. "That's how we got our start."

There's some evidence to back up Fountain's claim of victory. The Colemans helped get bookings for the Happy Lands in order to keep them solvent while working up material to record. Another epic struggle, "The Song Battle of the Century," took place on April 4, 1948, at Harlem's Golden Gate Auditorium, on the corner of 142nd Street and Lenox Avenue, an address that the Cotton Club had made famous in an earlier generation. An ad in the *New York Amsterdam News* proclaimed, "Between 5 Blind Boys of Mississippi vs. 5 Blind Boys of Alabama." The ad identified the Blind Boys of Alabama as "Acclaimed the World Champions."

The fates of the two blind groups intertwined. They stayed at the Coleman Hotel and battled around the East Coast for weeks while recording. Over the years, they would tour together, battle frequently, and trade members, while the two leading men, Archie Brownlee and Clarence Fountain, pushed each other higher.

The Blind Boys of Alabama still went by the name Happy Land Jubilee Singers and interchanged the names over the next decade, using "Blind Boys" in their battles with the Mississippi group and keeping Happy Lands on the bill where they'd drawn crowds by that title. They often used both names at once. Their first record is credited to "Happy Land Singers," though "Four Blind Boys" appears on the label as a subheading, similarly to how the name had appeared on billing for previous gigs and in the obituary for Velma Traylor. Seemingly, the group originated the "Blind Boys" name themselves while Ronnie Williams added their home state and a sense of buzz to the brand in conjunction with the Mississippi boys.

Melvin Coleman took a professional, hands-on interest in the Happy Land sessions. "Coleman rehearsed us over and over to make sure we had it right," Exkano recalled. "He'd cut a tape, play it back for us, and point out what we needed to work on. He really learned us how to record."

Exkano had to physically manage the group in the studio. "When you're dealing with a group of blind people, they gotta stand so far from the mike," he said. "Clarence had a loud voice, I had to back him up from the mike. I had to get them in position and everything had to be right. Olice, the baritone singer, moves. Clarence sings on his heels. It was hard getting them balanced."

At Coleman Records, the Happy Lands cut six numbers, the most enduring of which was the Coleman classic "I Can See Everybody's Mother but Mine." The veteran Exkano took most of the leads, but eighteen-year-old Clarence Fountain shined through. Beginning with his solo in "I Can See Everybody's Mother," Fountain would make a career of the dead mother song, though his own, Ida, was alive and well. Curiously, the first issue of "I Can See Everybody's Mother" carried a recording of Sister Rosa Shaw on its flip side, "The Lord Will Make a Way."

The Happy Lands developed material by attending church services, listening to the choirs, and covering the songs that went over on Sundays. As bass singer Johnny Fields explained, "This would give us a good reason to do the song, if the choir was singing it every Sunday. We'd change it a little. This has been very successful with us; quite a few of the numbers we've done was mainly choir numbers.

Choirs wasn't in demand. We'd go to church and hear them singing. If the morning worshippers enjoy it, then we'll sing it."

So they rearranged a choir song for quartet and crossed it over to a larger audience with some indication that people liked it, a classic formula anywhere in American popular music.

Coleman Records suffered from poor distribution, but Exkano took care of that business resourcefully. He recalled buying the group a second car with the seed money that had rained down on them from the East Coast crowds, and this became the chief retail vehicle for the early Happy Land sides. "I was taking records with me, selling them as I go along," he said. Nearly eighty years later, hand sales continue to make the gospel world go around.

Exkano didn't limit his side hustling there. "I made up a souvenir book, all about the boys, how they'd lost their sight," he said. "I sold more of the souvenir books than anything else, because everybody wanted to know about the blind boys." These moved for $1 apiece. Unfortunately, none are in circulation today.

In May 1948, the Happy Land Jubilee Singers performed at an unusual, high-profile event, the Cavalcade of Negro Artists, at the Diplomat Auditorium in Manhattan. The Harlem housing fund-raiser featured actor, vocalist, and activist Paul Robeson, jazz pianist Mary Lou Williams, blues guitarist Brownie McGhee, and harmonica player Sonny Terry. This seems to be the earliest example of the Blind Boys bringing a gospel message to a mainstream audience, the type of show that they would live on in future times.

The Happy Lands had turned around their fortunes completely in the span of a few months, from losing Velma Traylor in November 1947 to cutting their first records and playing the biggest stages in Newark, New York, and Philadelphia by May 1948.

CHAPTER 5

"OUR FATHER"

TWO YEARS AFTER THE Happy Land Singers' debut recordings, their friendly rivals from Mississippi made a hit that changed the game. With the unstoppable Archie Brownlee in the lead, "Our Father"—the Mississippi group's showstopper—would become the first gospel quartet record to reach the *Billboard* charts.

For Clarence Fountain, Reverend Paul Exkano, and company, "Our Father" proved to be the next best thing to a hit for themselves. Greater demand for the Blind Boys of Mississippi on the road resulted in more work—and greater exposure—for the Blind Boys of Alabama.

At one program in New York, Exkano met an executive from Palda Records, a Philadelphia-based indie that produced blues and country-and-western records. With the Blind Boys of Mississippi under contract to another indie, Peacock Records in Houston, Palda settled for the next best thing.

The Blind Boys of Alabama had no shortage of material thanks to their life of road miles. They made the most of countless hours in the car, as Reverend Exkano recalled. "As we were riding around from one place to another, that's when we rehearsed," he said. "We were riding around all the time. That's how we made up these songs. Trying to make something different from anybody else."

Exkano noted the importance of the other Blind Boys as their inspiration. "We had a lot of competition with Archie and them," he said. While the Blind Boys of Mississippi hit on "Our Father," the Alabama boys leaned in to the mother song during their sessions for Palda after finding some success with "I Can See Everybody's Mother but Mine" on Coleman Records. The theme had power to touch the coldest heart of the meanest scoundrel, the singer wondering if he'd treated his dead mother right, as Clarence Fountain did on "Since Mother's Been Gone."

Every gospel lead singer had asides they'd throw between verses—"child," "oh, Lord"—like an instrumental break; it didn't have to be fancy to be effective. In the 1951 recording of "No More Tears, No More Dying," Fountain uses one of his signature asides, which he'd embroider on many a tune and hear an artist on the sinful side make famous: "in the midnight hour."

The Blind Boys' 1951 Palda sessions offer rare examples of how the Happy Lands sounded during their jubilee days. George Scott, the strongest jubilee vocalist among them, sings lead solo on "I Have an Interest Over There." Scott strums a slow rhythm on his guitar, and his voice breaks into some sweet falsetto highs to punctuate the verses, a great record that must have suffered for its old-fashionedness. The group sings "What Manner of Man Is This" in tight harmony, hinting back to their school days as well. Their "Canaan Land," however, is modern, cutting-edge music. In perhaps the most ambitious of their early recordings, they sample the staggered phrasing of Queen C. Anderson as heard on her recording of "These Are They," also echoing the version of "I'm Bound for Canaan Land" that the Famous Blue Jay Singers had recorded. The Blind Boys of Alabama arrangement of "Canaan" spotlights the formidable dual lead of Reverend Exkano and Clarence Fountain. At age twenty or twenty-one, Fountain sounds fully mature, with his distinctive rasp, spirited improvs, and blood-chilling "Yeeeees!" in full effect. Scott frails manically on the guitar, and the backing vocals roll with sudden tempo shifts from hypnotic chanting to percussive humming. It's a version worthy of its heritage and thrillingly fresh.

Finally, "Living on Mother's Prayer" stands out among the greatest-ever recordings of the Blind Boys of Alabama. Like the finest in art and literature, the song evokes a world unto itself. Minimally religious, beyond the title prayer, the story pulls you into an atmosphere of desperation, deeper and more despairing than any blues.

Palda released the Blind Boys of Alabama on its Gospel Records label. Their sessions were part of a larger trend of independent record companies producing Black gospel. In the five years after the end of World War II, companies in New York, Philadelphia, Cincinnati, Chicago, Houston, and Los Angeles led the way. Many of the gospel indies also waxed the first generation of rhythm and blues rockers, plus so-called hillbilly music that ranged from traditional country to raw, electrified rockabilly. Palda, for instance, would go on to release Bill Haley and His Comets on its Essex imprint. King Records in Cincinnati released the Swan Silvertones and Spirit of Memphis quartets alongside a ribald blues shouter named Wynonie

Harris and, eventually, James Brown. The Blind Boys of Mississippi recorded prolifically for Black music mogul Don Robey's Peacock Records, as did Big Mama Thornton, with the original version of "Hound Dog," and Little Richard for his first solo recordings. So the Blind Boys were very much in the chaotic musical mix that resulted in the birth of rock 'n' roll.

The Blind Boys traveled among the nationwide roster of gospel talent, rising to prominence through this recording energy and the crackling feeds of a million AM radio channels. Other than steady work with the Mississippi boys, Exkano said they caught on with Rosetta Tharpe, the Harmonizing Four, the Ward Sisters, and the Dixie Hummingbirds. "See, our group was a pretty good drawing card," he said, due somewhat to novelty. "Everybody, if they couldn't get the other blind group, they got us. That kept us busy."

One report published in the nationally circulated *Pittsburgh Courier*—carrying probably the first nationally published photograph of the group—attests to the Alabama boys making a name for themselves in Black America even before they made their second batch of records. "These popular singers have appeared before vast audiences...[O]nly recently, a large number of persons were unable to obtain even standing room."

In action, the group played on its perceived handicap just as Archie Brownlee had with the Mississippi group. Brownlee, blind from birth, wearing his dark glasses and sharp suit while singing, invented the stage dive, a terrifying routine for a sighted person but an utterly shocking maneuver for him. He threw himself into the audience with only his faith to guide him.

To keep up with the Blind Boys of Mississippi, Clarence Fountain took the lead as an entertainer as well as a singer. Johnny Fields recalled, "Clarence was unusual—different. He was gifted for the stage."

Fountain began to understand how he could work an audience. On stage, he signaled to Exkano when he wanted to move. Fountain put a hand on Exkano's shoulder, and Exkano led Fountain, mid-song, out toward the crowd.

As Fields explained, they calculated their maneuvers to work up the crowd, with Fountain and Exkano sharing the lead vocal and pushing each other higher. "The guy who can see looks out where people are moving with the Spirit. He'd touch Clarence on the shoulder and let him know to go that way. They'd move over into that section and stay there awhile until the message, the feeling, or the Spirit, whatever you want to call it, catches that side. Like spreading flames from a match. They spread the flames from that area until the place is just about lit up. Once you get the front area started, automatically it spreads further."

Meanwhile, the backup singers caught the Spirit. "Once the program is well underway, then we were seated in chairs on stage," Fields said. "After it gets up to a point, all of us jump up at the same time from our chairs. This created a certain type of excitement."

Fountain worked his way back from the crowd to where the backup singers sat on stage. "We would sit Clarence down and he would refuse to stay down," Fields said. "Trying to sit him down, the background singers are up. They go up down, up down, constantly."

Their performance had everything to do with the moment, playing on their blindness, playing off the Blind Boys of Mississippi, but in so doing, they tapped into a deeply American style of worship. Gospel programs weren't just church. They united denominations for spiritual entertainment. The crowd didn't come to hear a sermon or message but to commune with the Holy Spirit and to see someone who possessed intensified spirituality. One of the greatest, most revered singers of the so-called golden age was Rev. Julius "June" Cheeks, best known for singing lead with the Sensational

Nightingales. As his daughter Judy explained many years later, his fans loved him more than his singing. "Even after he lost his voice, he was so anointed, people still came to see his programs." This "anointedness" gave spiritual entertainers another gift to share with their audiences, something above what a secular singer had.

The spiritual fire of these performances fed off a tradition of charismatic worship, of speaking in tongues, convulsing, and falling out. These personal expressions of Spirit possession are as old as Christianity itself but had been banished throughout millennia to the faith's outskirts. The impulse that the crowd felt at a Blind Boys of Alabama concert in 1950 is the same impulse that brought followers to the massive outdoor traveling revivals held in the South as early as the 1780s and that found expression and a new legitimacy in the Azusa Street revival of Black Pentecostalism in Los Angeles in 1906. Believers defined their faith according to the experiences of Christ's original disciples on the day of the Pentecost described in the New Testament, when the Holy Ghost descended and baptized followers in fire. These believers were, by their term, sanctified.

Black Pentecostal institutions like the Church of God in Christ began after Azusa Street, and in them sanctified worship found a house of its own after being shunned by Baptist and Methodist congregations. As pillars of the Black community, traditional religious institutions had concerned themselves with respectability. But respectability couldn't contain or satisfy the true feelings of the people. God filled them with ecstasy.

Ecstasy filled the churches and auditoriums where the quartets wrecked house. This passion overflowed into the personal life of a traveling Black gospel singer in the 1950s, challenging the very words issued from his mouth. Perhaps this illustrates why the more conservative congregations shunned the sanctified.

In 1952, Clarence Fountain's first child was born. "My mom was a singer as well, that's how they met," said Brenda Davis. "Her name was LaVerne. I was born in Sarasota, Florida. The Blind Boys were always on programs in Sarasota."

Brenda Davis's family attended New Bethel Missionary Baptist Church, where the Blind Boys performed. The family was friends with the local promoter. Davis's grandmother had a big house on the main street of Newtown, Sarasota's Black neighborhood. This became a stopover for groups traveling the gospel highway. "They ate at our tables," Davis said. "Olice, George, Mr. Fields, they were around all the time."

Davis's grandmother cooked collard greens, cornbread, and chitterlings. "My dad liked everything but macaroni and cheese, he didn't eat that," she said. "He loved food. Being at school and getting starved there and being on the road and not getting home-cooked meals, he enjoyed good food."

He would leave as quickly as he had appeared. When Brenda Davis was a little girl, her mother married a strictly local man. As years went by, and the Blind Boys returned to perform, Davis felt lucky to have both a father and a stepfather in her life. The men were clearly well aware of each other. "My step-dad sang with a local group, the Southern Echoes," she explained. "A lot of times he opened up for the Blind Boys."

Davis said that the two got along, much to the amazement of the neighbors. "My stepdad, Anderson Morris, he was a good man," she said. "He allowed my father to come to the house. That helped me understand and not be bitter, that my father traveled and wouldn't be around. I understood that the way he lived wasn't against me, it was to glorify God. I loved my biological father and loved my stepfather."

Within months of Brenda Davis's birth, Clarence Fountain married for the first time, not in Sarasota to Davis's mother but in North Carolina. Nine months later, his second child was born. Another daughter, she was also named Brenda, though Clarence did not name either child.

"My mother didn't really go to the programs," Brenda Johnson said. "Someone asked her to go and that was the first time she went. She was almost thirty. One of the men who was with him was friends with the lady she went with, and that's how my mom met my dad. She said she had dreamed about a man before she met him but could never see him. She realized she couldn't see him because he was blind."

Clarence remained consistent, if not a constant, in his second daughter's life, spending time with her when work brought him near. "I never lived in the same house with my father because he was always on the road," Johnson said. "My mom stayed in Hamlet, North Carolina. He wanted her to move to Detroit where his family had gone, but she didn't want to go."

As a young girl, Johnson traveled with her dad regionally during summers and learned about the more complicated and unglamorous details of his life.

"In Chapel Hill there was lady he'd go visit and stay with," she said. "Another in Durham. He had a place to stay in D.C. with a lady. These women were nice to me, and I was close to them."

She had the chance to observe him, to understand his life and appreciate his independence.

"Anytime he took his glasses off and I saw his eye, it looked like it didn't have an iris. His eyes look white," she said. "He would feel my face. He touched the cleft on my chin and said he had the same."

Johnson saw that her father could take care of himself. "He knew how to shave himself with that magic shaving cream. It smelled bad. He'd scrape it off with a butter knife," she said.

Though she heard his records on radio and saw crowds at Blind Boys programs, Johnson also observed the humble reality of gospel traveling. "They made money, but just enough to get them from one place to another," she said.

Another of Fountain's children has pointed out how the financial limits of gospel traveling on top of racial segregation pushed groups into much more intimate circumstances than they would have encountered in hotels. They stayed overnight in the homes of fans in many of the towns where the Blind Boys performed.

"These people didn't have a lot," Johnson recalled. "People living in so-called shotgun houses. They treated him so great. They would give up their bed for him to sleep in. That's how much they loved him. They must have met him during his programs and invited him to stay with them. They were good people."

As years went by, Johnson understood that Clarence got to know these places as well as his own home. "He was very independent in getting around and taking care of himself," she said. "Every house he stayed in, he could walk himself around, knowing where he was. He had all those layouts memorized."

Staying with her father also put Johnson in an awkward position. "You can imagine how hard it was for me, knowing he was still married to my mom," she said. "I was friends with his girlfriends while he was married to my mom. It didn't bother me. My parents were separated. The girlfriends were nice to me. But I couldn't let one woman know about the other women. I had to keep the secret. My mother would ask me things, my dad would ask me, 'Your mother got a boyfriend?' I'd say, 'I don't know, why you ask me that?' My mother knew I was staying with somebody, but she didn't ask."

Over time, she learned her father's secret weapon. "He was a sweet talker," Johnson said. "I watched him talk to the ladies later and was like, 'Oh my gosh.' He had a lot of ladies liking him." Johnson saw this not as a vice but as a survival tool. "I looked at it as he needed someone to take care of him on his down time. He had to be somewhere. Wherever he ended up at the end of the road, he needed someone. Especially having a handicap. Even if he didn't want to be in a relationship with a person, he needed them," she said.

As one of Clarence's traveling companions recalled, his pitch went something like "Would you take care of me? I ain't got no money, and we out here singing for the Lord."

Back home in North Carolina, Brenda Johnson lived in a Blind Boys bastion. Johnny Fields married and made a home in Henderson, North Carolina, that would serve as the group's headquarters. Johnson would write to her father at the Fields address and recalls receiving birthday cards from Johnny's wife, Mattie, who also wrote out Clarence's replies to his daughter's letters. Johnson said that her father never denied or ignored her financial needs, though he waited to get them expressed in writing.

Johnson got to know Olice Thomas, who lived in Chapel Hill with his wife, lovingly known as Miss Callie. "She was the one who told my mother that my dad wasn't being a truthful husband," Johnson said. George Scott and his wife lived in Durham. The Blind Boys of Alabama became a North Carolina–based family with the exception of its lead singer. Clarence Fountain had no permanent home of his own other than his family's base in Detroit.

In her hometown of Hamlet, Brenda Johnson kept a low profile concerning her famous father. "I'd see those old posters on the telephone poles," she said, notifying fans that the Blind Boys were coming to town. "Most of the time, I wouldn't even tell people he's my dad. People thought they had money. They were like superstars when I was growing up. I felt like he was just a dad working, doing his thing. I don't brag because people get jealous. People act strange and I didn't want that friction. I was proud of him for being able to do for himself. He never felt sorry for himself, no 'woe is me, I'm blind.'"

Nearly thirty years later, Clarence Fountain's daughters Brenda Johnson and Brenda Davis would meet for the first time, giving new meaning to the 1950 gospel title that had a part in bringing them into this world: "Our Father."

CHAPTER 6

"OH LORD, STAND BY ME"

Back to 1952.

WITHIN WEEKS OF CLARENCE Fountain's first marriage, in North Carolina, and his first child being born, in Florida, the Blind Boys of Alabama recorded their most enduring song and biggest hit—in California.

The group's run of high-energy, packed house battles with the Blind Boys of Mississippi brought them to the attention of Art Rupe, a self-described Jewish boy from McKeesport, Pennsylvania, who ran Specialty Records in Los Angeles.

Rupe's love of gospel went back to his small-town roots near the local Zion Baptist Church. "I think we were the only White family living in Tube Works Alley," Rupe recalled, of a narrow, densely populated residential lane. "Every Sunday morning, in the summer, when the church windows were open, I would sit outside on the curb just to listen to the fervent singing. It became part of my life as a preteenager."

This would have been around 1930. Rupe headed west after college, founded Specialty in 1945, and had himself a going concern on the strength of Roy Milton's 1946 hit record "R.M. Blues," clearly not a spiritual number. Two years later, Specialty entered the gospel field, just as the Happy Land Jubilee Singers cut their first sides for Coleman, and got rolling in holiness with LA's Pilgrim Travelers.

"The gospel groups were all familiar with each other," Rupe said. "The acts talked among themselves and they came to me. I had a reputation that I at least paid royalties. I made enough money that I didn't have to steal."

And so, Specialty soon added the Soul Stirrers, the Gospel Harmonettes, Brother Joe May, Sister Wynona Carr, and Birmingham-born Alex Bradford.

Rupe learned how the gospel record business differed from that for rhythm and blues. Without much radio support, big hits were rare to nonexistent. But with the way the groups constantly traveled, marketed themselves at the grassroots, and built relationships with fans, gospel sides sold steadily and over the long haul could outpace secular releases, which had a more feast-or-famine market. "The artists themselves promoted their records," Rupe explained. "We did very little."

Rupe began to see how the groups' traveling and making appearances were the key to their selling records and making a living. Rupe partnered with Specialty publicity director Lillian Cumber, the only Black woman thus employed in the country, to make this work for everyone. "We saw the problems of groups getting bookings, not getting paid, getting stranded," Rupe said. "Artists would telegram us and say they'd been stranded, so we bailed them out."

Cumber seems to have practiced the work ethic of doing ten times as much to get half as far as her White male counterparts. In the years directly preceding her appointment as Specialty's publicity head, Cumber organized a Black beauty pageant, ran a Black modeling school, tended bar at a fashionable LA cabaret, edited two Black Hollywood gossip rags, wrote a column for the *California Eagle*, and took a nightly red-eye shift as a disc jockey. In her minimal spare time, she schmoozed with Billie Holiday, Ella Fitzgerald, and Lionel Hampton and, with those notable artists, helped organize a program designed to curb juvenile delinquency with music. She came to Specialty through her freelance publicity work with Rupe's first R&B hitmaker, Roy Milton.

Cumber and Rupe identified exactly what the Blind Boys of Alabama could have told them about the gospel highway up to that point: "It wasn't run as a business," Rupe said. "We started Herald Attractions precisely for that reason."

The energetic and resourceful Cumber opened an office on Central Avenue, Black LA's Main Street, across from Club Alabam and the Dunbar Hotel. Under her stewardship, Herald Attractions became the first national booking agency for spiritual acts. "She was sophisticated in business and a good organizer," Rupe recalled.

She soon hit upon another quirk unique to the spiritual field. Unlike R&B acts, which could perform in any old joint, gospel singers could only play churches, schools, and auditoriums. Cumber made and maintained these contacts and dealt with them professionally, as if working in the pop market, selling advance dates only to ministers, promoters, or deejays who paid a deposit to ensure an act's bottom line for the show. With this guaranteed income, "gospel acts could make a living like the popular acts," Rupe said.

"She did a good job and had a lot to do with the popularity of our artists."

Cumber expanded the Herald roster in 1951 and 1952 to include groups that didn't record for Specialty, including the Spirit of Memphis, now with legend Silas Steele singing lead, and the Blind Boys of Mississippi.

By late 1952, Cumber's innovative efforts had drawn the attention of industry bible *Billboard*, which reported in its December 20 issue that Herald booked a thousand dates in forty-eight states over the previous year, among them a high-profile show for ten thousand fans at Brooklyn's Ebbets Field at $1.25 a head. She booked packages of three acts on four-month swings, estimating three to five hundred thousand tickets sold per junket.

Clarence Fountain said that Rupe tracked down the Blind Boys of Alabama on the road and signed them. Rupe, interviewed seventy years after the fact, could not specifically recall the Blind Boys' signing but cited his reputation in the business getting around among the quartets who came to him. Either way, the Blind Boys hit Hollywood in June 1952 with a lineup of Fountain, Rev. Paul Exkano, Rev. Samuel K. Lewis, George Scott, Olice Thomas, and Johnny Fields to record for Rupe's Specialty Records.

Reverend Exkano's importance to the group's sound had diminished greatly since the days he'd saved the Happy Lands after the death of Velma Traylor. Clarence Fountain now sang first—and often the only—lead. Reverend Lewis, a wheezy but fiery sanctified minister from Georgia, assumed the role of closer, launching into rough, hypnotic chants to take a song deeper toward its climax. This formula—Fountain leading, Lewis closing—characterized the group's first cut with Specialty, a song that would influence mainstream pop and remain a steady part of the Blind Boys repertoire for decades to come: "Oh Lord, Stand by Me."

The song features two key elements of the classic Blind Boys' sound as they continued to evolve from what Fountain has called the "correct harmony" they had grown up singing into a wilder style, emphasizing rhythm, texture, and spirit. Sam Butler Jr., who traveled with the Blind Boys as a child in the late 1950s and joined the group in the late 1970s, explained that while Fountain took care of the front, George Scott took care of the back. With Scott at his best, the Blind Boys' backing vocalists had a "jump sound," Butler said, a jagged, syncopated feel, sometimes startling in its volume, suddenness, and emotion.

A successful quartet put as much into its backing vocals as its leads, and the background style had to have an identity. Jojo Wallace of the Sensational Nightingales recalled how his quartet developed a high-volume, high-pitched sound, like a chorus of angels, in order to highlight and contrast their lead vocalist, Rev. June Cheeks, a technique heard best on the Nightingales' 1956 Peacock release, "See How They Done My Lord" and "Morning Train." The Blind Boys of Mississippi, with J. T. Clinkscales and Lloyd Woodard taking care of the back end, had a deep, smooth sound, often also providing some of the most animated and lively accompaniments on record. For the Alabama Blind Boys, George Scott created a backing vocal identity that would be with the group for decades to come. Scott, Thomas, and Fields sang resourcefully, driving the song's rhythm and changing the pace with sharp pauses, accenting and punctuating beats with sudden increases or decreases in volume.

Meanwhile, in terms of a stylistic breakthrough in the lead department, Clarence Fountain busted out what Butler called the "sanctified squall," years before Ray Charles, James Brown, Wilson Pickett, and Al Green brought the technique to the mainstream.

You can appreciate the Blind Boys' style at its best in the group's 1964 *Gospel Time TV* performance of "Too Close to

Heaven," available on YouTube. Core members George Scott, Olice Thomas, Johnny Fields, and lead singer Clarence Fountain are all there, joined by sighted singers Louis Dicks (seen at right in the video) and possibly baritone "Big" Bill Rash. Fountain's formidable stage presence is on display. He would hold his hand up beside his face while squalling, as if shielding the microphone from his own overwhelming power, a move only Clarence seems to have made. Musically, Fountain's sacred squall and Scott's muscular jump-style backing vocals push the song in classic Blind Boys fashion.

This sound had importance not only in distinguishing the group from other quartets on the road but also in authenticating them to listeners. In a world fraught with fraud and chicanery, in which phony singers and shady promoters would steal an act's identity and the public's money for a night, the signature sound made them tough to copy and easily verifiable to a public that, in the 1950s and 1960s, hadn't seen them on YouTube. On-the-level promoters made sure a group showed up early and performed a song over the radio to reassure fans of their authenticity. Still, imitators and sound-alikes worked their cons.

The Blind Boys' signature sound, particularly that strapping, syncopated back end, clearly influenced secular vocal quartets Billy Ward and the Dominoes and the Falcons. Two lead singers of the Falcons, Wilson Pickett and Eddie Floyd, were born in Alabama during the early years of the Happy Land Jubilee Singers. The Falcons' 1962 hit "I Found a Love" rides a rolling, lifting background vocal all their own, yet akin to the Blind Boys' style.

The Blind Boys' songs influenced pop music, just as their style and approach did. You can hear Ben E. King echo the Blind Boys' "Oh Lord, Stand by Me" in his 1961 release "Stand by Me." And if King's version is one of the five hundred songs that shaped rock 'n' roll according to the Rock 'n' Roll Hall of Fame, what does that say about the song that shaped the song?

On the flip side of "Oh Lord, Stand by Me," the song "When I Lost My Mother" was pure Clarence Fountain, with his dramatic timing and emotional storytelling building into the sanctified squall. The record seems to have been a hit. *Billboard* reviewed the release on March 14, 1953, in the same issue as Big Mama Thornton's "Hound Dog," an all-time classic. "Hound Dog" achieved a rating of eighty-two. "When I Lost My Mother" got an eighty, and "Oh Lord, Stand by Me," a seventy-eight. The song deepened Clarence's commitment to the "mother" song, a theme he hit on with the group's initial batch of releases with Coleman Records that fans would forever identify with Fountain.

The Blind Boys' work for Specialty was their best yet. Despite their commitment to emotional power, they had matured in their approach to a song, with a greater fidelity to rhythm and a more confident use of space than in their earlier material. They use pauses and breaths to underscore the beat and build the formidable emotional punch of their music. George Scott's electric guitar always surprises and satisfies, bringing a feeling more akin to fellow Specialty recording artist Guitar Slim than gospel peer Sister Rosetta Tharpe.

In his Sam Cooke biography *Dream Boogie*, Peter Guralnick reports that "When I Lost My Mother" sold nearly a hundred thousand copies, outdoing the combined numbers of Cooke's Soul Stirrers and the Pilgrim Travelers in 1953.

In August of that year, Herald Attractions announced the signing of the Blind Boys of Alabama to its roster, though the group had worked for the agency for some time already. Fountain recalled moving the Blind Boys into the Dunbar Hotel, across Central Avenue from Lillian Cumber's office. They would not call the Dunbar or any other place home for long.

CHAPTER 7

THE GOSPELCADE

AFTER HELPING TO CARRY the Blind Boys of Alabama to a new level while experiencing a diminished role in the music, Rev. Paul Exkano began to feel fatigued. His duties extended far beyond the obvious. "I done everything," he said. "[I kept track of] all the money, I had to check up on all the programs. We get a flat tire, they couldn't do nothing."

He also had personal differences with his younger charges. He had felt that the Blind Boys of Alabama behaved themselves well during their first few years together, particularly compared with the other group they traveled with, the hard-drinking and in-fighting Blind Boys of Mississippi. "They were nothin' but children when I met them," he said. "And I raised them. I raised them strict. I wouldn't let them do anything contrary or wrong. I taught them the Bible and made them pray. They didn't like that, but that was just my way of doing things."

Exkano felt that as the Blind Boys of Alabama enjoyed greater success and bigger crowds, they succumbed to common temptations of show business that, as a minister, Exkano could not abide. "I wouldn't let them have sex with certain kinds of women," he said. "They were nothing but prostitutes out there tryin' to make a dollar."

He felt uncomfortable being asked to judge the younger blind men's sexual prospects. "They couldn't see the women that they wanted to be with. I could see them. They felt them. They said, 'She look good to me.' And I know she wasn't clean, she didn't look good, and she just want to get some money out of 'em. I was looking out for my boys. They didn't like that."

The death knell rang. "They said I was old-fashioned," Exkano recalled. Exkano gave notice. He stayed on thirty days, until a July 5 program in Atlanta that the Blind Boys played with Mahalia Jackson and Brother Joe May. After the show, Exkano parted. "I told them they were on their own now," he said, feeling good about his tenure. "They were known all over the United States. I said, 'You can make it without me. I'm getting old, I'm getting tired.'"

They parted on good terms and remained friends. "We didn't fall out. We had no animosity," Exkano said. "I just had as much as I could stand. I had a good experience. I wouldn't take a million dollars for it—wouldn't do it over for a million dollars."

After leaving the Blind Boys, Exkano became a successful evangelist, crediting his time with the group with helping him to make a name for himself.

For its eyes, the group now had Rev. Samuel Lewis, the second lead vocalist, and Rev. George W. Warren. This role of eyes and second lead would be a revolving position with the Blind Boys for years to come.

Without Exkano, the group continued hard down the road, with constant work, both in small churches and big package shows. They played a West Coast swing immediately following Exkano's departure in a Lillian Cumber attraction known as the Gospelcade. This partnered the Blind Boys with two other top quartets, the Spirit of Memphis and the Soul Stirrers.

The Spirit of Memphis had begun in the 1930s as one of many neighborhood groups in Memphis singing for pure joy. The core of local men, featuring lead singer Jet Bledsoe, had since added two outside ringers, professional leads from the quartet circuit, the formidable Silas Steele and Willmer Broadnax, known in the business simply as Little Axe. With sweet, soulful Bledsoe, thunderous, superhuman Steele, and operatic Little Axe, the Spirit of Memphis had it all. The group's homegrown harmony section had been together for fifteen years, so the back end was every bit as locked down as the front.

Steele, formerly of the legendary Famous Blue Jay Singers, stole the lead right out of Bledsoe's mouth in the group's first professional recording, "Happy in the Service of the Lord," released in 1949. Steele's work on record with the Spirit of Memphis remained consistently excellent, peaking with haunting performances in "The Day Is Passed and Gone," a version of the Blue Jays' "Sign of the Judgment," and a wholly convincing rendition of "The Ten Commandments."

Veteran journeyman Little Axe joined up soon after Steele and sang his hair-raising best on "Calvary," with Steele backing him up one beat behind as the moon dripped away in blood on the scene of the Crucifixion.

The three leads shared a special chemistry together, each taking a turn on the finest Spirit of Memphis recordings, "How Far

Am I from Canaan," "If You Make a Start to Heaven," and a harsh but true Bledsoe composition inspired by life on the gospel highway, "Automobile to Glory." The group recorded for King Records out of Cincinnati, which deserves credit for producing one of the only two live recordings of gospel in the house-wrecking days, a Bledsoe slayer called "Lord Jesus," replete with fits of ecstasy from the crowd and a burst of laughter from the singer. Quartet gospel, while terrific on record, was a live music experience, with only "Lord Jesus" and an effort from Specialty's Art Rupe capturing the music in its heyday in the way it was meant to be experienced.

The Spirit of Memphis was possibly the most musically adventurous quartet, considering their dynamic approach with three leads and moody experimentation on songs like the Gregorian "That Awful Day."

But the Blind Boys' other traveling companion on the Gospelcade is better remembered. The Soul Stirrers, along with the Blue Jays, had been among the earliest nationally touring gospel quartets, going back to the late 1930s. More recently, though, the group had developed a young lead singer more graceful than Daddy Grace, more divine than Father Divine, whose charisma verged on cultish persuasiveness. This Soul Stirrers outfit embodied peak golden age gospel, featuring the biggest name that came out of the genre: Sam Cooke.

The clearest testament to Cooke and his power comes in the form of Specialty's *Great Shrine Concert* album recorded in 1955. The set features several acts on Art Rupe's roster, excluding the Blind Boys, unfortunately, though the Stirrers nine-minute "Nearer to Thee" brings the listener nearer to the thrills of a program in the golden age than anything else. The Shrine Concert also highlights what made the quartets special. While the great soloists like Brother Joe May draw out the emotional power of a song like no other group of American performers, they sound more like a church service. The quartets sound like a rock concert.

The Soul Stirrers' budding superstar brought a wild, sexual abandon to life on the gospel highway, or at least, a new level of it. "Sam Cooke had so many women coming at him, he would tell the women to go sleep with this or that other man, and the women would go and do it," Sam Butler said.

Butler, who traveled as a child with his father and the Mississippi Blind Boys during this era, laid awake many a night in motel rooms, listening to this activity.

"The guys on the road were singing gospel but not living it," Butler added. "When you're playing both sides of the fence, you're not really where you should be. My father was one of those. The Blind Boys of Mississippi drank liquor every day. They drank liquor from one program to the next. My dad driving down the road, if he saw a liquor store, he had to stop. Why? Because the men needed what they called their oil. 'I need my oil,' they'd say. They partied every day. They sang every day. They partied with women."

Despite such racy accounts of this time and its excellent soundtrack, Clarence Fountain said that reality didn't quite match the glitter of retrospect. As Fountain told Peter Guralnick in a 2001 interview for the Cooke biography *Dream Boogie*, "It wasn't really exciting. Like you come along and write about old times and that will be exciting to the people who read all this. But to us it wasn't really exciting. We had a good time and we were doing the best we could with what we had. And that's all you could do. You do the best you can with what you got and that's the way it went."

Offstage and after the party, Clarence Fountain perceived another side to Sam Cooke. The sensational singer used to jump in the Blind Boys' car en route to the Gospelcade's next stop and read aloud from a dime store western novel or the newspaper. Fountain marveled at Cooke's ability to bring the scenes to life. He was better than sitting in the movies. Little did the Blind Boys know, they'd soon meet Sam Cooke at a spiritual crossroads.

Still, these were the highest times yet for the music. As Little Axe told gospel scholar Ray Funk, "I went with the Spirit of Memphis just in the nick of time. Gospel singing was really coming up. Things started movin' in the '50s. Oh, you were just getting along in the '40s. But it started movin' in the '50s."

The Blind Boys' early 1954 Specialty Records release of the single "Marching Up to Zion" and "Does Jesus Care?" added to the group's glowing reviews from *Billboard*. The reviewer named "Zion" "one of the group's best," while calling the flip "wildly rhythmic and beautifully harmonic." That fall, *Billboard* rated "Alone and Motherless" and "Since I Met Jesus" even higher. Specialty used the old Happy Land Singers name, probably to avoid confusion with their counterparts, whom Peacock Records marketed as "The Original Five Blind Boys of Mississippi."

The sensation of movement that Little Axe described had much to do with Herald Attractions president Lillian Cumber. She built her company and established the gospel highway on a core of reliable promoters. From there, she would take it to new heights.

The Blind Boys of Alabama worked at least twice every year in and around the rich territories that promoters like Herman Nash of Atlanta and Goldie Thompson of Tampa had cultivated.

In Atlanta, Herman Nash based his operation on Auburn Avenue, the city's vital Black Main Street. In a highly unusual arrangement, Nash partnered with rhythm and blues promoter B. B. Beamon to host all of the big shows in town. They held court at Beamon's Auburn Avenue restaurant and staged concerts at the rented city auditorium. The partners shared an accountant named Annie

Durrah, who ran the restaurant after having done the books for the traveling Silas Green minstrels. Nash knew how to put on a show. Sandy Foster, longtime lead singer of the Mississippi Blind Boys, remembered Nash driving a new Cadillac on stage at one program. Just when the excitement from that stunt wore down into confusion, the great singer Rev. Julius "June" Cheeks popped out of the trunk.

Nash made Atlanta a Blind Boys stronghold for decades, bringing them in for big-ticket programs at least twice every year and booking them through smaller venues outside the city during the weeks leading up to and following the Atlanta anchor show. The Blind Boys routinely bounced from battling Sam Cooke and the Soul Stirrers before thousands in Atlanta to blowing out the Sons of Zion Singers at their little home church, the Spring Hill AME in Prattville, Alabama.

Disc jockey and promoter Goldie Thompson had three gospel shows on the air in Tampa: *Peace in the Valley* and *Old Ship of Zion* at 10 a.m. and 2 p.m. every weekday and *The Goldie Thompson Hour* on Sunday at 1 p.m. Thompson had introduced gospel promotion to the Sun Coast around 1940, when he and his wife, Sister Elizabeth, presented the Friendly Four at the St. Mark Missionary Baptist Church. The velvet-voiced Goldie—he claimed to have caught flak for sounding too White—emceed while Sister Elizabeth collected a dime at the door from each attendee, which one recollection numbered at less than a hundred. Goldie built the Tampa gospel fan base into a stronghold of the national scene through his electric pulpit, first buying radio time to advertise his attractions and before long getting a paycheck to play records, host live singers, and spread the Word.

After World War II, Thompson began holding programs at the Manhattan Casino in St. Petersburg and broadcasting from the Black-owned Robert James Hotel, where traveling performers stayed. The Blind Boys regularly filled the bill on Thompson's annual Watch Night celebration held on New Year's Eve at the Manhattan. Thompson would promote gospel concerts right up until his death in 1972.

Sam Butler, born in Florida, said that the two promoters were connected. "Goldie Thompson kept my group working a lot. He was a giant. He pushed us. Not only that, he had us go to Atlanta for Herman Nash. You're talking about powerhouses in the gospel world."

<hr />

Back at the Alabama School for the Negro Deaf and Blind in Talladega, the group of former students who'd departed in frustration had left a legacy. In late 1951 the local newspaper reported that another band of blind singers had started at the school. A six-person "glee club" working directly for the institute had gone out and given programs at a few nearby churches. Herman C. Morris, a supervisor at the school, acted as the group's spokesman and manager, saying that they were open for engagements and would be pleased to render programs wherever called upon. Clearly the school planned to make some money off of the singers and piggyback on their disgruntled former students. "The members are desirous of organizing in such a manner as to be able to travel extensively during the summer months. They have been inspired by the outstanding success of the Famous Blind Boys of Alabama, who began their career at the local Blind institute."

Jimmy Lee Carter had remained at the school for the blind after his old buddies left.

There he joined a quartet along with Jasper Lee Culliver. Jimmy met another up-and-coming blind musician in school as well. Clarence Carter, no relation, enrolled after the Blind Boys had hit the road. He would begin his musical education in Talladega, eventually learning composition, guitar, and piano. As a vocalist in the soul era, Clarence Carter recorded a number of hits, including "Patches," "Slip Away," and, later, "Strokin.'"

Though Jimmy had grown up and learned all he could about mop making, his mother kept him at school. "I wanted to quit, but my mama kept me going," Jimmy said. Finally, in 1953, at age twenty-one, Jimmy got his wish. After leaving school and spending some time at home in Birmingham, he relocated to Montgomery.

"I got with Jasper," Jimmy explained, "and we had a little group going called the Blind Boys of Mobile. We sang at churches and when the Blind Boys of Mississippi or the Blind Boys of Alabama came through, we opened up for them."

He spent little or no time reuniting with his old classmates at these programs. "They didn't particularly hang around us. Once we opened up, that would be it." Jimmy said. "We traveled the gospel circuit. Solomon Grant, who was in the group, managed us."

A press clipping from 1953 announces a Blind Boys of Mobile appearance at the St. Mary's Methodist Church in Hogansville, Georgia.

The group stuck together for a few years, going through some changes. "This group evolved into the Dixieland Blind Boys of Mobile," Jimmy said. "I was one of the leads. The other lead was Norman Hutchinson, from Philadelphia."

Jimmy recalled that the group made it to New York and had its biggest opportunity yet. "We recorded for United Artists, for Joe James and Joe Medwick," he said.

One record by the Dixieland Blind Boys appeared on the Ascot label in 1963. Jimmy sang lead on "I Found a Friend." The record could have been their big break, but for the Dixieland Blind Boys of Mobile, things never quite broke. By the time "I Found a Friend" came out, Jimmy had moved on.

CHAPTER 8

"IN THE GARDEN"

THE BROTHEL AND THE church are opposing cornerstones at the foundation of Western music. From Johann Sebastian Bach on the organ at Thomas Lutheran in Leipzig to Jelly Roll Morton on the piano at Mahogany Hall in Storyville, the church and the brothel have employed and inspired numerous important musicians over the past five hundred years. The institutions not only shared opposite-corner proximity but a tension bordering on mutual obsession and, it must be said, a secret underground tunnel through which members of each passed in both directions. Their conflict formed a moral universe in which musicians, like the rest of us, have grappled for truth.

The success of the gospel world brought it nearer to temptation from the other side. "Hallelujah!" shouted a 1954 headline in *Billboard*: "There's Money in Religion." Through the efforts of Herald Attractions boss Lillian Cumber, the Blind Boys of Alabama's booking agent, numerous spiritual acts were grossing $100,000 per year. With greater ticket sales came greater opportunities to sell tickets. In late 1955, Cumber booked a package of religious acts for the first time into the ultimate venue for Black music, the Apollo Theater in Harlem. Though New York City promoter Thurman Ruth publicly got credit for the breakthrough, reaching the Apollo had been part of Cumber's long-term vision for growing gospel, and she booked every act on this historic program.

Clarence Fountain recalled two things about playing the Apollo: the grueling five-show-a-day schedule and the money he made. He caught pneumonia and felt that he nearly died singing that much on a Saturday and Sunday, but he pulled in $1,500 that weekend.

Playing the Apollo wasn't the only foray of gospel into the secular world. Fountain remembered being in Richmond, Virginia, to play a program with the Soul Stirrers when he learned that Stirrers lead singer Sam Cooke had made a pop record, "Lovable," based on the spiritual "He's So Wonderful." This happened in 1956, months after Cumber and the Gospelcade broke through to the Apollo. Though Cooke had switched the title and lyrics from the song's gospel roots and released the record under an assumed name, the gospel public knew better than anyone the sound of that voice. Fountain recalled that thousands in the Richmond crowd walked out as the Soul Stirrers were announced, in protest of the secular record Cooke had cut.

In the coming year, Cooke would leave gospel entirely and become a singular voice in pop music when "You Send Me" hit the top of the pop chart in 1957. Nothing comparable had yet happened in the gospel world. Rosetta Tharpe had gone back and forth through her own revolving door between the Church of God in Christ and Café Society, but she never approached Sam Cooke's fame in popular music.

A key figure in Cooke's crossover became a key figure in the Blind Boys of Alabama's story during this time: Robert "Bumps" Blackwell. During the early 1950s in his hometown of Seattle, Blackwell had recruited both Ray Charles and Quincy Jones into his big band. In 1955, Blackwell joined Specialty Records, where the Blind Boys and the Soul Stirrers made their records, not as a recording artist but as a producer. He supervised the live recording at the Shrine, witnessing Sam Cooke's magic and predicting, so he later said, Sam's mass appeal, should the singer perform mainstream music. According to Peter Guralnick, Blackwell left the Shrine Auditorium to produce a recording session in New Orleans that yielded a rock 'n' roll breakthrough, Little Richard, and his hit "Tutti Frutti." Clearly, Blackwell had a feel for talent, a grasp of the moment, and a dual perspective on the pop and gospel worlds.

Clarence Fountain reported many years later that Blackwell had become the Blind Boys' manager during this period, though exactly when remains uncertain. According to Fountain, Blackwell encouraged them to record rock 'n' roll, saying that the Blind Boys could make much more money in pop than they could in gospel. Guralnick described how Blackwell persuaded Cooke that every person in a church on Sunday had to make the best living they could somehow, whether or not that living celebrated God. A cobbler didn't make shoes strictly for the Lord, but this secular activity in no way jeopardized his spirituality. In other words singing pop, making the best living one's talent could afford, needn't compromise one's soul. As Fountain explained to Guralnick, Bumps "showed you the rock 'n' roll map and he showed you the gospel map. Pick your choice. Rock 'n' roll map was big and wide as this room. The gospel map was a little old trail, you know."

According to Fountain, Bumps never pushed terribly hard; he simply stated the economic facts and asked if they'd like to make more coin. It was no big argument. The Blind Boys, according to Fountain, meant to stay true to their early promise to sing only for the Lord. "So I said no," Fountain recalled. "I'll just stay and sing the gospel."

The Blind Boys' eternal embrace of gospel occupies a high place in their mythology. Truthfully, the group's potential crossover had come much closer than a single conversation and a symbolic map drawn for a blind man. Though the Blind Boys have maintained for years that they declined many offers to sing rock 'n' roll and make more money, evidence suggests a longer, more tantalizing flirtation with the other side of the street.

Rev. Paul Exkano, the eyes of the group and co-lead singer from 1947 to 1953, said that secular temptation helped drive him from the group. In his interview with Lynn Abbott, Exkano talked about the group's womanizing and drinking as flash points but said their interest in unholy music was the last straw leading to his departure. "Then they wanted to make some blues," Exkano said, citing a Louis Jordan number. "'Choo Choo Ch' Boogie,' and like that. They thought they could make more money...I said, 'Man, you can't do that. Not with me, I'm a preacher.'"

Figurative sour grapes seem as likely a cause of these comments as the Blind Boys' partaking of actual wine. The group's bass singer, Johnny Fields, though, told gospel historian Ray Funk that the Blind Boys dabbled in pop. "Our group was unusual because we did 'Caldonia,' Bing Crosby numbers. We learned it just in case we had to," Fields said.

Why they would have to perform such material remains unknown. People attending a gospel program would have no interest in Bing Crosby or "Caldonia." It may be that Fields referred to an early period of the group's evolution: "Caldonia" was hot in 1946, well before the group had really defined its path. Picking up a few nickels on the fly with whatever an audience wanted meant the difference between life and death in those early days. But both the pop influence and the temptation of the other side remained strong.

In early February 1956, the Blind Boys did a session for Specialty at Roy's Record Shop in Hollywood. They recorded several versions of an upbeat Latin-style tune called "In the Garden." The group also recorded several takes of a purely secular version, replacing "in the garden" with "oh my darlin'." George Scott seems to be singing lead on the darlin' takes. The version Specialty released, with Clarence Fountain singing lead, is barely spiritual. Though superb, the lyrics sound like pop awkwardly transformed into gospel, the opposite of what Sam Cooke pulled by turning "He's So Wonderful" into "Lovable" for his first foray across the line. Though Clarence and many others have noted that pop songs simply substitute "baby" for "Jesus" in many cases, the reverse isn't so magical. The romantic, up-tempo accompaniment to the story of meeting Him in the garden creates a certain confusion.

The same Specialty session yielded a brilliant George Scott lead, also minimally spiritual, called "Swinging on the Golden Gate." Again demonstrating Scott's superb vocal talent and cutting-edge electric guitar chops, this and both the brothel and church versions of "In the Garden" seem to support the notion that the Blind Boys had rehearsed pop arrangements before, as Fields said. Both songs come off as smooth, streetlight a cappella more than the intensely soulful, sanctified squalling hard gospel they'd spent nearly ten years developing. These pieces have both a spiritual and an artistic versatility. As Bumps said, the cobbler needn't make shoes for the Lord in order for himself to be holy.

George Scott also sang lead on "Darling Come Home" at these sessions, a purely secular romance ballad. On other tracks, Scott's guitar style echoes that of his secular Specialty labelmate Guitar Slim, a star-crossed alcoholic picker whose stinging leads and distortion sound fundamental to rock 'n' roll. Unlike vocalists, George could get away with borrowing licks from sinful colleagues. What respectable, churchgoing community member would have heard Guitar Slim? Scott seems to have been the Blind Boy who sang closest to the other side.

Another edgy concept from the Blind Boys' Specialty run deserves notice. "The Sermon," recorded in 1953 but unreleased until 1993, mocks highfalutin, hypocritical preachers. As gospel scholar Opal Nations pointed out, Louis Armstrong helped popularize this theme on record with his 1938 release "Elder Eatmore's Sermon." Sam Cooke explored the concept in an ill-fated project on his SAR Records label. The downhome authority figure seems to have worked best not from the pulpit but from court, with Pigmeat Markham's "Here Come the Judge." Though the Blind Boys had earned the right to criticize jackleg men of God, wisdom likely prevailed in leaving "The Sermon" out of circulation.

The tension between sacred and secular within the Blind Boys resonated also in the relationship between Fountain and Scott. Sam Butler, who worked closely with the two, said, "There was always competitiveness between Clarence and George. Clarence didn't want George to come out front. George didn't sing more lead because he wasn't allowed to. Not because he couldn't do it. Clarence had a thing about being the star of the Blind Boys of Alabama."

Though Butler and Fountain collaborated on many important projects for the group, Butler's respect for George Scott ran deep. "George was a *bad* man. He carried the group. Clarence carried the front. George was hell on wheels in the background. He brought that jumpy guitar style to fit what they were doing vocally. George remained astute on learning what was going on."

Historically, the February 1956 and March 1957 Blind Boys Specialty sessions predate Sam Cooke's complete, no-turning-back crossover with "You Send Me" in the fall of 1957, though the group's manager, Bumps Blackwell, certainly would have known which way the wind was blowing for Cooke. The Blind Boys had their own path and their own journey.

These sessions, the latter of which took place in New Orleans at Cosimo Matassa's historic studio, where numerous early rock records had been made, were the Blind Boys' last for Specialty. Specialty president Art Rupe, who'd championed gospel and discouraged Cooke from crossing over, became disillusioned with the record business and directed his formidable energies elsewhere. Lillian Cumber left the booking business she'd built at Herald Attractions to launch her own agency. Though she continued to work in the gospel field for a few years, she ultimately transitioned to motion pictures and television, creating the first Black movie actors agency accredited by the Screen Actors Guild.

The Blind Boys' recordings for Specialty merit consideration as the group's finest. The body of work from 1952 to 1957 includes the group's bestsellers, most flavorful arrangements, greatest artistic breadth, and most influential pieces, including not only "Oh Lord, Stand by Me" but another catchy spiritual classic destined for pop adaptation, "The Last Time." The Rolling Stones added some dissatisfied-lover lyrics around the traditional chorus for their own

1965 single "The Last Time." Although the Stones cite a 1954 version by the Staple Singers as an inspiration, the Blind Boys recorded the tune a year before the Staples did.

The end of the group's affiliation with Specialty proved bittersweet. The early 1956 release of "Here Am I" snagged the "Review Spotlight" in *Billboard*, alongside Fats Domino. Among their last batch of Specialty releases at the end of the year, "Broken Heart of Mine" received the Blind Boys' highest *Billboard* score yet, an eighty-five, well above the marks of the Soul Stirrers and Sister Rosetta Tharpe recordings reviewed, as well as the Blackwood Brothers Quartet songs covered in the same column. "The group outdoes itself with each release," remarked the scribe. Just when their trajectory headed upward and onward, the Blind Boys' Specialty releases ended.

While moving on from Specialty Records and Herald Attractions, bidding farewell to people like Art Rupe and Lillian Cumber, who'd taken the Blind Boys to new heights, the group stayed close to Bumps Blackwell. Bumps would produce numerous future sessions for the Blind Boys. Considering his clout, it's probable that he deserves credit for the Blind Boys' prolific recording run in the years to come, for indies Savoy, Vee-Jay, and HOB Records, among others.

CHAPTER 9

"THIS IS YOUR PURPOSE"

THE ROAD NEVER ENDED for the Blind Boys of Alabama regardless of who planned the trip. December 1956 had found them in Memphis playing on a mixed ticket—brothel and church—featuring Ray Charles, B. B. King, the Soul Stirrers, and the Spirit of Memphis. This annual Goodwill Revue, sponsored by radio station WDIA, benefited local charity for the city's Black population. Oddly enough, this seems to have been the one time that the group was billed with a mashing of its two names: the Happy Land Blind Boys.

The night made history not for who performed but for who crashed the show. Elvis Presley briefly appeared on stage, reportedly shaking a leg—like the quartets had been doing—while he shook hands with WDIA disc jockey Rufus Thomas, causing his typical level of pandemonium, although for a predominantly African American crowd.

A year and a day later, the Blind Boys were sharing the bill with another founding father of rock 'n' roll. As the *Atlanta World* of December 5, 1957, previewed, "Little Richard got his 'call' while on a tour in Australia and stripped himself of diamonds, money, and other worldly possessions in order to preach."

What compensation Atlanta promoter Herman Nash offered instead went unmentioned, but the description followed of Richard as a "preaching and singing evangelist in the style of the Rev. C. L. Franklin" (Aretha's dad), and the anonymous scribe noted, "A record crowd is expected to hear Little Richard preach the gospel here."

Despite such novelty, most nights for the Blind Boys of Alabama consisted of bread-and-butter battles with their visually impaired counterparts from one state west, the Blind Boys of Mississippi. Sam Butler remembered an unusual tension among the Blind Boys of Alabama. "They were always at each other," he said. "They loved one another, but it was crazy to see two blind men fight, swinging at one another. Olice [Thomas] and Clarence [Fountain] got into it and Olice started yelling, 'Speak, so I can hit you! Speak!' But Clarence just sat there in silence so Olice couldn't find him."

Fountain tried in another terrifying way to overcome his impairment. "Clarence used to try to get up under the wheel and drive all the time," Butler said. "I was just a little kid, but I remember." Fortunately, that experiment did not go far.

At this point, ten years since the first Mississippi versus Alabama Blind Boys battle in Jersey, promoters still milked the old rivalry, as one ad wondered—though you'd think they might have learned Archie Brownlee's correct name—"Can Archer stop Clarence?"

The quartets squared off in an Orlando high school auditorium during an event known as the Body and Soul Program, sharing the bill with another pair of entertainers, "Old Chief Silver Cloud, better known as Rattle Snake Bill...and magician Old Chief Thunder Cloud," with no alias mentioned for the latter. You could purchase tickets at Ned's Grill in Orlando or from the Sunlight Gospel Singers over in Apopka.

In October 1959, the groups performed in slightly higher-profile fashion at Norfolk, Virginia's Center Theater in an event billed as the World Series of Gospel.

Around the time of this fall classic, Archie Brownlee brought two new singers into his group. One, Willmer "Little Axe" Broadnax, came from the Spirit of Memphis. The other, Roscoe Robinson, was traveling with another quartet when Brownlee contacted him through an intermediary.

"The Blind Boys of Mississippi did a show in Philly," Robinson recalled. "I was there eating in a restaurant, and one of Archie's runners came to me and said, 'Say, Archie'd like to see you.' I said, 'I imagine he do,' 'cause he's blind. So, I went down to the Carlisle Hotel where they're staying. Archie told me, 'Man, I'm sick. I'm supposed to go see a doctor in New Orleans and I got this tour.' He wanted me to sing lead with him. So, he talked me into it."

Roscoe Robinson, then thirty-one, felt honored to be in Brownlee's company. "I never heard anybody out-sing him," Robinson said, and sixty years later, no one had caught up. "In my lifetime, I've never heard anybody better than Archie Brownlee."

Brownlee, though only thirty-four, had been on the road for his entire adult life and a few years more. Though many quartets featured multiple lead vocalists, Robinson doubted that Brownlee needed the help. Truthfully, years of severe alcoholism had caught up with Brownlee. He drank at least a fifth of scotch a day, and on some he drank two.

On the road, Brownlee took time after hours to rehearse with Robinson. "We'd sit in his room going over lyrics and him telling me things," Robinson said.

On New Year's Eve of 1959, both sets of Blind Boys played Goldie Thompson's annual Watch Night program in St. Petersburg, Florida. Goldie had been around so long he still called the Blind Boys of Mississippi the Jackson Harmoneers, and the Alabama boys forever were the Happy Land Singers.

The groups worked from Tampa to New Orleans in January 1960, where Brownlee saw a doctor. After learning that his condition required hospitalization, Brownlee broke it to Robinson. "I want you to take the group and finish the tour," Brownlee said.

"Man, I can't take the group," Robinson replied.

"Why do you think I've been teaching you?" Brownlee asked. "You're going to tell me you can't? C'mon, man."

Robinson still felt unprepared and overwhelmed.

"I can't do it," he said.

Brownlee lifted Robinson's spirit. "You're good enough," he said. "I'm telling you, man."

Reluctantly, Robinson and the Blind Boys of Mississippi went on to fulfill their bookings without Brownlee. They did the shows and called back to New Orleans every night to check on their leader. One night, Robinson and Little Axe stood outside the phone booth as the group's blind manager Lloyd Woodard made the call. They saw Woodard drop the phone. Robinson went in and picked up the receiver. New Orleans promoter Rev. Herman Brown was on the line.

"Archie died," Reverend Brown told Robinson. "He's passed."

The news devastated Robinson and Little Axe, while Woodard seemed paralyzed.

The next wave of news only reinforced the leader's importance to the band: promoters canceled contracts for upcoming shows. Though the cancellations left the Blind Boys of Mississippi without guaranteed income, they were invited to sing anyway and take up an offering, and the spirit of Brownlee carried them through those dark days.

"I sang his songs, 'Leave You in the Hands of the Lord,' 'Our Father,'" Robinson said. "We were still living day-to-day, even as established artists. If you don't get paid one day, you don't eat like you should. We scrape together change from each member of the group, go get some bologna, crackers and some Kool-Aid. We'd get peanut butter. We survived on the cheap because we had no money."

Robinson and Little Axe shared treacherous driving duties behind the wheel of a fluky 1942 Ford. "Something was wrong with the front end of it," Robinson said. "It'd jump over to the side."

They encountered racism in cafés and at gas pumps, often being denied service on empty. "We got used to that," Robinson said. "Got used to that word. Nigger don't mean nothing to me. We'd see signs in towns that said, 'If you can read this, nigger, run. If you can't read, spell it.' What can you say? I went through stuff."

As the road went on, the Blind Boys of Mississippi shared a few laughs over the unpredictable. As if they needed further humbling, Robinson recalled of one performance, "We were in Greenville, Mississippi with the Swan Silvertones, Sensational Nightingales, Swanee Singers. It was my time to sing. I heard the people holler. They hollered when I hit the stage. I said, 'Looka here.' I took my coat off, threw it aside. They hollered again. I said, 'Look what I'm fittin' to do with these Blind Boys.' The women stood up and screamed and hollered. I'm thinkin' I'm killin' 'em. Then I see an armadillo running down the aisle."

Of course, Robinson and company remained close with their longtime rivals.

"While singing lead with the Blind Boys of Mississippi, I battled against Clarence Fountain with the Blind Boys of Alabama. Sometimes I win, sometimes he do," he said. "After the show, they come up and shake my hand, say, 'Boy, you were tough today.'"

Rather than pulling the quartet tighter together, the loss of Brownlee and trials of the road created tension. "There were people in the group who didn't want me to be lead singer," Robinson said. "Little Axe was one of them because he was there before me."

The diminutive, baby-faced Little Axe cut an odd figure on the gospel circuit, particularly beside the rather dashing Roscoe Robinson. Robinson felt that Axe had an advantage over him as a passionate lead. "He wasn't nothin' to play with," Robinson recalled.

The story of Little Axe has become the most sensational in gospel history. Both Robinson and Sam Butler, who traveled with the Blind Boys of Mississippi during this era, stated that Axe had male and female genitalia. After Axe's death in 1992, an autopsy reportedly identified Axe's sex as female. The state of Pennsylvania, where Axe died, releases autopsy reports only to family members of the deceased, and so I could not obtain documentation. Since Axe's death, other gospel artists have said that Axe was secretly a woman.

Axe had the respect of peers, regardless of what they thought they knew. "Shit, main thing was, Little Axe could sing," Robinson said.

Sam Butler, who traveled with the Blind Boys of Mississippi, recalled, "Little Axe had range. He could sing, and he could sell. A lot of people may have a voice but don't know how to sell. He was good."

Born in 1915, "Little Axe" came up singing lead in a series of quartets, an intense tenor sounding "almost vicious" to a top gospel historian. Axe identified as male, remarking to an interviewer about his wife and daughters, while marriage and divorce records documenting Axe's legal relationships with women attest to the same. He registered for the draft as a man as well. "He was straight up and honest," Butler said. "If you wanted to know, he told you. Back then, people were accepted for who they were. James Cleveland was gay. He was open. Sister Rosetta was open about her sexuality. She was bisexual."

As an artist, Axe made some sublime recordings as one of three formidable leads with the Spirit of Memphis in the 1950s before joining the Blind Boys of Mississippi just prior to Roscoe Robinson's tenure, which began late in 1959.

Robinson said, "We shared leads, and people accepted both of us. We sang together." Robinson's vocal range and technique sound more polished and wide-ranging than Axe's. But for sheer power, in a genre in which power equals glory, few have ever matched Little Axe.

Creative tension between the two spurred Robinson to write one of the classic, all-time gospel hits. In so doing, he probably saved one of gospel's greatest franchises.

"My daddy was a lumber contractor, back in Arkansas," Robinson said. "They would take logs and send them on the river to the next stop where they could be picked up and put on a truck. They called what they were doing 'sending up my timber.' That's how I got the idea for my biggest song."

The Blind Boys of Mississippi's recording of "Sending Up My Timber," with Robinson's scorching lead, sold nearly as well as

Brownlee's biggest hit, "Our Father." Robinson's poetic lyric refers to doing right in this world in preparation for the next—sending up timber to build a mansion in heaven.

It seems that Robinson will have to wait for his fortune there. "Lloyd Woodard was highly educated," Robinson said. "He took credit from me for my song. A lot of things I didn't know, he knew. I didn't know nothing about copyright. He did. A blind man. I'm taking him around, feeding him, leading him to the bathroom. He got the credit, and I didn't."

Really, the composer credit on the record is "PD": public domain.

Robinson calls Sam Cooke his God-brother, and you can hear how the sweet Sam style affected Roscoe, but he can get rough, too, and cut loose a hair-raising wail on the order of Fountain or Brownlee.

Though "Sending Up My Timber" saved the Blind Boys of Mississippi from the loss of its longtime leader, Roscoe Robinson would not stick around long to establish himself as that voice, instead becoming embroiled in a nasty contract dispute that split the group he'd just saved.

Within months after Brownlee's death in 1960, Robinson had taken the Blind Boys of Mississippi to record with Chess Records in Chicago. Robinson believed that the group was between contracts with its longtime company, Don Robey's Peacock Records. Robinson had a relationship with Chess and, as lead vocalist, made it his prerogative to record where he wanted to.

When Robinson and the group returned to Peacock to record "Timber" in spring 1961, Robey found out about the Chess session. Robey had competed with the Chess brothers in the rhythm and blues business for years and hatched a scheme to damage his rivals. Robey enticed three of the Blind Boys of Mississippi—longtime group manager Lloyd Woodard, J. T. Clinkscales, and Lawrence

"Shorty" Abrams—to sign a fraudulent predated contract that would have legally prevented the group from recording with Chess back when they'd done so. According to Robinson, they were offered a piece of the winnings should the suit prove successful.

Robinson refused to go along with the scheme and left the group. Though Robey initially won a $350,000 judgment against Chess, Robinson helped Chess prove the falseness of the fraudulent contract. Woodard, Clinkscales, and Abrams had testified in the hearing Robey initially won and, with Robinson's proof, had to admit that they'd perjured themselves. A federal appellate court reversed the decision against Chess. Robey, a man of high temper, warned Roscoe Robinson on two points: one, that Roscoe was finished in gospel; two, that Roscoe could never again safely set foot in the state of Texas.

Robey was not a man to cross. Even to singers of God's word, he promised vengeance. Joe Ligon, who recorded for Peacock with the Mighty Clouds of Joy throughout this period, recalled that a member of the group received a letter from Robey's partner, Evelyn Johnson, who had heard a rumor that the Clouds intended to sign on with another company. As Ligon told gospel scholar Jerry Zolten, "This letter said, 'If you leave Duke-Peacock, I've got five black boxes for all of you.'"

Roscoe Robinson largely followed Don Robey's advice out of the gospel business into a run of successful R&B singles throughout the late 1960s and early 1970s. Blues was neither Roscoe's first love nor his first choice, and he would return to the music of the Lord once the Don went on his way. As gospel scholar Opal Nations has pointed out, Robinson did have a few spiritual numbers released during the period of his feud with Robey but did so laying relatively low as a member of the Blind Boys of Ohio as well as the Clefs of Calvary.

Like Robinson, Little Axe left the Blind Boys of Mississippi, though seemingly without the curse of Don Robey. Axe, pushing fifty, recorded a series of breathtaking singles for Peacock Records as leader of the Golden Echoes, part harmony vocal group and part hot R&B band, with bass, piano, and electric guitar. The Golden Echoes played a more aggressively modern style than any of Axe's counterparts in the upper echelon of quartet gospel. In 1963, they very slightly spiritualized the classic "You Are My Sunshine" as "The Lord Is My Sunshine" by adding a "Jesus" to one chorus. Axe delivers the vocal at his "almost vicious" best, smoky and laid back until he's peeling the pearly shine from the gates of heaven, reshaping the lyric to touch on his "bed of affliction" rather than the bouncy joy evoked in the original. The Golden Echoes offer high-energy backup, probably hitting their best on a frenetic Little Axe lead called "So Soon" that predicts the sort of unleashed funk that would dominate R&B in a few years. Peacock Records last advertised a Golden Echoes release in 1965.

Not much was heard from Little Axe until gospel scholar Ray Funk interviewed him in 1986. Their correspondence led to the 1989 release of a Little Axe compilation album, *So Many Years*, through Jonas Bernholm's Swedish imprint Gospel Jubilee. The collection presents Axe's lead work recorded with the Spirit of Memphis and Fairfield Four quartets. The tour de force, however, is a rare cut from the Coleman Records catalog, made around the time of the Blind Boys of Alabama's debut at the same label: "Lift Him Up." Credited to the group Golden Echoes, the song features a first solo by Little Axe's brother William, known also as Big Axe. Little Axe makes a chilling, banshee-like entry into the song before delivering an impassioned vocal on a par with or above anything else the great singer recorded.

According to published reports, in late May 1992 Little Axe argued on the street in South Philadelphia with his former girlfriend. He pulled a knife. A bystander disarmed Axe, and the ex stabbed Axe in the chest. Axe lingered for nine days before dying at the University of Pennsylvania hospital at age seventy-five.

———◆———

After falling out with Robey, the Blind Boys of Mississippi needed a lead and a second tenor. They hired "Big" Henry Johnson to fill the lead, and during the first part of 1964, in Columbus, Georgia, they found a tenor background vocalist who also happened to be visually impaired—a graduate of the Alabama School for the Negro Deaf and Blind and a veteran of the Dixieland Blind Boys of Mobile named Jimmy Lee Carter.

"It was a privilege to be with those guys," Jimmy said. "Big Henry was a good lead singer."

Jimmy also got to work closely with two of the finest backing vocalists in the business. "It was great to be there with Lloyd Woodard and J. T. Clinkscales," he said. "I guess I'll claim that I coordinated the background vocals."

The road went on for Jimmy as it had for his old friends from Talladega: scrappy food, dodgy money, and good times. "A lot of times, you had to get bologna and bread to eat because we couldn't get anything else," he said. "We made do with what we could get. We would harmonize to pass the time. We loved sports and listened to baseball on the radio. We had a good time on that. I used to ride with other groups to be with someone else."

Carter quickly got a feel for the ups and downs of road life. "We did a show in Denver, Colorado," he said. "Our next show was in

Philadelphia, Pennsylvania. We had to drive. Wasn't doing no fly-ing then, we drove in cars. When we got to the church, we found out that the guy that promoted the show was gone! And had all the money, too. We didn't make a dime on that trip. All those miles and made nothing. We were in fair shape and didn't get stranded."

He also experienced a sense of adventure, visiting places and meeting people a long way from home. "The Blind Boys of Missis-sippi would go to California at least once a year, sometimes twice a year," he said. "I met Howlin' Wolf in Los Angeles. We were all staying at the Dunbar Hotel. We were talking, he gave me a recipe for if I got a hangover, what to do about that. I forgot what it was and didn't ever try it. I never met him again."

The mind pretty well boggles at the possibilities of a Howlin' Wolf hangover cure, both as a commercial opportunity and a Nobel Prize contender. Unfortunately, a pioneering Black artist like Wolf would have to do something as miraculous as defeating the hangover to be remembered to his deserved extent.

Carter also spent a moment at the Dunbar with one of Wolf's colleagues. "I met 'Big Mama' Thornton the same time," Carter said, of the underappreciated rock originator. "They got a room to jam in. She was gonna play the harmonica. I didn't get too close to her. She was a very good harmonica player and a singer. She came from Montgomery, Alabama."

While feeling blessed, Carter still wanted more. "I thought I had the power to be a lead," he said. "During my time with the Dixieland Blind Boys, I sung lead. I thought I was qualified. Blind Boys of Mississippi didn't, because they kept me mostly in the background."

Despite the challenges of the road, Jimmy began to understand what God meant for him. "It was hard for me to understand why He would take my sight," Jimmy recalled. "I had five brothers who could see. I was the youngest of all and I couldn't see, so I questioned that.

But He knew further on down the road and that this was the best way for me to go. I asked Him why did He take my sight, and He said, not in so many words, 'This is what I'm calling you to do. This is your purpose.'"

God gave him no other choice. "He looked after me in a personal way," Jimmy said. "I had to depend on Him."

Jimmy's promotion came at a time of great stress on his hometown. "With the Blind Boys of Mississippi, I lived anywhere and everywhere," Jimmy said, but as he followed the news closely, he felt shocked by what was going on in Birmingham. "I wasn't in Birmingham," he said, "but they had a police commissioner called Bull Connor. He was the one who sicced the dogs on people and turned the fire hose on everybody."

During the spring of 1963, local civil rights activists partnered with Dr. Martin Luther King Jr.'s Southern Christian Leadership Conference in a massive campaign against segregation in Birmingham. King, under arrest for parading without a permit, issued his famous "Letter from a Birmingham Jail" in response to local White clergy who'd spoken out against the movement. Terrorists bombed the Gaston Motel, where King stayed, a landmark owned by the biggest supporter of quartet gospel in the city, A. G. Gaston. They also targeted the home of King's brother. On September 15, 1963, a bomb exploded in the basement of the 16th Street Baptist Church, killing four Black children, all girls.

Gospel quartets experienced every facet of segregation in every southern state. Though they supported the fight for civil rights, "the Blind Boys of Mississippi never got a chance to work with Mahalia Jackson on those programs," Jimmy said of the movement fund-raisers that gospel's brightest star headlined. Quartets traveled the same roads as activists. Roscoe Robinson recalled staying at the Lorraine Motel in Memphis, site of the murder of Dr. King in 1968, and performing on programs at Mason Temple, where King delivered his "I've Been to the Mountaintop" speech the night before he died. But as quartets had no visibility or mainstream clout on the order of Mahalia Jackson or Harry Belafonte, they seldom if ever participated in high-profile events. Nevertheless, the quartets and the movement traveled different paths toward a similar destination, nourishing their spirits and those of their communities with the word of God.

PART II

EXODUS

CHAPTER 10

MASHED POTATOES FOR GOD

AS A LITTLE GIRL, Brenda Johnson looked forward to spending time with her father, Clarence Fountain, in the summer. She felt elated to see the Blind Boys of Alabama parked outside her school in their green Fleetwood Cadillac to pick her up. She remembered that sighted singer Louis Dicks was driving.

She hopped in, and they headed from Durham to Detroit, where Clarence's mother and siblings had relocated and which had become the closest thing he had to a permanent home.

"When I rode in the car with them, Mr. Olice, Mr. Fields, I could tell they were very close to God," Johnson said. "I could feel their spirit."

Though they kept quiet most of the time, the blind men occa-
sionally discussed matters that they wanted to keep among themselves. "They would speak this language," Johnson said. "They didn't
want me to understand what they were saying. It wasn't pig Latin. I
thought it was unique."

The Blind Boys had matters of the utmost seriousness and
importance to settle: a breakup was looming.

The group had continued to garner high-profile recording and
performing opportunities since leaving Specialty Records at the
height of their powers in 1956. Their next major recording session
had taken place in 1959 with the Savoy-Gospel label. As with their
Specialty sides, *Billboard* raved, awarding their 1961 Savoy LP four
stars. The single "Hop, Skip, and Jump" is particularly classic, with
Clarence and the backing vocalists finishing each other's sentences
like partners in a happy marriage.

Their 1964 performance on *Gospel Time TV* shows them still at
their best, twenty years since they'd hit the road. During the same
period, they recorded for Vee-Jay, a Black-owned independent in
Chicago, and in summer 1966, they landed a weeklong gig at that
city's Regal Theater, playing alongside Gladys Knight and the Pips,
the Manhattans, and Tammi Terrell, as apparently the only sacred
act on a pop bill. Later that summer found them in Central Park,
performing at a weeklong festival that also featured Lionel Hampton
and Bo Diddley, among others, another early example of the Blind
Boys reaching the secular market.

The Blind Boys' time with Vee-Jay is unusually well documented
thanks to gospel scholar Jerry Zolten's acquisition of business records
pertaining to Blind Boys sessions at Vee-Jay and correspondence
including royalty statements and sales figures for 1963 and 1964.
Johnny Fields had become the group's in-house business manager
by this time. The lineup included sighted singers Louis Dicks and

Jimmy Evans, as well as George Scott, Olice Thomas, Fields, and Fountain. Each blind man marked a shaky X beside his name to sign the recording contract.

Vee-Jay backed the Blind Boys with top-notch studio musicians for the 1963 LP *You'll Never Walk Alone*. Drummer Shep Sheppard had worked with Bill Doggett, cutting the classic "Honky Tonk." Alfred Bolden became known as a great gospel organist, maybe or maybe not for his work here, and bandleader Barbara Webb stands out as the rare woman in a man's world.

The album's title track, originally from the musical *Carousel*, came from the Rodgers and Hammerstein songbook. The Blind Boys' recording represented a possibly—probably with good reason— unprecedented mash-up of gospel and show tune. One would guess that the Blind Boys had Jesus in mind as the ghostly companion implied in the title, while the plot instead referred to a dead robber named Billy who came back to earth invisibly for a day to right wrongs he'd left behind.

The Blind Boys' recording features Broadway musician Zane Paul Zacharoff on flute, the early notes of which indicate that you are in for something you've never before heard from the great quartet. Odd as it may seem, the single outsold every other 45-rpm platter Vee-Jay issued on the Blind Boys in 1963, hitting the low thousands in sales. "You'll Never Walk Alone" certainly outperformed their version of "Danny Boy" at the cashbox. Additionally, the group recorded a Brook Benton number, "Looking Back," though otherwise the album contains mostly George Scott arrangements of spirituals. "Rock, Sword, and Shield," with Scott singing lead and Zacharoff zinging the flute, remains well worth a listen.

The Vee-Jay business records show that the group received an advance of $2,200 for their *The Original Blind Boys* album. Vee-Jay charged the session musician fees to the group's account as well. According to their royalty statement covering January 1, 1962, to June 30, 1963, the Boys had sold just under ten thousand singles and just over twenty-five hundred LPs from the recordings; at a royalty rate of .035 percent, they were $3,377.66 in the hole. It's entirely possible that the company didn't mind showing a loss through verified retail statistics while the group moved volume by hand sales on the road.

Overall the group's Vee-Jay singles generally sold in the hundreds and their albums sold in the low thousands, at least in documented numbers. By 1966, the Blind Boys had moved on to HOB Records. HOB was the gospel division, or rather the "devotional line," of Scepter Records, which had found success with the Shirelles, Dionne Warwick, and the Guess Who. John Bowden produced HOB's gospel records at the company's Manhattan studio, where the Blind Boys almost certainly passed near Andy Warhol and Lou Reed, who made parts of the *Velvet Underground & Nico* album at Scepter in 1966. Though Reed and the Boys would meet down the road, more relevant at this point was HOB's work with artists like Shirley Caesar and her group the Caravans, as well as quartet veterans the Swan Silvertones.

In May 1967, the Blind Boys recorded a live album in New Orleans for HOB.

"Put your shoutin' shoes on," Fountain tells the crowd. "Let's have a good time tonight, in the name of the Lord."

Fountain banters expertly between songs, bringing his fire to the audience.

"If this was a rock 'n' roll show tonight," he preaches, "you could hear the people screaming from blocks away...If Ray Charles was here tonight, if Jackie Wilson was here, you couldn't get close to this place. I wanna tell you that if you can go out there, on the rock 'n' roll floor...and see them doin' the mess around for the devil, then I feel like it's all right. It's all right. It's all right if I stand up here and mashed potatoes for God."

The Blind Boys deliver their patented, hearty jump style in the back, led by George Scott's soaring tenor. Fountain unleashes the sanctified squall in full fervor. Louis Dicks jumps in and pushes Fountain higher. The crowd sends it back with "all right" and "amen." The Blind Boys classics "Too Close" and "I Can See Everybody's Mother but Mine" scorch. Fountain sells the songs hard. Even "Just a Closer Walk with Thee" struts along with zeal.

"I don't like to sing to a dead audience," Fountain exhorts. "Anybody dead need to be buried."

The Blind Boys go out strong on a breakdown titled "Lord's Been Good to Me." No one listening to the record would think that this is a group on the verge of ending it all.

⬥

Breakups and shakeups are virtually unavoidable for an outfit as long-lived as the Blind Boys were even at that point in time—thirty years since their first glee club get-togethers at school, with nearly a quarter century of constant road life. Clarence, George, Olice, and Johnny had lived closer than most families, and on some level had just grown plain tired. Understandable as fatigue is, the Blind Boys' shakeup involved more than that. Of course the group later reunited. But in telling their long story to mainstream media in the 2000s, they seldom if ever mentioned this phase. They talked about their beginnings, their glory days, and life on the road with Sam Cooke. It's fine to smooth over a few rough patches in the story. But this one lasted for eleven years. And leader Clarence Fountain did a lot more than leave the group.

So begins the most mysterious era of this history. One man who is still around was close to the situation, and he offers the best perspective on what happened. "I joined the Blind Boys in 1966," said Robert Weaver, a singer from Chapel Hill, North Carolina.

Living in the Blind Boys' home base, Weaver got to know Olice Thomas. "He took my name back to Clarence, Johnny, and George. Then he got back to me and said, 'The fellas want to give you a tryout,'" Weaver said. "Olice told me, 'George not gonna like you too good because you seem to talk quite a bit. But if you get by with Clarence, you'll make it.' So, Clarence took a liking, Johnny took a liking, and that's where we started."

Weaver soon realized that his tryout amounted to a month of gigs on the road. "All the rehearsing I did with them I did on stage," he said. "I was able to pick up on parts and voices."

George Scott, true to Olice's word, came at Weaver with some tough love. "George told me, 'Sing or drop out,'" Weaver recalled. "I said, 'Hey man, what's that supposed to mean?' George say, 'When you're not singing, you're hollering—you're singing too hard. When you sing, don't sing too hard.' And that was one of the greatest things ever blessed my life. That was a great lesson to begin to learn how to control output, to sing and not to holler. I sang second lead, tenor, baritone. I learned how to sing all four parts."

Of all of the group's many former members and close colleagues, few have expressed such sensitivity to the special talents and insights of the blind that Weaver has. He marveled at the extravisual capabilities of the singers. "One of the things that really amazed me about all of them, they had the ability to develop sight through sound—vibrations through voice," he said. "They told me I had a vibration, that my voice vibrated differently from other folks and they picked up a kindness...They usually picked up more harshness than kindness. They could see faces through voices."

Their extrasensory perception extended into another direction as well. "Once they were able to touch your shoulder, they were able to guess your weight almost to the pound," Weaver said.

"George had a wee bit of sight flash in now and then. He never knew when it would come, but there were times when he could see red or yellow, and when he looked back again, he'd say, 'I wonder where that red went.' He was not able to see pictures, but he could pick up action."

Weaver offers a deep explanation of how blindness affected their sound. "Everybody couldn't sing Blind Boys stuff," he said. "The sound required a different kind of inside substance. The Blind Boys were feeling for something they could trust in in their sound, when a sighted man would go more at what he could see in the audience. They would be singing from a place where sight didn't matter. The Blind Boys didn't sing to faces, they sang to spirit."

Louis Dicks, the Blind Boys' longtime sighted singer and driver, was still there too. As Weaver and Dicks shared the wheel, Weaver realized that he'd joined the Blind Boys at a tense time. Their gigs were mostly not of the lucrative variety. "It was touch and go," Weaver said.

Despite the unique chemistry of the Blind Boys, financial uncertainty increased old divisions within the ranks. "Olice and George were very close together, and Clarence and Johnny ran the group," Weaver observed. "Olice and George were the silent ones who had to go along with Clarence and Johnny. They had that little friction ever since they were boys."

As pickings slimmed, "George and Olice wouldn't go on certain long engagements if the money wasn't right," Weaver recalled.

"They said, 'We're not going no four, five, six hundred miles for no chicken feed.'"

Scuttlebutt outside the group had the split emanating out of long-suppressed tension over the death of lead singer Velma Traylor. A lady who had attended school in Talladega with the Happy Lands told Mississippi Blind Boys singer Sandy Foster that Traylor's death was no accident. "[She] told me Clarence killed Velma Traylor to get him out of the way," Foster said. "Clarence was the baritone singer at that time. Traylor was the lead singer. They said Traylor was *bad* like Archie Brownlee."

Along these lines, Olice had started the group with Velma Traylor and never forgiven what had happened. Sam Butler certainly saw the tension between Thomas and Fountain on the verge of getting physical. Robert Weaver, who was with the Blind Boys at their breakup, however, said it wasn't quite so confrontational within the group. The official final word was that only one source knew the truth.

"Velma Traylor came up when I was around," said Weaver. "All of them were together that day Velma got shot. They were playing with this gun, and the gun went off. George used to say, 'I had it but I gave it to Olice.' Olice said, 'I had it too, I gave it to Clarence.' Clarence said he gave it to Johnny. None of them ever admitted to pulling the trigger. They say it was either Johnny or Clarence who pulled the trigger. Clarence said, 'All we know is the gun went off.' It was either Johnny Fields or Clarence Fountain who pulled the trigger, but they don't really know. They said, 'God knows who did it.'"

Though the precise timing and exact moment of the separation remains unclear, the core Blind Boys broke apart in the late summer or fall of 1967. Clarence Fountain spent most of his time apart from the group pursuing a solo career, but immediately after leaving the group, he joined his longtime competitors in the Blind Boys of

Mississippi. This would compare to Mick Jagger leaving the Rolling Stones for the Beatles, except that it really happened.

———◆———

The first time I heard about Fountain joining the Mississippi boys, I thought it had to be a mistake. But the fellow I heard this from isn't prone to mistakes. In fact, he's rather jarringly precise.

Donald Ray Hutton's father, Elder J. T. Hutton, had sung with the Happy Land group back in Talladega and left to start a family even before the death of Velma Traylor.

The Huttons remained part of the Blind Boys' extended family.

Standing across the street from the 16th Street Baptist Church, Donald Ray said, "The Blind Boys never came to Birmingham without stopping at my house. When the Blind Boys came to our house my dad served them peanut butter and syrup. That was their main menu, they loved it so well. My mama and my daddy kept them fed with pinto beans, neck bones, sweet potatoes. They stayed real close to us. They might just show up at four, five, six in the morning. Clarence and George just wanted mama and dad to feed them, like two old puppies."

Donald Ray is totally blind and, like his father and the other founding Blind Boys, attended the Alabama School for the Negro Deaf and Blind in Talladega. As we talked, he rattled off dates, names, and song titles, all with impeccable accuracy. Like seemingly everyone I've spoken to about Fountain, Donald Ray loves imitating Clarence's low, grumbling voice, recalling especially a request for one of Elder Hutton's famous sandwiches. "I'm hungry—y'all got peanut butter and syrup?"

Donald Ray impressed me with his warm, personal familiarity with Fountain and the Blind Boys as well as his sharp, factual memory. Still, he surprised me, saying, "[In] 1967, Clarence left and Billy Bowers, one of my schoolmates, took his place." When I asked what happened, Donald Ray said, "Clarence decided he was gonna depart from the Alabama Boys and go with the Five Blind Boys of Mississippi," adding, "Clarence didn't stay with the Blind Boys of Mississippi no more than a year."

Black gospel history is community history. As a *Gospel News Journal* correspondent wrote in 1968, "Gospel remains an underground music, unknown to almost all but the people who now listen to and enjoy it. It scarcely matters that any time a good gospel singer appears anywhere, he steals the show...Gospel has no sizable white following; it remains the one music performed almost exclusively by and for black audiences."

The day-to-day events of this world made no headlines. The Black gospel version of "Jagger defects to Beatles" completely escaped any media notice. To be fair, this event took place during the infancy of American music journalism, as *Crawdaddy* magazine and *Rolling Stone* published their first issues. An increase in newspaper feature coverage of so-called roots music would take another decade or more to flourish.

Instead, Black gospel history relies entirely on people like Donald Ray Hutton. What he said checks out. Two brief notices in small-town Louisiana newspapers that appeared in late 1967 and mid-1968 advertise Clarence Fountain with the Blind Boys of Mississippi.

One member of the gospel community recalls a more momentous occasion in Clarence's brief run with the other guys. Sandy Foster joined the Blind Boys of Mississippi as a lead singer in 1971, by which time Clarence had gone on his own. But when Foster joined, the Mississippi boys still had original members J. T. Clinkscales and Lloyd Woodard in the lineup, serving as institutional memory. They filled him in on recent events. "Clarence Fountain won a gold cup singing with the Blind Boys of Mississippi in Houston, Texas," Foster said. "All the big groups were on that show. He didn't work with the Blind Boys of Mississippi long, but he went out and got that gold cup. Clarence was a *bad* man. The audience loved Clarence."

According to Foster, the Mississippi boys had a need for Fountain due to the legacy of Don Robey's fraudulent lawsuit involving the group. Out of bitterness at his scheme going awry, Robey tried to break up the band by poaching its lead singer. "Don Robey paid Big Henry [Johnson] $10,000 to quit the Blind Boys of Mississippi," Foster said. "That was a whole lot of money. After that, they got Clarence."

Though the Blind Boys of Mississippi had recorded prolifically up to that point, there is an unusual, lengthy gap in their discography from 1965, during Big Henry Johnson's tenure as lead singer, to 1972 and Sandy Foster's time. This means that Fountain never recorded with the Mississippi boys. Furthermore, this seven-year void would seem to indicate a Robey-esque fatwa on one of the top-selling recording acts in the business. By comparison, the Blind Boys of Alabama released eight albums through two labels during the same period. These circumstances may also explain why Fountain remained with the Mississippi boys but briefly.

Clarence's foray with the other Blind Boys stands out for bringing Fountain and his former classmate Jimmy Lee Carter back together, an event that would gain heightened significance years later.

As Jimmy recalled, "He wanted to come, and we needed a lead singer, so we told him to come on. The Blind Boys of Alabama and Mississippi had been friends for a long time. We all got along. I'm sure it was a surprise for the audience, but it was no controversy for us. Clarence fit the group very well. We didn't lose anything with Clarence singing lead. When Clarence came with us, he did our songs. He did Archie Brownlee songs, and he was great with them. He did 'Leave You in the Hands of the Lord.' Another old Archie song Clarence did was 'Save a Seat for Me.'"

Clarence being Clarence, "he still wanted to be the boss," Jimmy said. Though he got along well with elders J. T. Clinkscales and Lloyd Woodard, singing Archie Brownlee songs and leaving his own identity behind felt wrong. "I don't think Clarence's heart was with the Blind Boys of Mississippi."

But, as Weaver recalled, "Clarence left the Blind Boys of Mississippi about m-o-n-e-y. Tour dates and all. I was with him when he went solo. Money was the contributing factor to all of it."

Johnny Fields, the other lifer who left the Alabama boys in 1967, became a record producer and expanded his role as the group's booking agent into a business. "After Clarence and me left I was what you call freelance," Fields told gospel scholar Ray Funk. "I produced Clarence and other groups. I had a lot of help from Bumps Blackwell, got a lot of tutoring from Bumps." On the booking front, as Weaver explained, "Every group knew about Johnny Fields and his ability to book engagements. Everybody had his number. That was the basic booking number for Slim and the Supremes, the Swans, the Nightingales, the Swanees. Johnny had the ability of a computer to remember names. He booked all the acts, all the dates. People knew if they wanted certain groups, they could call Johnny and he could hook them up. He booked from New York down to Florida. Everyone had annual dates, Mother's Day, Father's Day, church anniversaries, when they would put packages together. Johnny handled major bookings for Shirley Caesar for years."

Within days of one of Fountain's publicized appearances leading the Blind Boys of Mississippi at a show in Alexandria, Louisiana, Johnny Fields presented a huge gospel festival at the Durham Athletic Park. Clarence Fountain emceed the event. Virtually every major gospel group appeared, with one major exception: the Blind Boys of Alabama.

Even without Fountain and Fields, their formidable lead singer and their remarkable business manager, the Blind Boys of Alabama never went out of circulation. George Scott and Olice Thomas carried the Blind Boys through their darkest days.

CHAPTER 11

THE SIAMESE TWINS
AND THE MIGHTY CLOUDS

D URING THE LATE 1960S and early 1970s, mainstream pop embraced
gospel as Aretha Franklin brought the sound of the Black
church to millions of ears. "Oh Happy Day," an ancient hymn
modernized by the Edwin Hawkins Singers, became an international hit. Anne Murray's version of "Put Your Hand in the
Hand" and Judy Collins's rendition of "Amazing Grace" reached
the *Billboard* top fifteen. Mahalia Jackson, long recognized as a
national treasure, proved to be a global sensation when touring
abroad. Her death in 1972 prompted an outpouring of appreciation for her life and recognition of her genre, including from

President Richard Nixon; he was perhaps not exactly the champion of Black culture, but his office nonetheless conveyed the grand stature of the artist. In 1973, maybe the most enduring gospel-pop collaboration mixed the Dixie Hummingbirds, a quartet older and longer traveled than even the Blind Boys of Alabama, with Paul Simon on the timeless hit "Loves Me like a Rock." The Hummingbirds' own version also made the *Billboard* Hot 100 and won the group a Grammy in 1974.

None of this momentum impacted the Blind Boys of Alabama in the least.

Had you asked gospel quartet fans in 1955 for an opinion on which of the top acts would still thrive in 2005, maybe a few would have offered the Blind Boys. They were hot on the road, and their Specialty releases gained a lot of attention. In 1975, on the same question, no one would have guessed that the Blind Boys would be enjoying mainstream success in another thirty years. During the 1970s, the group's fame arrow pointed downward.

Still, these circumstances don't make this era uninteresting or unimportant. The Boys' perseverance through these days is a critical aspect of their legacy. Their current renown was not improbable or unlikely at this stage; it was inconceivable—impossible. So, how did they survive?

The Blind Boys stayed solidly on the grassroots gospel circuit, touring constantly and recording almost annually. Their arrangements had gone stale with Clarence Fountain, and new voices brought different dynamics to a group that had fallen into a few particular sonic patterns. Now with co-lead singers Billy Bowers and Louis Dicks, they put out some high-quality material and received acknowledgment from the music industry, if not enough love from the general public. The 1970s Blind Boys, without Fountain, produced a series of compelling recordings, not only drawing on the group's traditional strengths of passion and rhythm but adding contemporary dimensions. Shag carpet, ball-fringe gospel, and a cover of George Harrison's "My Sweet Lord" characterize this obscure but not unsatisfying era of their music.

"The War in Viet Nam," recorded in 1970, features the intense Billy Bowers on lead, with bluesy piano and funky organ accompaniment on top of a classic George Scott jump-style backing vocal. The lyric stresses awareness and support for the boys fighting, along with a subtly phrased civil rights message in the hope that someday we might all be free. Like Clarence Fountain, Bowers had a sanctified squall, though more reminiscent of B. B. King's whoop. The "War" track leads on a self-titled album that garnered the Blind Boys' first Grammy nomination, losing out to their HOB Records labelmate Shirley Caesar.

"So Sweet to Be Saved," a Louis Dicks lead, features some of the most impassioned singing the group ever recorded, with Dicks straining to his breaking point and the backing vocalists hitting notes they may not have known they had. Dicks interacts differently than Fountain with the background singers, on some verses coming in behind the beat and sometimes ahead of it, creating a rising and falling sensation, heightening the dramatic intensity of the lyric.

Dicks was the longest-tenured sighted singer to work with the group during this era. On YouTube, you can see Dicks take a lead on the Blind Boys' 1964 *Gospel Time TV* appearance in the hard-driving "Something Got a Hold of Me" and perform a quick rendition of the "Let's Go Down" bit from the Boys' stage act.

Dicks, a North Carolinian, first recorded with the Blind Boys as a second tenor on a 1963 session for Vee-Jay, beginning a ten-year run that culminated with an entire Blind Boys album of Dicks leads,

Jesus Rose with All Power in His Hands, a work that features fresh, if not always sensational, vocal arrangements.

Dicks certainly showed best in person, as both a singer and key straight man to the blind men's physical antics. "I saw Clarence act like he's gonna jump off the stage," said a longtime gospel fan and performer. "Louis Dicks had to grab him. The people went wild. Clarence acted like he was getting ready to fly, Louis Dicks carried him in the air, and his legs were kicking. People had a fit."

Some who knew Dicks personally admired his wit and street smarts while feeling wary of his accounting practices. Sandy Foster, with whom Dicks would work in the Blind Boys of Mississippi, said, "Louis Dicks was a con man. Everybody loved Louis, because he could work on your mind. He didn't have an education, he couldn't read or write. Anybody that knew him loved him, but he was a snake in the grass."

Foster continued, "At the Met, in Philly, I was the money man, collecting from the promoter for the group. While I was changing clothes, somebody went in my pocket. It wasn't but a three-hundred-dollar split because it wasn't that good of a show. Bill Moss, of the Celestials, saw Louis Dicks go in my pocket and get the money. The group decided I had to pay back the money. Every checkup after that, Louis would bring up, 'What about that money that Sandy owe the group?' After he's the reason I didn't have it."

Outside of Louis Dicks, Billy Bowers, and longtime members Olice Thomas and George Scott, the Blind Boys' lineup fluctuated. In 1971, they hired Charles Porter, a sighted young singer from Detroit. "I thought when I joined the Blind Boys, I was gonna make a million dollars," Porter recalled. "That's how crazy I was."

Porter had grown up a legacy fan of the group. "The Blind Boys of Alabama were legends in the Black community," he said. "I heard stories from my mother about how the Blind Boys performed, the way they coordinated their movements, the rhythms they made. She described them pretty well. For me to have the opportunity to sing with them I never could have dreamed of."

Porter and his family had attended big gospel programs at King Solomon Baptist Church, and Porter had become a solo singer locally. The Fantastic Violinaires, one of the top touring gospel groups of the day, were based in the city, had heard Porter sing, and recommended him to Louis Dicks.

Soon after a call from Dicks, Porter hopped a Greyhound bus and rode to New Orleans, where he met his new colleagues at Mason's Las Vegas Strip Motel, a favorite among Black entertainers. The group's bass player took Porter around to make introductions. Porter walked into Billy Bowers' room and saw the singer laying on the bed with his head hanging upside down off the foot, watching TV. "If he got himself just right, he could see a little," Porter explained.

That night, the Blind Boys baptized Porter by fire at the municipal auditorium. Without rehearsing, he had to perform on stage with them in front of a highly engaged audience. "You had to be there to hear the excitement that group generated," Porter said. "The crowd roared to see those Blind Boys. As Olice used to say, 'Boy, they was havin' a hissy fit.'"

Porter jumped right into the group's unique sound and energetic stage show. "George Scott had the sound that made the Blind Boys," Porter said. "'Oh Lord—Oh-Oh-Lord!' He created the vamps. We'd be into them with that hard beat. Louis Dicks put out chairs for the blind members. He'd sit each one of them down and then they'd pop back up like they couldn't sit still with so much Spirit. Louis would go back through and try to sit them, with George jamming on the guitar, Olice tapping his feet and jumping up, his feet left the floor, his knees hit his chest. Billy would do his thing, and by the time those guys were jumping up and down, the house would be in an uproar. People cheering, hollering, screaming, and enjoying, it was phenomenal. They were performers."

Porter kept up with the Boys on the fly, and they took him on to the next show. He started off as a background singer and, after a trial period, became an essential member of the Blind Boys' retinue: a driver. They traveled in a white van, bought secondhand from another quartet, with "Original Five Blind Boys of Alabama" painted on it in colorful lettering. Porter learned that he couldn't easily hide mistakes made behind the wheel.

"Olice, having traveled all over the United States, knew every road," Porter recalled. "When I started driving them, he'd tell me the directions. He knew the interstate and highway systems by memory. I asked how he did it, and he said, 'I just do it.' There were times when I got lost. Olice would be so upset because when I first got lost, I wouldn't say anything. He knew that for as long as we'd been driving, we should've gotten to where we were going. When he got mad, instead of cussing, he'd say, 'Mister': 'Mister, where are you?' I told him. He said, 'Mister, you done went ninety miles out the way!' I would be so embarrassed. A blind man knew the way better than me."

Porter the driver eventually earned the Blind Boys' approval. "The way you know a blind person trusts your driving is when they go to sleep," he said.

Porter got to know Scott and Thomas intimately, and as much as their music moved him, their humanity impressed him more. "George could see just enough to make him mad," Porter said. "He always wanted to see, but he still had a sense of humor about it. One time in New York, there was a naked woman, and we said, 'Man, look at that lady, she's butt nekkid.' George had impeccable timing. He spoke up and said, 'Where?'

"There were times he was funny. And times when he didn't want to talk. He'd get mad and didn't want to talk for two or three days. He'd get mad at Clarence. He'd get mad at Olice. He'd get mad at the world."

When Porter drove Scott home on a layover, he stayed for dinner and learned of Scott's painful history. "George had a beautiful home," Porter said. "He had a fridge full of steaks, and I'd go over there and cook for him. He lived alone, but it hadn't always been that way. His wife was killed by her boyfriend in that house. George never got over that. He tried to wash her blood off the walls, but if the weather got wet, you could see where the stains were. He never moved from that house."

George had married Althea Cynthia Lewis, known as "Thea," in Tampa, Florida, in 1953. She died on August 12, 1968, in the home she and George shared, as the result of knife wounds to her chest and neck. The Blind Boys, as always, were on the road when the tragedy occurred. George reportedly showed little outward emotion during a period of mourning and afterward sank deeper into his shell. Always quiet and moody, he became even more withdrawn.

Knowing the men on such a deeply personal level, Porter realized he had to keep things light, and he grew comfortable enough to prank the Blind Boys on pit stops. "At the gas station, they'd get out to go to the bathroom, and put each other's arms on each other's shoulders," he said. "I'd guide them around the gas pumps. It wouldn't be long before they'd get mad and say, 'Hey man, you're leading us around in a circle.'"

Porter loved the genius of George but credited Olice Thomas with stabilizing the group during these trying times. After Johnny Fields left, Thomas took over management of the Blind Boys, booking their shows, planning their routes, arranging accommodations, and handling the all-important "checkup"—collecting a night's payment from the promoter. More than one colleague of Olice Thomas saw this gentle, level-headed, totally blind man grab ahold of a scoundrel deejay or promoter and enforce the code of business ethics with his fists. He'd wrestle them to the floor and use his weight advantage until the full, agreed-upon amount appeared.

"I had lots of questions about things they did," Porter recalled. "Him and George, every time they gave me money to go to the store, they knew exactly what they gave me and wanted exact change. They memorized the bills when they got paid and kept it organized in their pocket and in their mind. You couldn't trick them. I tried to."

Porter also admired the Blind Boys' secret language. "George and Olice used to talk around me," he said. "They used their code when they didn't want me to know what they were talking about. They called women 'pins.' So I would hear them say 'squins,' and I caught on."

Billy Bowers recalled, years later, how he too had caught on to the code. George and Olice talked around Billy about much more than "squins." He thought he heard them say they planned to pay him a "squndred squollars" less than they kept for themselves.

In 1972, a little more than a year after Porter joined, Billy Bowers left the Blind Boys. Porter, at age twenty-one, stepped in and became lead singer alongside Louis Dicks.

Porter is the most overlooked of the Blind Boys' lead vocalists, as his name never appeared on his recordings with the group. He is not mentioned in the surviving news clippings about the band during that time, though his photograph was grafted onto a 1950s group shot of the Blind Boys to display on advertising placards. No film footage of Porter leading the Blind Boys has surfaced, and his name is scarcely mentioned in interviews that touch on the group's history. But Porter had his moment, and as a young man of his time, he encouraged a funky sound from the band as he covered contemporary hits of a spiritual nature. Witness his "My Sweet Lord"—sans the Hare Krishna chants heard in George Harrison's original—and "Put Your Hand in the Hand," a hit first for Anne Murray. Both had demonstrated mainstream appeal, something that the Boys had never gone after. Though no one has credited Porter with this innovation, the technique of spiritualizing popular tunes became a key ingredient of the Blind Boys' formula during their American icon phase beginning in the 1990s.

The Porter-era arrangements are a total departure from what the Boys had recorded even just a couple of years earlier with "The War in Viet Nam" and "Too Sweet to Be Saved." Still, distorted guitar and ex-Beatle covers could never get the Blind Boys totally out of their own shadow. "We ran into Clarence on the road," Porter said. "It was kind of odd."

Clarence Fountain and the Blind Boys often played, separately, on the same programs. Promoters usually listed the two distinct acts as if they were one to avoid spooking fans. Long behind them were the days of performing alongside Sam Cooke, of sharing the bill with Little Richard, of Elvis hopping on stage. Cooke and Silas Steele were dead and gone. Some of the long-running groups from the so-called golden age had reduced their travel and gigging, if not totally hung it up: the Spirit of Memphis and the Swan Silvertones appeared infrequently on the big programs. Other than the two Blind Boys outfits, groups like the Mighty Clouds of Joy, Slim and the Supreme Angels, the Fantastic Violinaires, the Gospel Keynotes, Bill Moss and the Celestials, and the Gospel Caravans had become the hard-traveling, full-timers on the Lord's highway. To be clear, this wasn't a time of diminished interest on the Black gospel scene but an era of new acts leaving some of the old quartets behind. Charles Porter is quick to point out that hot records and radio play dictated popularity, and the Blind Boys didn't have a hot record.

Since Fountain worked as a single act accompanied by his guitarist and a pickup drummer, he usually went on before the quartets. This played to his advantage against his former group, on whom he exacted a special form of entertainment vengeance. "Clarence would do his old Blind Boys songs and sold them better than the Blind Boys could without him," said Sam Butler, Fountain's guitarist. "People wanted to hear the Blind Boys, but Clarence came up before the big groups. They put us on first and he'd always kill. Doing his mother songs, all them old songs. Charles [Porter] had a more upbeat sound, which was really grooving. But if Clarence sang one of those songs, the Blind Boys might as well go on down the road. That's what people wanted to hear."

Fountain also had his mighty stage presence, something the Blind Boys couldn't quite match in his absence. Butler remembers Clarence executing his famous move, opening his blazer and popping his hip, which his own daughter said did not seem very Christian. Clarence maintained a strong visual connection with the audience. He had an aura.

Fountain not only tore the heart out of the Blind Boys' set but also poached opportunities that would have gone to the group. Fountain performed on Atlanta promoter Herman Nash's big programs in the late 1960s, a spot that had traditionally gone to the Blind Boys.

At the same time that Charles Porter stepped up to sing lead for the Blind Boys, Sam Butler Jr., known on the road as "Junior Butler," became Clarence Fountain's accompanist, thanks to Clarence's recruiting tactics. "I was with the Swanee Quintet," Butler recalled. "Clarence was on my tail every night. 'How much you makin', Junior?' I told him. He said, 'Boy, look, you make that in one night with me.' I went with him. Sure enough, he was making money."

Butler, born in St. Petersburg, Florida, had entertained professionally since age six. Brought up in the Church of the Living God, a Pentecostal denomination, he had learned to play guitar on the road with his father, a lap-steel player in that church's tradition, one that current music fans associate with Robert Randolph.

Butler knew quite well what he was getting into by working with Clarence. Though only around twenty years old at the time, Butler had opened for the Blind Boys of Mississippi as a kindergartner, learning pointers on the road from Archie Brownlee, Sam Cooke, Rosetta Tharpe, and Mahalia Jackson, before fronting Little Junior and the Butleraires as a preteen. When the Butleraires opened for the Blind Boys of Alabama, Little Junior had seen Clarence Fountain's jealousy up close.

"Louis Dicks and another sighted singer had this thing where they played off each other on stage, singing, 'going on down...can we go down?' and they would work that thing," Butler recalled. "By the time they came back up, it was like they threw fire out, it was so magical, and the people just loved it. Clarence told them, 'Y'all can't do that no more. I'm the star.' He could be that temperamental. That was Clarence's holdback, because it stopped the group from being its best."

For young Junior Butler, life with Clarence Fountain was an endless party. They played music, made money—much more even in lean times with a fifty-fifty split over a five-way—and did it again in the next town on the next night. "We sold records, outsold everybody, because Clarence didn't mind selling his for three dollars each," Butler explained. "He undersold everybody. He got 'em wholesale and made a buck on each. He did very well. Clarence was one man making as much as a group was making [per show]. My split was much bigger than it would be with a five-piece. Clarence made the same as the Blind Boys as an act but had only two people to pay."

They typically worked a double on Sundays but had Mondays off. Venues ranged from the Knoxville Civic Auditorium, to the Martin Luther King Jr. Community Center in McComb, Mississippi, or the

Truth for Youth Center in Lima, Ohio, to, as ever, churches and school auditoriums. One program traveling as the Gospel Train had Clarence on the bill alongside a novelty act, a gospel singing set of Siamese twins, Yvette and Yvonne McCarthey, billed somewhat accurately, if not tastefully, for a 1974 stop in Orangeburg, South Carolina, as "two bodies, one head"—the women were conjoined at the top of the skull.

Butler said, "They were the worst singers in the world. I made money working with them, because I played guitar on the show with them. It was the novelty of them being Siamese twins, the people wanted to see them. Clarence and Johnny Fields promoted them around the country. They made so much money, people crying, coming to the stage and throwing twenties, fifties, in the bucket. They had a big bucket to get that money. They didn't need to make a living—the government paid them a check every month. They both got a check."

After the show, the twins hit the party room where artists gathered to drink, gamble, and unwind. Butler enjoyed their company to a certain extent. "Yvonne and Yvette each had their own personality," he said. "But if you got along with one, you got along with both. When you speak to one, the other would talk back too. They were always talking about getting naked and doing the nasty. A couple guys were talking about dating them. I said, 'Man, you got to be crazy.'"

A few drinks got the twins going. "Let me see what you got," they told Butler. "What you got in your pants? Junior, you coming over here tonight?"

"They were typical human beings," Butler explained. "I believe that Percy from the Swanee Quintet went to bed with them."

Another novelty act graced the stage of the gospel express in these days. "We had a lady named Gloria Spencer, the six-hundred pound woman," Butler recalled. "We went all over the country with Gloria. When we didn't have one novelty, we had another. Now, she could sing. I played with her, too."

Clarence and Butler bonded more closely with a group that many consider among the greatest quartets of all, the Mighty Clouds of Joy, with perhaps the most highly regarded lead singer of the day, Joe Ligon. Born in Troy, Alabama, in 1936, Ligon found inspiration at an early age. "One night Clarence Fountain and the Blind Boys were singing in Alabama," Ligon recalled. "They were young, young men, and I was like about ten years old. My dad said, 'I'm going to hear the Blind Boys tonight, you want to come?' I said, 'Yeah.' He took me to the concert. I met Clarence Fountain. I met George [Scott]... I talked to George—I was scared to talk to Clarence. I told my dad that night, 'I want me a quartet.' And I prayed and asked God to give me a quartet. And thank God, He didn't just give me a quartet...he gave me *the* quartet."

Thanks to this history, Ligon respected Clarence deeply. More importantly for the moment, as Butler pointed out, "the Mighty Clouds were hot at the time." Seen as pioneers of gospel soul, the Mighty Clouds dressed and sang more like a contemporary pop group. Their appeal to an audience became Clarence and Junior's meal ticket. The Mighty Clouds had come together in the mid-1950s after the big wave of golden age quartets and recorded prolifically for gospel's leading label, Peacock, throughout the 1960s. By the 1970s, they had emerged as the premium headliner gospel quartet. The group toured on mixed tickets (brothel and church) with James Brown and Al Green. In a time of newer acts on the gospel highway, Fountain's relationship with Ligon gave him a huge advantage that his former group simply did not have.

CHAPTER 12

THE TWO FACES

CLARENCE FOUNTAIN RECORDED HIS solo albums for Jewel Records, an R&B- and gospel-oriented indie based in Shreveport, Louisiana.

His first, titled *Soul Gospel*, teamed Clarence with producer Ralph Bass and arranger Sonny Thompson. Both knew a few things about great records. Bass had produced James Brown's hit debut "Please, Please, Please" and worked with Muddy Waters and Howlin' Wolf at Chess Records. Thompson, a pianist, never reached the James Brown level of hit, but his "Long Gone" and "Blues for Nightowls," among others, are cool, confident, evocative slices of the long-gone night.

Soul Gospel rehashed much of the more mystifying material from the Blind Boys' 1963 Vee-Jay album *You'll Never Walk Alone*, including, yes, another rendition of the Rodgers and Hammerstein show tune, plus "Danny Boy" and "Looking Back." But the songs feature Fountain, singing without backing vocals, which seems to have been the main point. The liner notes, credited to Johnny Fields, promise, "For the first time in his career, you will hear the real Clarence Fountain." And, in a bit of a reach as awkward as the phrasing, "There are modern arrangements in this album that will attract the attention of teenagers." Touted as "the master key that will unlock the remaining doors for gospel music to be accepted by the general audience," the record did not achieve—musically, critically, or commercially—the lofty hope of its producers.

A subsequent release dropped the pretension, showcasing Fountain in his element, performing live. A later product, the 1974 LP *Soul, Spirit, and Song*, shows Clarence on the cover decked out in a salmon-colored suit of knee-length jacket with matching pants. This super-fly look embodied Fountain's mid-1970s self-image. "Clarence always wanted to be pimpy," Sam Butler said, "because the women were after him."

———◆———

Butler describes his and Fountain's womanizing as a total addiction. "He had a woman in every town," Butler said. "It was fun, but it was a job. You never have a night off with Clarence, because if you're not working, you're taking him to one of his women."

Fountain nevertheless had a wholesome side. When he wasn't touring, Clarence spent most of his nights in Chapel Hill with a lady named Faye Alston. It was a happy home in a friendly neighborhood. Robert Weaver, a friend of Alston and colleague of Fountain, had introduced them and lived nearby. Alston and Fountain regularly kept Clarence's second daughter Brenda overnight. Other family members and friends stayed in the area, as did George Scott and Olice Thomas.

The woman with whom Fountain made this home is a formidable figure in her own right. As a high school student in the early 1960s, when civil rights activists made news in nearby Greensboro, Faye Alston and her friends had demonstrated outside Colonial Drug Store in Chapel Hill to protest the store policy barring Black customers from the lunch counter. She graduated high school in 1962 and attended North Carolina A&T State University, where students had carried out the sit-in campaign against a local Woolworth's that had inspired Alston and made national news. She joined student marches against segregation in Greensboro, noting that A&T football players were stationed around the marchers and caught rocks hurled at the students.

Ten years later, Alston read the daily paper and often told Clarence, "You should hear this," before reading an important news story aloud.

Her memories of Fountain are less of the leisure-suited singer whom Junior Butler lived with and more of a gentle soul. "Clarence was a talker," Alston recalled. "He was a very friendly person. I introduced him to my family and my friends. I had a daughter very young, and she loved her Uncle Clarence."

Clarence made Faye and her daughter part of his life as a singer. "When they had programs, we would take her with us and she worried him crazy to go on stage with him," Alston recalled. "It was fun times with him. I went with him many times."

Alston remembers how Fountain pushed the boundaries of the blind world.

"Clarence wanted to drive," she said. "Robert Weaver let him get in a place where it was no cars and they let him drive a little short distance. I wouldn't have been near that car."

Off the road, Fountain was a big part of Alston's home life. She laughed, remembering a time that she redecorated without telling Clarence. "Not thinking that he was blind, I moved things around. When he came in, he walked into everything and he said, 'Now when you move furniture, you need to let me know.'"

He could get a little too comfortable in these surroundings. Alston once came home from work and smelled smoke outside her house. She ran in and found Clarence in the kitchen trying to cook. "I said, 'Boy, you better be glad I got off work early,'" she said.

The two built a life together throughout the early 1970s. "When I bought my house, Clarence helped me financially," Alston recalled. "If ever I needed anything, he was there."

Just as Alston's daughter adored Clarence, Faye became close with Clarence's second daughter. "I formed a friendship with Brenda," Alston said. "She is a nice young lady. She and Robert Weaver's children and my daughter were always into something in the neighborhood."

Alston visited Clarence's family in Detroit and welcomed them into her home as well. "He had a brother named Chester, who I liked. He came to my home. They had one older sister who was very protective of Clarence. His younger sister, she also looked after him. His mama and sisters teased with him all the time. He came up in a very nice family. I got along with them fine."

Plenty of others knew the same Clarence Fountain. He cared for his friends, loved his family, and stayed as active in the lives of his children as his circumstances allowed. When he arrived in Detroit, his mother greeted him gleefully, "Boonanny come home!"

This side of him simply couldn't help in the gospel world. Competition and survival dictated his conduct at work. Fear, suspicion, and the knowledge that total uncertainty and extreme financial pressure awaited his blind self around the next corner, maybe on the next day, motivated him. He had only considered leaving the road once, and at that point he found an opportunity in a box factory. That wouldn't do. The road was his life.

By the mid- to late 1970s, as he approached his fiftieth birthday, Clarence Fountain had six children. Those children and their mothers consistently report that Fountain did his best to take care of them and never declined a request for financial help. One of his exes later recalled him wishing her well in a marriage but warning that if her husband mistreated her, that man would have the Blind Boys after him.

At home, Faye Alston never knew the extent of Fountain's financial responsibilities beyond the cash in his wallet. That, she put in order from big to small bills so that Clarence could keep track of what he had.

Over time, Fountain's fondness for women became clearer to Faye. "He would always feel a woman's face," she said. "That's how he saw you. It didn't matter about your size. What impressed him is what sighted people would say about the ladies who were attracted to him. He just had a knack for women, he could draw women to him. Clarence stayed into something all the time."

Fountain's other lives finally caught up to him. "Clarence and I dated for about twelve years," Alston said. "He was strollin' other places I didn't know about. I had really thought that Clarence and I were going to get married. I guess it really wasn't meant to be, because I got this strange telephone call from this female that was asking for Clarence. She said that she and Clarence were supposed to be getting married. After that, me and Clarence started separating. I don't even remember us arguing."

Faye asked Clarence who the woman was, and he claimed he didn't know. "I didn't believe him at all," Faye said.

Faye Alston was right to disbelieve Clarence. He was leading a double, if not a triple, life.

In 1974, Fountain's son Chris Hay was born. "He came to Augusta, Georgia," Hay said, "to do a show, and met my mom at the show. One thing led to another. He wasn't ashamed of his life. He told the truth. He had kids by different ladies because he traveled a lot. They couldn't stay in hotels. People invited him to stay in their home, they made friends, and sometimes it turned into a little romance. That's just the way it was back then."

Hay appreciated Fountain's effort to stay close. His comments echo those of Fountain's children born twenty years earlier in other states. "He wasn't a person who would go around having kids and just forget about them," Hay said. "He always reached out, he always provided. He wasn't around physically, because he stayed on the road, but I knew who he was, I never had any negative feeling toward him. We laughed and talked about anything as I got older."

<hr />

The white van, colorfully painted with the name "Original Five Blind Boys of Alabama," became even more like a family home during the mid-1970s.

Just as Johnny Fields's sighted wife, Mattie, had taken an interest in the Blind Boys' business while her husband managed the group, Olice Thomas's wife, Callie, sought to help her husband after he took over the business end. In 1974, she went out on the road with the group. With Miss Callie in tow, George and Olice would have to develop telepathy to keep up their discussion of "squins"—their code word for road women.

Along the way, Olice and Miss Callie introduced lead singer Charles Porter to their granddaughter Pam. Charles and Pam married and had a child. And so Olice and his wife, granddaughter, grandson-in-law, and great-grandchild all traveled with the band.

The caravan trucked on despite hard times, for the group and the country at large. The 1973 oil embargo raised US gas prices and decreased the available supply, leading to long lines of cars at gas pumps and fuel rationing.

The Blind Boys had their own twofold economic issues. Neither their recording career nor their performances were paying off. Porter believed that HOB Records released bad product on the Blind Boys. "There was something going on," he said. "HOB put an album out but they didn't produce it properly. Tracks were running into each other. It didn't sound professional. It was terrible. I couldn't believe they put it out like that. The worst."

As Porter well knew, a hot record could propel a group down the road even in times of fuel rationing. Without a current hit, and with Clarence Fountain competing with them, they had longer jumps from one show to the next. "Sometimes we'd be the only ones on the road in horrible weather, icy roads, trying to make that next gig," said Porter. "When the money gets smaller, the gigs get farther apart."

He had begun to feel the effects of road life, the exhaustion and cynicism. He saw things that didn't square with his upbringing or the message of the music. "There were shows where we went into checkup," Porter said. "That's when you go into a room with the promoter to collect your money for the night. He would call each group to meet, one at a time. I heard that guys would go into checkup with pistols because the promoters were crooked. I remember many times Olice would come back from checkup and say that the promoter didn't have all the money. George would hit the ceiling. He felt that Olice was too easy in checkup. He would get talked down."

Especially in checkup, the power of the hit record prevailed. "The groups that had hits, they would get all their money and they would get called in first. As they work down the list, the promoter would find ways to cut the groups who didn't have the hot records. We were one of the groups that didn't have hot records," Porter explained. "This happened more times than I'd like to remember."

They'd sit and wait to get stiffed at checkup, then head out and wait at the gas pump to fill up and get going. Sometimes they sat there all night until the gas station opened, too close to empty to roll on.

Business got so tough, Porter remembers, that the great Rev. Julius Cheeks worked gimmicks on audiences in order to shake loose a little donation. "He said we had to pawn the car battery to make the show," Porter recalled. "I thought I was a real Christian when I first got out there," he added. "The way my mother raised me didn't look nothing like what was going on."

Porter saw the audience dwindle as inflation kept people away in 1974 and 1975. "There were nights when we made just enough money to get the baby Pampers and milk," he said.

Porter realized that he and Pam couldn't raise their son in such a way. They left the road and returned to Detroit, where they still live. Porter came out wiser. "The people don't really know what you have to go through," he said. "They see you on stage, dressed in flashy colors. Entertainers wear two faces: they've got one on stage and the real one."

CHAPTER 13

DON'T LET THE DEVIL
SEPARATE Y'ALL APART

DURING THE LATE 1970S, cryptic little notices popped up in newspaper want ads in the Deep South.

"Come with us, see Doctor Dallas Moore, and receive a blessing."

"For a Few Days, a Spiritual Encounter with Doctor Dallas Moore."

"Carpool with me to Donalsonville, GA, to see Rev. Dr. Dallas Moore."

Practically every weekend Greyhound charters left Atlanta, Macon, Fort Lauderdale, Miami, and Orlando, all headed to

Donalsonville in the southwest corner of Georgia, much nearer Tallahassee than Atlanta. There lived Dr. Dallas Moore, a man of renowned divine power. On a sandy lot outside town, not far from the Chattahoochee River, Moore owned a compound consisting of a small hotel and restaurant, his home and office, and a few outbuildings. Thousands of visitors flocked to him there to receive blessings.

Dr. Moore performed what some believers could only describe as miracles. His lucky court date anointments were particularly popular, boasting a hit rate comparable to that of an all-star baseball slugger's batting average. Moore practiced herbal medicine with some visitors, applying botanicals he'd dug from the ground—making him truly a root doctor—but his gifts went well beyond the tangible into the deep mystical. He could behold a vision showing the future of a visitor.

One of them was Clarence Fountain. Clarence could have used a little good luck and guidance. His life had grown almost endlessly complicated. He'd had another child, probably his last, and gotten married, though not to the child's mother, not long after he and Faye Alston went their separate ways. He had financial and personal entanglements across the map and increasing challenges on the road. Things got rocky with another of his longtime partners, guitarist Sam "Junior" Butler.

"He thought that his wife slept with me," Butler said. "Well, she was like a mother to me. I wouldn't do that, I didn't need that. It's not worth it. From that point, we were not as close. We had a few dates in Jersey, and I had made up my mind to get missing for a minute."

Butler went to New York and hooked up with keyboardist Bob Telson. They formed a rhythm and blues club band called Night & Day. This connection would pay off in time, but at the moment it yielded nothing bigger than bar gigs for Butler and left Clarence to fend for himself.

Without a band and with dwindling opportunities and headaches in his personal life, Clarence Fountain took the trip to Donalsonville. Clarence soon came to believe in Dr. Moore's powers. And changes took place.

———◆———

Elder J. T. Hutton had left the Happy Land Jubilee Singers in June 1946 to start a family. Hutton and his wife, Margaret, bought a home in Birmingham and had nine children. Hutton also remained part of the Blind Boys' extended family, housing and feeding the group whenever they passed through.

Hutton made the most of his partial eyesight. "My dad had worked for the city a while," Donald Ray Hutton said. "That's when old Bull Connor decided he's gon' fire all the Black folks, which he did."

Elder Hutton went back to school in Talladega and learned to run a small retail establishment. He returned to Birmingham with his new skill. "My dad had a little store, little concession stand at the housing projects in Ensley," Donald Ray said. "He ran that for twelve years."

Gospel remained a prominent part of Elder Hutton's life. He preached at the Trinity Church of God in Christ and sang at revivals, featuring his own creative compositions, titles like "Come On in This Ark It's Gonna Rain" and "If the Lord Would Call You Tonight You Had Your Chance." Having called her husband home from the road, Margaret encouraged him to follow his dream later in life. "Mama told him, 'Come on out of that snack bar,'" said Donald Ray. "She encouraged him to run his own revivals." Father and son traveled around the state for five or six years, by Donald Ray's recollection.

Elder Hutton felt bothered by the breakup of his old buddies. So, in 1978, he called a summit. "My dad decided he wanted to get the group back together—Clarence, Johnny, Olice, and George," Donald Ray said. Hutton gathered the Blind Boys in his living room, a place where they'd often grabbed a few winks of sleep during better times, and told them, "The Lord been too good to y'all to let the devil separate y'all apart."

In the city where they'd first gone professional almost thirty-five years before, in the Jerusalem of the quartet world, the Blind Boys of Alabama reunited. "That was my daddy's main concern," Donald Ray said. "He wanted to see the old group get back together."

Above and beyond Elder Hutton's best intentions, the Blind Boys reunited out of necessity rather than sentiment. Clarence had no band, and the Blind Boys had never replaced him as a lead. So here they were: Clarence, with his steely exterior protecting an increasingly heavy heart; George, the brooding genius who never quite put it together as a lead voice; and Olice and Johnny, who, by substantial accounts from this time, often had their mikes turned off during performances. As much as they had made things difficult for each other, they also looked out for one another, keeping men on the payroll who might not necessarily carry equal weight musically.

They got back together in time for a World Series of Gospel event promoted in Memphis, remembered as a successful outing and a good performance for the reunited singers. As Johnny Fields recalled, "After three or four appearances together, we decided to go all out and try it again." By March 1978, they were back on the road, performing in tiny, out-of-the-way venues, double-billed with the Siamese Twins.

Clarence and Sam Butler reconnected, and Clarence promised to never let a woman come between them again. Butler joined the Blind Boys as a guitarist and driver, and he brought his Night & Day partner Bob Telson with him on some gigs. A White piano and organ player, Telson would be a pivotal figure in the most important moment of the Blind Boys' career. But first: rock bottom.

CHAPTER 14

TO BE BLOUNT

THOUGH CLARENCE FOUNTAIN AND Sam Butler hadn't been apart for
long, Sam couldn't help noticing something different about
Clarence.

"Clarence was walking around with a skull tied to his waist,"
Butler said. "He was believing in roots."

In 1979, the reformed Blind Boys of Alabama recorded *I
Found a Friend* for the ALA label, their first album with Foun-
tain in the lead since 1967. This time the group was billed as
Clarence Fountain and the Blind Boys.

"They couldn't draw flies to a dead body," Butler said. "We
went on some dates with Shirley Caesar in New York and New
Jersey. Olice, George, and Johnny stayed at the President Hotel

downtown. Clarence stayed out with his girlfriend in the Bronx. The program bombed, we had no money."

In total desperation during this era, Clarence brought a new member to the team, not a musician but a full-speed hustler he'd met through his root doctor connections named Aubrey "Lamont" Blount.

As far as Butler could ever determine, Blount had worked in a family-owned funeral home and dabbled in the occult, learning under masters like Dr. Dallas Moore and Rev. Roosevelt Franklin of Macon, Georgia.

Other musicians who worked with the Blind Boys during this time agree that Blount's hustling went beyond witchcraft.

As Blount became the group's manager, it became clear that Clarence feared him as a root worker and that Blount had a psychological hold on Clarence. With limited contacts in the music business as such, Blount used Clarence and his gospel highway connections in a more resourceful manner.

"Blount and Clarence were moving stolen cars," Butler explained. "Clarence had enough people across the country to buy the cars. Promoters, fans, other groups. He'd peddle them cars, 'I got a Thunderbird, I got a Lincoln.' Clarence was the contact man. Blount was the robber. Blount stole the cars in Detroit. One robber [working for Blount] got shot stealing cars. He'll never walk again. This thing was serious. A couple groups almost went to jail for getting pulled over in these vehicles."

According to a version of events that Sam Butler and others heard, Clarence and Blount were at Blount's place in Atlanta one day in late 1981 or early 1982 when police came to the home. Clarence—always able to blindly navigate his way through familiar surroundings—slipped into a bedroom and hid underneath a bed while the police arrested Blount.

Apparently Blount confessed to his role in the car heist scheme. The September 9, 1982, *Montgomery Advertiser* reported that Blount had been sentenced in federal court.

> Blount received two concurrent three-year sentences after he pleaded guilty to two counts of a four-count indictment that charged him with the interstate transportation of a stolen vehicle.
>
> The three-year sentences are to run consecutively with a sentence Blount is already serving in Georgia.

There are, however, competing visions of Clarence Fountain, as a whole and specifically in these circumstances. Donald Dillon, who would become a fixture in Fountain's life in 1987, said that Fountain, innocently of the purpose, loaned Blount the seed money for this scheme and received repayment from Blount, seemingly from the ill-got gains. Fountain, Dillon attests, had nothing more to do with the stolen-car caper.

"Blount had told Clarence he had a deal, something in the pot cooking," Dillon said. "He told Clarence that if he would loan him a certain amount of money, he would double it. That sounded like a deal to Clarence. If you call me up and say, 'Give me five hundred dollars and I'll give you a thousand in two days,' why wouldn't I make five hundred dollars in two days, if I could?"

Dillon said that falsehoods about Clarence's involvement started with Blount. "When Blount got caught, he wanted to say that it was all because of Clarence," Dillon explained. "Everyone want to think Clarence was involved and that Blount took the fall. Blount tried to make people think that. I was in their presence one time. This matter came up. Clarence said, 'Blount, you know I wasn't involved in none of that.' Blount told him, 'I never said you were.' Clarence said,

'You're trying to destroy my character and credibility, and that's not gonna work.' Blount said, 'I ain't told nobody that.'"

Just as the bracelets closed on Blount, the Blind Boys released a new album, the most ambitious recording project of their career, one that welcomed two important new members to the lineup. Roscoe Robinson, who'd left gospel after crossing Don Robey in the early 1960s, joined up as the latest in a long line of sighted co-lead singers.

"Don Robey couldn't kill me forever," Robinson said. "I started back with the Blind Boys of Alabama with Clarence Fountain. Me and Clarence were friends. I used to process his hair. One day he said, 'Why don't you come in the group? Sing with me.' I didn't think the Blind Boys of Alabama were as big as the Blind Boys of Mississippi. I didn't think they had the prestige. But I loved Clarence, beautiful guy."

Nearly forty years after staying behind at the Alabama School for the Negro Deaf and Blind in Talladega while the Happy Land Singers hit the road for good, Jimmy Lee Carter reunited with his schoolmates. He had been in the more prestigious Blind Boys of Mississippi for nearly two decades.

Both Robinson and Sam Butler Jr. recorded tracks featuring the new lineup, Robinson producing his in Birmingham and Butler working in Tampa. Robinson said that he sent his tracks to Tony Beck, a gospel producer affiliated with the hit-making production team of Kenneth Gamble and Leon Huff in Philadelphia, and Gamble and Huff signed the Blind Boys. In addition to the songs cut in Tampa and Birmingham, they recorded in Philadelphia. A variety of producers, writers, arrangers, and engineers worked on each track, with Gamble and Huff themselves chipping in, as did Bobby Womack's brother Cecil, guitarist Eddie "Spanky" Alford, and bluesman Cash McCall. The whole deal got the Blind Boys closer to the big time than they'd been since leaving Specialty Records a quarter century earlier.

I'm a Soldier in the Army of the Lord featured almost all new material, with the exception of the title track. Though credited to Gamble and Womack, "(I'm a) Soldier (in the Army of the Lord)" covered a Blind Boys of Mississippi song from back in Archie Brownlee's days, "I'm a Soldier." Song arrangements incorporated string sections, horns, and a feeling of late disco, carried forward on the cover with a photo of Fountain, Robinson, Carter, Johnny Fields, and George Scott decked out in white suits with gold trim, looking a bit more like the cruise ship staff of the Lord.

The album launched a new offshoot of Gamble and Huff's Philadelphia International Records, focused on gospel: Peace International. The release made news in *Billboard*, which reported that the first pressing of five thousand had sold out, another pressing was imminent, and the Blind Boys were on a thirty-city tour to promote the record. Gamble said he hoped that Peace International could rival the impact of the Philadelphia International enterprise.

Truthfully, though, Philadelphia International was on the decline. The company ended or lost its long distribution deal with CBS Records during the same year as the *Soldier* release. Peace issued maybe a total of three albums, and this ambitious return of the Blind Boys today is a collector's item, a remnant of another stillborn dream. With their would-be manager in jail and their breakthrough album dead on arrival, the Blind Boys seemed destined to wander the desert.

Little could they know, salvation awaited in the form of a shaggy, bearded Jewish guy.

PART III

RESURRECTION

CHAPTER 15

THE GOSPEL AT COLONUS

N 1973, I WAS a hippie trying to play R&B, living in Tribeca," said Bob Telson.

The keyboard player had found inspiration in Aretha Franklin's 1972 live gospel album *Amazing Grace*. Realizing that he could hear music like Aretha's in person, Telson took the A train to Harlem and visited a big church on 123rd Street one Sunday.

Mingling with hundreds of sharply dressed worshippers, Telson witnessed drama, spectacle, and spirit, plus a full band with a horn section and a choir. At one point the minister paused his sermon to welcome visitors. He asked them to stand and testify about what Jesus had done for them.

"I stood up," Telson recalled. "I'm not only Jewish but was brought up a staunch Atheist. It was not the most obvious question for me to answer. Up there in my ill-fitting suit and tie with my long hair, I said, 'I'm a musician and the music really moves me.'"

Further prompted by the preacher, Telson said he played piano, to which the minister replied, "We have a piano, come up here and sing us a song."

Telson headed up front, figuring out what to do as he walked. "I had discovered a tape of some obscure gospel group who did a version of Sam & Dave's 'When Something Is Wrong with My Baby,' and the version they did was 'Nothing Is Wrong with My Jesus, Something Is Wrong with Me,'" Telson recalled. "I had played it a couple times and learned the lyrics, so I played and sang that song in church."

He won over a politely encouraging flock. "By the last chorus the entire congregation was standing on its feet, clapping and singing along with me," Telson said.

After the service, people congratulated Bob and told him he'd better come back. "I realized that the doors of the Black church are open," he said. "There was not only great music there, but a spiritual message that is not easily attainable in our society. I started going to Black churches quite a lot."

Telson also frequented nightclubs, and in one such Harlem establishment he encountered Sam Butler, who had decided to "go missing for a minute" from Clarence Fountain. "Sam would bring the band down in the middle of a song and tell a story, or preach as it were," said Telson. "It was powerful, his ability to take a song and tell a story the way a preacher would take scripture and make a story out of it, with a lesson."

Telson and Butler became friends and formed a band, Night & Day. They played clubs off and on for five years during the mid- to late 1970s. Butler also brought Telson along to cut some spiritual music. "When Sam was living in Newark, he had me play on a few gospel recordings with local groups, the Stephens Singers among them," Telson said.

When Night & Day hit a slump, Butler went back to Fountain, who by this time had reunited with the Blind Boys of Alabama. Butler once again brought Bob Telson along. "I played a bunch of gigs traveling around the Northeast, playing small Black churches," Telson said.

Telson felt elated just to be there. He savored the experience of playing with the Blind Boys in an authentic setting and soaked up the powerful singing he heard. The Blind Boys, on the other hand, were all business, and business was not always good. "The money was funny on about one out of every three gigs," Telson recalled. "The experience was wonderful for me. Meanwhile, the Blind Boys are all pissed off because the promoter's giving lame excuses for why he isn't paying them what he's supposed to pay them. The Blind Boys would be reluctant to go on until they could get paid properly. The fans were out there waiting, clapping their hands, and some agreement would be made, probably for less than the original amount, and we'd go on, the place would go crazy, and afterwards I'd be in heaven. But they'd be pissed off."

Telson saw the Blind Boys turn it on for the people. "Clarence had this schtick where Sam would lead him off stage and he'd come crawling back to sing some more and the crowd just went crazy," he said. "They really knew how to work the crowd, and it was spectacular."

Meanwhile, Telson had worked with playwright Lee Breuer on a doo-wop opera, *Sister Suzie Cinema*, which opened in New York and Los Angeles in 1980. Breuer, who had also based a play on a Samuel Beckett poem, began developing an extraordinary musical version of Sophocles's ancient tragedy *Oedipus at Colonus*. The show debuted in Europe during the summer of 1982, playing festivals with a scaled-down book and the group 14 Karat Soul, who'd starred in *Sister Suzie Cinema*, in the footlights. The *London Observer* reviewed the production favorably, but Breuer and Telson kept working.

Though seemingly unbeknownst to Breuer and Telson, a figure long associated with the Blind Boys had done some pioneering work in the Black gospel musical genre.

Throughout the 1960s, Bumps Blackwell, who produced the Blind Boys at Specialty Records during the 1950s, had directed Black gospel shows for nightclubs. His 1960 production *Portraits in Bronze* ran successfully in Las Vegas and Los Angeles. His gospel rock musical *Bicycle of the Lord* played in 1970, featuring his longtime protégé Bessie Griffin. Meanwhile, the Langston Hughes play *Black Nativity* had opened off-Broadway in 1961, creating something of a legacy for Black church productions.

After returning from Europe, Telson invited Breuer to a Blind Boys concert in Harlem, not far from the church where Telson himself had found the Spirit. Breuer came out of the show with a bizarre new vision for his take on Sophocles. "After the show Lee said that Clarence and the Blind Boys were going to be Oedipus," Telson recalled. "That had never occurred to me in any way."

Telson said that he and Breuer met with Sam Butler and Clarence Fountain after the show in a Cadillac parked behind the venue. The two men agreed to give it a shot.

With the *Observer* review building interest for *The Gospel at Colonus* in American theatrical circles, and with the Blind Boys on board, Breuer got a two-week residency at the Walker Art Center in Minneapolis to prepare for the opening at the Brooklyn Academy of Music (BAM) in November 1983.

Happy Land Jubilee Singers. Left to right: Johnny Fields, Clarence Fountain,
J. T. Hutton, Olice Thomas, George Scott, Velma Traylor. Circa 1944.
Photo provided courtesy of the Alabama Institute of the Deaf & Blind archives

The Five Blind Boys of
Alabama promotional photo.
Front, left to right: Johnny
Fields, Olice Thomas.
Back, left to right: George
Scott, Rev. Paul Exkano,
Clarence Fountain.
Circa 1948–1952.
Courtesy of Lynn Abbott

1955 advertisement for a "Battle" between the Five Blind Boys of Mississippi and Five Blind Boys of Alabama. Top right photo: Happyland Singers / Blind Boys of Alabama. Bottom left photo: Jackson Harmoneers / Blind Boys of Mississippi. *Photo provided by Preston Lauterbach*

The Blind Boys in 1955. Bottom, left to right: George Scott, Johnny Fields, Clarence Fountain. Top, left to right: Rev. G. W. Warren, Olice Thomas, Rev. Samuel K. Lewis. *Photo provided by Preston Lauterbach*

The Five Blind Boys of Alabama promotional photo hanging inside the Apollo Theatre in Harlem, New York. Left to right: Rev. Purcell Perkins, Clarence Fountain, Olice Thomas, Johnny Fields, George Scott. Circa 1957.

Photo of the photo taken by Charles Driebe

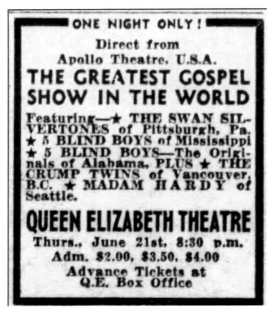

Ad for an early international Blind Boys concert in Vancouver, B.C. *Photo provided by Preston Lauterbach*

Longtime Blind Boys of Alabama lead singer Clarence Fountain. *Photo by Dave Peabody via Getty Images*

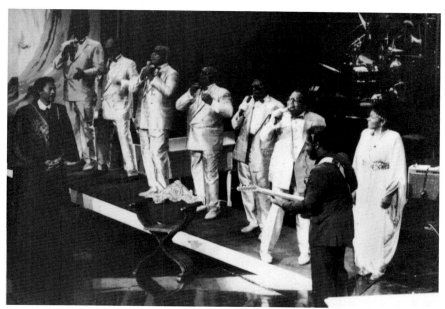

Morgan Freeman and the Blind Boys in *The Gospel at Colonus*.
Photo by Star Tribune via Getty Images

Jimmy Carter performing in the crowd on the Blind Boys
first UK tour in Brighton at the Event in 1992.
Photo by Charles Paul Harris from Michael Ochs Archives via Getty Images

George Scott showing Joey Williams some guitar licks.
Photo by Monica Lewis-Williams

Jimmy Carter meeting Hillary Clinton on the Blind Boys first
White House visit in 1995 for the National Heritage Fellowship Awards Ceremony.
Photo provided by Kevin Morrow

The Blind Boys performing at the Bottom Line in New York City in 2001.
Left to right: Bobby Butler, George Scott, Clarence Fountain,
Jimmy Carter, Joey Williams.
Photo by Hiroyuki Ito via Hulton Archive and Getty Images

The Blind Boys
performing
at the Belly Up
in Solana Beach,
California, circa 2001.
Left to right:
David Lindley,
Charlie Musselwhite,
Clarence Fountain,
Jimmy Carter,
Joey Williams.
Photo by Steve Sherman

The Blind Boys recording with Ben Harper at Capitol Studios in Los Angeles, California, circa 2003. Left to right: George Scott, Jimmy Carter, Ben Harper, Clarence Fountain. *Photo by Steve Sherman*

Jay Leno with the Blind Boys following a *Tonight Show* performance on February 3, 2003. Left to right: George Scott, Clarence Fountain, Ricky McKinnie, Jay Leno, Jimmy Carter, Joey Williams. *Photo provided by NBC Universal and Getty Images*

Stevie Wonder presenting a Lifetime Achievement Award to Jimmy Carter and the Blind Boys at the 34th Annual Vision Awards—honoring those who have made significant contributions to the ongoing fight against degenerative blindness—at the Beverly Hilton in 2007 in Los Angeles, California.
Photo by John M. Heller via Getty Images

The Blind Boys in *The Gospel at Colonus* on tour in St. Paul, Minnesota, at Ordway Center for the Performing Arts, August 2010. Cast of the musical with Jimmy Carter, Bobby Butler, Ben Moore, Sam Butler, Joey Williams.
Photo by Melissa Gaul

The Blind Boys of Alabama and team at the White House in 2010 to perform as part of "In Performance at the White House: A Celebration of Music from the Civil Rights Movement." Left to right: Mike Kappus, Ben Moore, Chris Goldsmith, Billy Bowers, Michelle Obama, President Barack Obama, Jimmy Carter, Charles Driebe, Ricky McKinnie, Joey Williams, Sue Schrader.

Photo provided by Sue Schrader

Willie Nelson, Jamey Johnson, and the Blind Boys on May 6, 2011, at New Orleans Jazz & Heritage Festival. Left to right: Mickey Raphael, Jamey Johnson, Willie Nelson, Ricky McKinnie, Joey Williams, Jimmy Carter.
Photo by Marc Millman Photography

Robert Plant and the Blind Boys while on tour together in Australia in 2013. Left to right: Tracy Pierce, Ben Moore, Ricky McKinnie, Robert Plant, Jimmy Carter, Joey Williams.
Photo by Willie Chuck Shivers

New Orleans Music Royalty and the Blind Boys at a tribute to Dr. John in New Orleans at Saenger Theatre on May 3, 2014. Left to right: Ricky McKinnie, Ben Moore, Jimmy Carter, Irma Thomas, Joey Williams, Chuck Leavell, Dr. John, Allen Toussaint, Aaron Neville. *Photo by Charles Driebe*

Taj Mahal and the Blind Boys at the Capitol Theatre in Port Chester, New York, in 2014. Left to right: Paul Beasley, Ricky McKinnie, Taj Mahal, Jimmy Carter, Ben Moore, Joey Williams. *Photo by Charles Driebe*

Congressman John Lewis and the Blind Boys at the 50th Anniversary of "Bloody Sunday," the crossing of the Edmund Pettus Bridge in Selma, Alabama, by civil rights marchers in 1965. Left to right: Ben Moore, Paul Beasley, Ricky McKinnie, Congressman John Lewis, Jimmy Carter.
Photo by Willie Chuck Shivers

Tom Jones and the Blind Boys at Byron Bay Bluesfest in Australia in 2016. Left to right: Ricky McKinnie, Ben Moore, Tom Jones, Joey Williams, Jimmy Carter, Paul Beasley. *Photo by Willie Chuck Shivers*

The Blind Boys in studio recording for their album *Almost Home* in Seattle in 2016. Left to right: Ben Moore, Jimmy Carter, Paul Beasley, Ricky McKinnie.

Photo by Charles Driebe

The Blind Boys *Almost Home* promotional photo. Left to right: Joey Williams, Ben Moore, Jimmy Carter, Ricky McKinnie, Paul Beasley.
Photo by Jim Herrington

The Blind Boys bowing after a set in South Australia at WOMADelaide in 2020.
Joey Williams, Ben Moore, Jimmy Carter, Ricky McKinnie, Paul Beasley,
Ray Ladson, Austin Moore, Matt Hopkins, Willie Chuck Shivers.
Photo by Charlotte Lucy Emily Sawbridge

The Blind Boys 2020 promotional photo. Left to right: Joey Williams, Ben Moore,
Jimmy Carter, Ricky McKinnie, Rev. Julius Love.
Photo by Michael Weintrob

Amadou & Mariam and the Blind Boys on the Bamako to Birmingham Tour playing Stockholm, Sweden, March 19, 2022, at Konserhuset.
Left to right: Yves Abadi, Amadou Bagayoko, Mariam Doumbia, Sam Dickey, Joey Williams, Jimmy Carter, Ricky McKinnie.
Photo by Danish Saroee

Though the concept generated tremendous enthusiasm, pulling it off required intensive preparation. Fountain and the Blind Boys had never performed in a play and faced certain disadvantages as blind actors finding their marks and learning their lines. The music, though, flowed naturally. "I would work with them and teach my ideas," said Telson, "but they would take those parts and interpret them their own way to sound rootsy and real. They understood my ideas and personalized the stuff."

Sam Butler felt that the contributions of other musicians to *Colonus* deserved more notice. "Bob took credit for everything I, Butch Hayward, and J. D. Steele added," Butler said. "The music evolved with us." Butler also had to assemble a crew of background singers on the fly as the Blind Boys' lineup changed. J. T. Clinkscales and Joe Watson from the Blind Boys of Mississippi joined the *Colonus* cast after Johnny Fields and Olice Thomas left.

When the curtain rose in Brooklyn, however, they were ready. Mostly. "During the first shows at BAM, Clarence had an earpiece in and somebody feeding him his lines," Telson said. "He quickly learned his lines and spiced up the way he delivered them. He ad-libbed, and stuck his hip out with a big smile on his face. It added a playfulness to the story."

The Blind Boys' stage presence added instant gravity. "The power of seeing the men walk out on stage with their hands on each others' shoulders, and seeing them sing together so well brought a magic to the show," Telson said.

As if having five singers play Oedipus wasn't complicated enough, the character's narration often shifts to a more conventional actor playing a preacher addressing a congregation with tales of his tribulations. Oedipus at this moment faces the end of his life after impregnating his mother and killing his father—thus the famous complex—and blinding himself as punishment. For the role of the preacher, Breuer had chosen an up-and-coming actor then known, if at all, for appearing on *Sesame Street*: Morgan Freeman. In delivering the life of Oedipus in sermon form, Freeman flashed his ability to channel a godlike voice, for the first though not the last time. "I had never heard of Morgan Freeman," Telson said. "It was a stroke of great fortune to have him in the show. He was wonderful. He did the entire run at BAM and did other runs. He came back to do Broadway in 1988, by which time he was well known. Morgan got along with the Blind Boys beautifully."

Breuer cast Robert Earl Jones, James Earl Jones's father, and for good measure added the Soul Stirrers, the J. D. Vance Singers, and the Steele Singers, in addition to a full choir.

The production must be seen to be properly believed, and fortunately the 1985 PBS *Great Performances* version featuring the classic cast is a search and a click away. Freeman holds the play together, but Clarence Fountain and the Blind Boys steal the show. The talent of Sam Butler, longtime Fountain and Blind Boys collaborator, shines throughout. Breuer, Telson, and Butler create magic in the "Stop Do Not Go On" number, mixing the words of Sophocles with the guitar style of Pops Staples rendered with Butler's brilliant talent.

A review published in the November 14, 1983, *Newsday* gushed. Praising the ambition, spectacle, and musical texture of *The Gospel at Colonus*, Peter Goodman urged, "If you read no further in this review, hurry to BAM to see it." As Goodman notes, the Blind Boys fit their role in one sense because Oedipus, by this late phase of his life, had lost his eyesight, and the *Colonus* story translates well to Black gospel. The reviewer hurled but one tomato, seemingly not familiar enough with its target: "Freeman Morgan, far too tentative, is the weakest link."

The Gospel at Colonus thus began a long but jumpy run, playing off and on in theater residencies across the country for the next several years. "Getting this thing with *Colonus* was much bigger and better than anything we were doing on the road," Sam Butler said. "We were making six bucks a night, thirty bucks a night. We were not making any money. We started seeing four hundred dollars a week."

In November 1984, a *Baltimore Sun* critic wrote of a performance in Washington, DC, "It scores its first hit when we see Oedipus portrayed by five blind black men in sunglasses and tuxedos, leading each other down a celestial staircase. When Clarence Fountain, a frenzied, raw-voiced singer leads his mellow quartet of backup singers in 'A Voice Foretold,' the worlds of ancient Greece and contemporary gospel music meet on common ground."

The DC run of *Colonus* proved momentous for Clarence personally as well as professionally. His second daughter, Brenda Fountain Johnson, recalled, "I was in my thirties and thought I was the only child." After joining the military in 1971, Johnson spent time in Washington, DC, often visiting Sarah, her dad's girlfriend there. Sarah brought Brenda to the theater to see her dad in the play. Backstage, Sarah told Brenda, "I got a surprise for you."

Sarah brought Brenda to where Clarence was seated with another young lady beside him. "This is your sister," Sarah said, introducing Brenda Johnson to Clarence's first-born child, Brenda Davis.

"I felt kind of weird," said Johnson. "My dad never said a word." Despite the silence of King Oedipus, the ice broke pretty quickly. "We have the same first and middle name," Johnson quipped.

The two Brendas got to know each other, became friends, and started piecing together their dad's personal life, a maze of complications that makes Sophocles seem like Dr. Seuss.

Though Clarence had remained silent at this first meeting, he grew from the experience, managing a complete sentence when introducing Johnson to her brother at a program in Savannah. "This is Chris," Clarence said.

Now all of Clarence's children are in touch with each other and with the Fountain family roots in Detroit. They are close, friendly, and helpful to one another in processing their father's unusual family history. Brenda Davis said, "In later years, my father wanted to know whether me and his other children were communicating. That meant a lot to him."

Whether performing as Oedipus, a man destroyed by ignorance of his own complicated family situation, nudged Clarence to make his own children known to each other remains a mysterious but powerful connection between actor and character.

In 1984, *The Gospel at Colonus* won an Obie—honoring off-Broadway plays—for best musical, and that same year it was a finalist for the Pulitzer Prize in drama.

On stage, the production thrived. A reviewer in Los Angeles in late 1985 called *Colonus* the most fun you could have at a musical west of New York City.

As *Colonus* made its way from LA to Atlanta, Minneapolis, and Des Moines, newspapers often led their previews or reviews with Clarence Fountain interviews. Now when the Blind Boys performed, word got out. The *New York Daily News* called the Blind Boys on their own "a show that can't be recommended highly enough." The Associated Press story on the opening of *Colonus* on Broadway in 1988 focused almost entirely on Fountain and the Blind Boys' history. It led off the Saturday entertainment section of the *Philadelphia Daily News*.

As the *Colonus* run faded a bit after over five years, Clarence and the Blind Boys regularly received premium newspaper coverage for their expanding radius of gospel shows—in Vancouver, Albuquerque, Spokane, and Wichita. The media now treated Clarence and the Blind Boys as American icons, above and apart from their role in the musical. Many of the features focused less on *Colonus* and much more on the Blind Boys' history, going back to Talladega.

The Gospel at Colonus brought together an unprecedented combination. An avant-garde theater dramatist, an eclectic musician, Darth Vader's father, and a pre–Miss Daisy Freeman changed the Blind Boys' lives and legacy forever. You could say that *Colonus* introduced the Blind Boys to a new audience or opened new doors to them, but to put it more directly, the play made the Blind Boys of Alabama White-people famous.

⬦

Looking back forty years later, it's clear that the Blind Boys' crossover and endurance are without equal in American music history for a Black gospel quartet. Now that we know the beginnings of how it happened, how truly random and borderline miraculous it all was, we have to wonder why it took so long for a Black gospel quartet to go mainstream.

Gospel's brothel-born brethren, the blues, crossed over early and often, initially as a pop music fad under its own name in the 1910s, as a key ingredient of jazz in the 1920s and 1930s, as the seed of rock 'n' roll in the 1950s, and in the 1960s embrace of older roots artists in the so-called blues revival.

Though a largely White group of music scholars have mined the blues for limited and relatively insignificant political content, there has always been something bigger happening in gospel, something more important to Black culture and millions of Black lives. Gospel helps people to spiritually overcome life's pain and to face death courageously. White music fans relate to the outcast bluesman. They don't quite connect with the profound hunger for spiritual nourishment that gnaws at the gut of African American history. Gospel music is Blacker than blues—and therefore a tougher sell to secular Whites.

The message, like the philosophy, isn't exactly tuned to the White mainstream. Gospel, by definition, spreads the word of Jesus. Whether one believes in the divinity of Jesus or not, the historical figure's message of humanity and valuing the lives of the poor and downtrodden was so dangerous as to get him executed and so powerful and enduring as to form a new moral universe. Though used today too often as a force of conservatism, Jesus is truly more of a founding rebel of Western civilization. To African American culture, the story of Jesus is revolutionary, inspiring individuals and groups against being dominated body and soul.

Bringing this message to a secular, White audience not only created a challenge for the Blind Boys but gave them an opportunity. Forty years since their young voices crackled over Birmingham radio station WSGN, this new opportunity would define their next forty years. As Clarence Fountain said, "Our object in the first place is to get to the masses. This came along at the right time."

After seeing the Blind Boys squabble for a few hundred dollars to sing in small churches, Bob Telson—the bearded Jewish guy trying to make Black music—felt gratified to help them get over. Telson passes along credit to the Blind Boys' prodigal son for making *The Gospel at Colonus* and its massive impact on the group possible. "We couldn't have done it without Sam Butler," he said.

CHAPTER 16

WHITE PEOPLE ARE GOING TO . . . WHEN THEY SEE THIS

THE GOSPEL AT COLONUS period brought changes to the Blind Boys of Alabama lineup and some additions to the group's extended family. Jimmy Lee Carter, who first sang with the group in its earliest days and first recorded with them on *I'm a Soldier in the Army of the Lord*, began sharing leads with Clarence Fountain and eventually played Fountain's part in the play. "It's hard to explain *Gospel at Colonus* because I never understood it," Carter said. "I just showed up and did my job."

The rhythm of a musical took some getting used to. "It felt odd not to get any 'Amens,'" said Carter, "but it's a different type of audience. You got a standing ovation when the play was done, but that's it. In gospel, we feed off the audience throughout the performance."

Carter nevertheless appreciated other differences between the theater and the gospel highway. "It was nice not having to drive from one place to the next every night," he said. "The pay was good. It was a sure thing, you knew you were going to get that."

Fountain brought more help to the band as well. In 1987, he hired guitarist Donald Dillon, who ended up being Fountain's close companion and an all-around help to the aging group. Entering their sixties, several of the men had been diagnosed with diabetes and required extra care on the road. Dillon took a class to learn how to care for diabetics. "I made sure they ate at the right time, took medicine at the right time, put on the same uniforms," he said. "I accompanied Clarence everywhere he went."

The latter responsibility put Dillon in the awkward position of caring for an aging Casanova who had no health-related plans to scale down. "Many times his blood sugar would drop, females that he was around would panic and want to call 911," Dillon said. "I didn't have to do that, because I knew what to do. He kept peppermints or a Snickers in his medicine bag. You could tell when his sugar was dropping. All I would do is stick some peppermints in his mouth, give him something with sugar. Wait a few minutes and measure his blood sugar. He'd be back to normal in no time."

The Blind Boys also added a new bass player whose responsibilities went beyond music. Caleb "Bobby" Butler, no kin to Sam, went way back with the Blind Boys as a gospel highway traveler. "My career started with the Highway QCs back in 1962," Butler said. "I was a guitarist, a vocalist in the background, and I did a lot of writing and arranging. About 1964 I joined the Brooklyn All-Stars. I was lead guitarist for them until 1978. I had written a lot of songs with them. I was fortunate to have gold records with them. One of them was called 'He'll Bring Peace to You,' and the other one was 'The Windows of Heaven Are Open.'"

Butler, sympathetic toward the blind men in any event, had to intervene when he saw their own manager robbing them. He said, "They were blind already. Lamont Blount robbed them even blinder. I always have been sentimental about handicapped and blind people. When I was with the Brooklyn All-Stars and we toured together, I told them, 'Y'all gotta get away from that guy. Every time I see him with your money, he steady rippin' you off.'"

The Blind Boys trusted Bobby for this, and Fountain asked him to manage the group on the road. He collected money at checkup, helped arrange food and accommodations, and, like everyone, took Clarence around to visit women. Having talked to Sam Butler about this chore, Bobby knew what he had coming—to some degree. Sam had told him about once having to retrieve Clarence when a hookup had gone terribly wrong, leaving Clarence on the street with no clothes on. "You got to come and get me, man," Clarence had told Sam. Everybody but Clarence laughed about these stories. He seemed to think it was fairly normal. Bobby would soon get caught up in another Clarence caper.

"The woman usually says she doesn't have anybody, that's standard," Bobby recalled. "At one woman's apartment, we stayed overnight and got a call that her husband was coming home. It took Clarence a half hour to put on one shoe. I said, 'Come on, we got to go!'"

Fortunately, Sam Butler was outside the same apartment building looking for Clarence and Bobby. Sam knew the husband, and when the man came home, he and Sam stopped to chat outside the building. "If it wasn't for that, we'd have never gotten out of there," Bobby said.

With Donald Dillon and Bobby Butler on board, the Blind Boys had caring, responsible people around them at all times.

They had also lost an original member when Olice Thomas left the Blind Boys. Meanwhile, Johnny Fields traveled with them only part-time. Most who were close to the group concede that neither man could sing anymore, and both had stayed as long as they did—with silent microphones in later gigs—for appearances and for tradition's sake. Neither had recorded with the group since the mid-1970s, though both came back for spot starts in the *Colonus* lineup and experienced that phenomenon. And, according to most who have been close to the group, the Blind Boys have a tradition of paying retired members, formally or informally.

In the aftermath of *Colonus*, the Blind Boys gained many more opportunities to travel, perform, and slip away from husbands. In 1989, the group signed with Falk & Morrow, a talent agency based in Solana Beach, California, north of San Diego. Falk & Morrow fit the Blind Boys. The agents specialized in blues and had connections to overseas markets for American roots music. Kevin Morrow became the group's first fully dedicated manager who could channel them toward the mainstream and offer a professional level of guidance and perspective on how to build a bigger, better Blind Boys.

The relationship began randomly when Morrow contacted the booker at O. T. Price's, a club in Santa Cruz, California, about a date for Little Charlie & the Nightcats. The booker already had the date filled. Morrow asked with whom. Told it was the Blind Boys of Alabama, Morrow initially felt shocked that the group was out touring. He asked to be put in touch with them and had a conversation with Clarence Fountain.

Morrow and Fountain hit it off, and Morrow invited the Blind Boys to play a gig down in San Diego at a nightclub called Smokey's, purview of former San Diego State University basketball coach Smokey Gaines. Morrow took a week or so to promote the event.

Chris Goldsmith had recently joined Falk & Morrow as a booking agent. He went to Smokey's that night with Morrow. Goldsmith hadn't been to the club before and took in the decor—brass railings, mirrored walls, and a disco ball up top. The room could hold three hundred people, but he looked around and saw maybe fifty or sixty. Goldsmith and Morrow knew that such a dynamic could be awkward for performers. As soon as the Blind Boys appeared, marching in line with hands on shoulders, dressed in matching lavender tuxedoes, the place began to buzz.

"Once they started," Goldsmith said, "it was like being in an arena with ten thousand people. The electricity was incredible. It was the most amazing thing I'd ever seen live. We were all struck by lightning."

Morrow recalled, "I kept thinking to myself, 'White people are going to shit when they see this.'"

Though Morrow himself might not say so, that spicy little phrase served as his campaign credo for the next several years. In addition to the group's crossover potential, Morrow recognized their core strengths. "There's truth in the Blind Boys music," he said, "and they're insanely talented."

Goldsmith said, "I remember Kevin telling the Blind Boys, 'We don't know what we can do for you, but we'll figure it out, you're just too good. There has to be a path to somewhere else for you if you're not happy where you are.'"

Goldsmith felt that this pleased the Blind Boys. "I think that after *Gospel at Colonus* slowed down, their profile faded," he said. "They were at the mercy of church promoters, who are not the most scrupulous. They weren't getting paid what they were promised; sound systems aren't always good. So, they agreed to work with us and that began this long episode. I worked as their booking agent while Kevin managed them."

Fountain and Morrow agreed on how their relationship would work. They shook on it and never had a contract in what ended up being a nearly ten-year relationship. Morrow wanted to introduce the Blind Boys in Europe, Asia, and Australia. He also recognized the importance of keeping the Blind Boys' base energized. This dual outlook required two creative directions. "We talked about what each audience wanted," Morrow said. "For the White audience, Clarence sang older stuff that he'd mostly moved away from. He knew that they wanted to hear 'If I Had a Hammer.'"

With the Blind Boys' Black audience, Morrow witnessed something else. "The first time I saw the Black show, we were at a church in Inglewood," Morrow said. "The opening act was Tutu and the Truthettes. Four Aretha Franklins. All four of these church girls could sing their asses off. They slayed that church. I walked back to talk to Clarence and said, 'Man, I don't know how much meat is left on the bone.' He cackled and said, 'You ain't seen our church show yet.'"

Morrow continued, "He walks in and they start whipping into this set with the heavy backbeat drumming and at one point they ripped their glasses off and tilted their heads back and women are running up trying to touch their eyes, people were speaking in tongues, it was insane."

Not long after the "insane" church show, Morrow booked the Blind Boys into a small venue that holds big prestige. McCabe's Guitar Shop in Santa Monica contains a cramped backroom, jammed with folding chairs and cluttered with guitars and banjos hanging on its walls. The Blind Boys performed there to an intimate crowd that included, as Morrow recalls, Anthony Kiedis of the Red Hot Chili Peppers, Bette Midler, and Faye Dunaway. After the show, Midler reportedly told the Boys that she wanted them to sing on her next record, while Dunaway bowed at the feet of Clarence Fountain.

"I wanted to create some buzz," Morrow said.

With this mission accomplished, another person who saw the show got serious about working with the group. "The guy who booked McCabe's, John Chelew, said that Ry Cooder wanted to produce a Blind Boys record," Morrow said.

"This was before *Buena Vista Social Club*," Morrow added, in reference to Cooder's hit collaboration with a group of Cuban musicians that resulted in a hugely successful album and a widely seen documentary film. Morrow and Clarence Fountain met with Cooder, who, in Morrow's words, "wanted to do the old stuff."

Fountain, though happy to tweak his stage show per audience demographics, felt strongly about recording modern material. According to Morrow, "Clarence said, 'Ry, I wanna do stuff with synthesizers like they do at Philadelphia International.' Ry said, 'Clarence, that's poppy stuff that's gonna go away as peoples' tastes change. You will never go away, you're an institution.'"

Ultimately, Clarence did not feel like an institution just yet and allowed Cooder to head on down the road to Havana. "That was a missed opportunity," Morrow said. "To this day I kick myself, I should have gone a little harder at that."

Morrow felt too much reverence for Clarence and too much racial, historical awkwardness to tell a Black man from the Jim Crow South what to do. Though the Bette Midler collaboration never progressed past lip service, all was not lost from the McCabe's gig. In years to come, the guitar shop's booking agent, John Chelew, would become a force in the Blind Boys world. And Morrow's vision for the Blind Boys was not long in materializing.

In 1988 or 1989, the Blind Boys played the San Francisco Blues Festival. On the bay, with the Golden Gate Bridge as a backdrop, they marched on stage, in silver suits this time, as Goldsmith watched from a crowd of ten thousand. "Having that experience at Smokey's, we wondered, is it just us?" Goldsmith said. "But in San Francisco, I saw thousands of people react the same way. We knew this would work."

They found immediate success on the blues festival circuit: nice paydays, a receptive and built-in audience, and a low pressure "soft ticket," where the Blind Boys didn't have to carry the business side of the show and draw the whole crowd on their own. "They were seen as a treasure from an era when gospel was visceral, exciting music," Goldsmith said.

Just when all began feeling right with the Blind Boys, an old associate reemerged: former manager Lamont Blount got out of prison. His sentence had begun in 1982, the year before *The Gospel at Colonus*, and he came out around 1988, during which time the Blind Boys' fortunes had improved dramatically.

Considering his history with Clarence Fountain, Blount returned to the Blind Boys and assumed he'd manage the group once again. Bobby Butler, though, had seen Blount steal from the group. Butler stood up to Blount in a motel room that contained just the two of them and Fountain. "We argued toe to toe, nose to nose," said Butler. "Blount had a little small pistol, a .22. It got kind of touch and go for a minute. Clarence got between us, I don't think he knew Blount had his pistol out. We had some wild adventures with that guy."

According to Butler, Fountain either believed that he owed Blount the job or that Blount could ruin him. Butler said, "It's my assumption that Clarence said, 'If you do this time for me, I'll give you the group.' Blount indebted Clarence to that." If Clarence had not been part of the auto theft ring that got Blount put away, Blount could still tell people that Clarence had been in on it and that Blount had taken the rap.

Butler stepped aside as road manager in favor of Blount while staying in the band, but he felt an even greater need to look after Clarence. "Blount took the reins with Clarence's permission," Butler explained.

Blount tried to create suspicion and uncertainty elsewhere. "Lamont Blount tried to say untruths to Clarence about me," said Blind Boys sideman and road caretaker Donald Dillon. "He succeeded one time and Clarence fired me. I had been away from the group for two weeks, and I had gotten a job when Clarence called and asked me to come back and meet him in Chicago. I said, 'OK, I'll do it.' I packed up and left and that was history." Dillon from that point worked for Clarence personally. "I accompanied Clarence everywhere he went."

Despite their misgivings, both Dillon and Butler acknowledge the usefulness of a person like Blount in the entertainment business. Clarence didn't entirely mind the idea of having a conman work for him rather than against him. If only it could have shaken out that way.

"Blount was a good businessman," said Dillon. "These were Clarence's words to Blount: 'If you can make it work, do it.' He was a negotiator. When it came down to record contracts, he could get more money in deals."

This might explain why the Blind Boys cut three albums between 1989 and 1990 for labels outside Kevin Morrow's sphere of influence during the same period that Ry Cooder put his offer on the table. These records featured the dreaded synthesizers and drum programs and are probably not remembered among the group's classics.

Even if they made a little more on small record deals thanks to Blount, his scheming to help the Blind Boys ended up hurting them. "Blount for many many years kept the Blind Boys individually from paying taxes," said Dillon. "In the end it caught up with them. Clarence Fountain had to pay a lot of money back to the IRS."

Jimmy Carter put it more bluntly. "Being blind, I felt worried about being taken advantage of with money. Blount stole everything from us. We knew it, too. We never could stand up to him for some reason. We didn't appoint him to be our manager, he took it."

Kevin Morrow and booking agent Chris Goldsmith, meanwhile, tapped into another lucrative market for the Blind Boys. "We showcased them at a performing arts center conference in 1990," said Goldsmith. "The Blind Boys had the same impact they always did. To me, that was like putting Babe Ruth in the lineup, almost too easy. They crushed it there and we had a great run in the performing arts world where the Blind Boys were seen as culturally important artists who were also very entertaining. With that audience they had the tie-in to *Gospel at Colonus*."

With *Colonus* still driving media interest in their gigs, the Blind Boys continued to make headlines, now as the gospel group that played nightclubs. As Don McLeese wrote in the March 5, 1991, *Austin American-Statesman*, "If a gospel group has ambitions beyond preaching to the already converted, it must eventually sing of sin where the sinners are." As Fountain put it to Tom Moon at the *Philadelphia Inquirer*, "You take the Word into the Devil's sanctuary... Jesus said, preach to the sinners as well as the Christian people, so that's what we do."

Their crossover would soon reach new shores. "The UK was our first foray into the European market," Morrow said. "We flew to London, played Birmingham, Morecambe, that's where we played for Peter Gabriel, who ended up signing them later, and came back and played London. We had another eight shows, festivals in Belgium, Amsterdam, Montreux, we had twelve shows in total. This was around 1990. The reception was huge. The Blind Boys that went over there had like seven lead singers and five of them were like James Brown. It was the craziest show, and the international folks ate them up."

CHAPTER 17

THEY SLAYED EVERYBODY

K EVIN, LET'S GO TO Mickey D's," Clarence Fountain said.

An artist's manager must dutifully handle a variety of requests, whether for a certain extra financial perk in a contract or an excuse to elude a potentially troublesome personal liaison. A fast-food run, however, shouldn't have been a problem.

Except that Kevin Morrow and the Blind Boys were on a bus driving through Amsterdam.

"We're in a foreign country, let's eat something different," Morrow said.

Clarence's bandmates chimed in as if singing background. "Yeah, let's go to Mickey D's."

Morrow said, "I don't think they have one here."

No sooner had Morrow said this than the blind men all turned their heads in the same direction at the same time, as if they could smell something.

One declared, "There is a McDonald's that is close."

The van turned the next corner, and there appeared the arches of gold. "Alright, there's a McDonald's," Morrow told them. "If you guys really want it, I'll go in and get it."

He recalled, "So, we had McDonald's. The road was fun with those guys."

Between May and September 1992, the Blind Boys toured the United Kingdom, returned to Los Angeles to record a breakthrough album, and conquered Australia.

"They were good to go, traveling long distances," Morrow said. "The only challenge was that they had diabetes and would have to give themselves insulin shots in the craziest places. We're at the airport in Sydney. Everyone's staring at them, walking with their hands on each other's shoulders. We get to the gate. We're sitting there, and all these kids are staring at them, and the men needed their insulin. They pulled out their hypodermics and shot up into their sides. One little kid started talking about it, and other people started looking."

Abroad, Clarence Fountain continued to garner most of the headlines, but from his formidable shadow emerged a secret weapon, in the words of a *London Independent* critic. "Jimmy Carter...holds a note for what seems like an eternity before slipping, amid cheers, into a bit of testifying, 'I can't see you...I need to hear you'...eliciting a sensational response when he goes walkabout through the crowd, raising excitement to fever-pitch with a driving call-and-response routine."

Jimmy's crowd walks are a callback to the house-wrecking days, which, of course, he never saw but felt, as Archie Brownlee blindly leaped from the stage, as June Cheeks opened his mouth and women fainted, as ambulances carried away the fallen. Now the man who'd stayed in the background got out front and brought a palpable sense of hard gospel history to fans who really had no idea of all that Jimmy was bringing them but loved how it felt. "Going out into the audience is part of our show," he explained. "We don't rehearse it, though. When I feel it, I just go. The guy who leads me out knows, when I give him a certain signal, it's time. He looks to see where the crowd needs us, and that's where he goes."

Carter credited his old friend Fountain with providing him the confidence and the opportunity to step up. "I would have to say that Clarence is the cause of me coming forward as a lead," Jimmy said. "He had an idea of what I could do. He said, 'I don't know why the Blind Boys of Mississippi let you get away.'"

Touring Europe put the Blind Boys into some of the venues in which Christian music had its beginnings, as they performed in ancient cathedrals. Guitarist and bass player Bobby Butler, who'd joined the group in the mid-1980s and made the international tours, jokingly said he didn't like performing in the middle of a grave-yard, as many churches sit at the center of old burial grounds. "I'd say, 'We singin' in the cemetery tonight?'" The acoustics inside, however, added power to the word of God. "That sound is phenom-enal. It carried, you didn't really have to have a microphone. We had to dial it down some."

In one town, the Blind Boys had a show at the same time that guitarist George Benson was scheduled to perform nearby. Bobby Butler remembered a gloomy outlook prevailing among the Boys in this competition, until someone saw Benson in their audience. "He didn't draw," said Butler. "He had to shut his show down and just come on and see us. Clarence was amazed, he said, 'You mean to tell me George Benson shut down his show and came to see our show?'"

In Morecambe, as Kevin Morrow recalled, Peter Gabriel caught the Blind Boys show. The former Genesis lead singer and solo hit artist of "Solsbury Hill," "Shock the Monkey," and "Sledgehammer" fame, to name just a few, had founded Real World Records to produce new work by artists from eclectic genres across the globe. Gabriel's interest in the Blind Boys would lead in years to come to another of the group's landmark recordings.

After three or four years of Morrow's management, the Boys had a nice system going. "We worked the blues festivals, the European festivals, and the arts circuit," said booking agent Chris Goldsmith. "Kevin Morrow did a great job breaking them over there and they played many times to huge crowds, ten, twenty thousand people and just crushing them."

Morrow worked to address the other major facet of the Blind Boys' career: recording. He found a deal with Elektra Nonesuch. After a European swing, the Blind Boys returned to Los Angeles during the second week of June 1992 and gathered at Record One, a storied studio on Ventura Boulevard. The Sherman Oaks hit factory had scored with Kim Carnes's "Bette Davis Eyes," Don Henley's classic album *Building the Perfect Beast*, and, most recently, Michael Jackson's *Dangerous*, among many other notable recordings.

Clarence Fountain and Kevin Morrow sat in the control room, listening to a playback of a backing track for their album led by one of the great studio bandleaders of all time, Booker T. Jones.

Fountain remarked to Morrow, "It ain't got that sanctified church sound."

Unbeknownst to Fountain, the control room microphone shared his comment with Booker T. and the band in the studio.

"Booker T. looked at the musicians in the room," Morrow recalled. "Without a word, they broke into the most energetic churchy thing with the heavy backbeat. When Clarence really listened, he'd tilt his head back. He had his head tilted back. When the band stopped, Booker goes, 'Is that sanctified enough for you?' Clarence started laughing and said, 'I hear you, Booker! Booker, I hear you!'"

Booker T.'s involvement came about through Elektra executive Steve Ralbovsky. Morrow finally convinced Fountain to do what Ry Cooder had suggested four years earlier and cut a rootsy gospel album. After contemplating going back to Cooder with the concept, Ralbovsky suggested Jones. Morrow loved it. "I'm like whoa, only the greatest session bandleader in history," Morrow said. "He was perfect. And he came from the church. He fit naturally." Fountain clearly remained somewhat skeptical until he accidentally pushed Booker T. back into church via the hot mike.

The *Deep River* album encompasses traditional quartet songs like "Brother Moses," classic numbers like "Every Time I Feel the Spirit" and "Just a Closer Walk with Thee," and more modern arrangements—without synth and drum machines but with that heavy backbeat—such as the bluesy "Reminiscing" and the contemporary gospel of "Don't Play with God." The Blind Boys cover Bob Dylan with their rendition of "I Believe in You."

Fountain embraced the idea of "reaching the masses of people," as he explained it, and wanted to sing in a style and to develop a repertoire that would achieve that goal.

The new material had become part of the group's live repertoire by the time they hit Australia in mid-September. After seeing the Blind Boys in Melbourne, a reviewer wrote for *The Age*, "In slow, graceful songs such as 'Deep River' their voices blended in close harmony, producing sounds both sweet and surprising." This artistic direction, emphasizing sweet harmony rather than fiery fervor, represented a return to the group's 1940s jubilee roots, as did the Golden Gate–flavored "Brother Moses" cut on the *Deep River* album, probably evidence of the Blind Boys' outreach to Americana, or, more simply put, White audiences.

As Morrow explained, the appeal of the Blind Boys overseas lay in the foreign appreciation of American roots music, a trend that the savvy Booker T. Jones was well aware of.

Another crucial development to the Blind Boys' sound was as apparent to *The Age* in Australia as it had been to the *London Independent*. "Fountain sang the lead part on most songs, by turns smooth and fervent…But it was Carter who stole the show. He got the crowd on its feet and brought cheers with his exciting vocal efforts and unabashed showmanship."

Carter's increasing popularity may also have to do with the group's new audience demographics. In the Black community, Clarence Fountain was a star and had been for forty years, while Carter had sung backup with the Mississippi Blind Boys. Though Fountain received top billing at crossover shows and handled spokesman duties with the press, his legend did not precede him on the festival circuit to the extent that it did on the old gospel highway.

Fountain, with his reputation for jealousy, would have to deal with Carter becoming a showstopper and share the spotlight as he had never comfortably done in the Blind Boys. Fortunately for fans, insecure stars can make great music.

Bobby Butler saw Clarence differently from the way that Sam Butler had seen him in the 1960s and 1970s. "Clarence liked to share the stage, he wasn't in competition," Bobby said. "He felt Jimmy was doing his own thing in his own way. I felt like Clarence had gotten lazy, really. He could get over better than Jimmy, but he laid back and let Jimmy do his thing. Jimmy is a great performer. He really came into his own."

Clearly, both Jimmy and Clarence had grown—Jimmy as a performer, Clarence as a leader. And so Jimmy Carter's intensely spiritual delivery and his beloved crowd walks became an integral part of the Blind Boys show.

The Age noted a few upcoming tour stops in lesser known Geelong, Ballarat, and Albury, while Morrow recalled hitting every big city down under. "It was the first year of the Byron Bay Blues Festival," he said. "It's huge now, they do thirty-thousand people. Back then they had about two thousand in a nightclub. The Blind Boys headlined. We played Melbourne, Perth, Sydney. They slayed everybody. I never saw a Blind Boys show where everyone wasn't going crazy by the end."

<hr />

Elektra Records released *Deep River* in early 1993. "The record was Grammy nominated, an artistic success, and did well commercially," said Goldsmith.

Back in those days of robust newspaper coverage, *Deep River* was reviewed widely and well, while the Boys toured the West Coast from Vancouver to San Diego. "We were able to tour a little more traditionally and sell them as a hard ticket that people pay to see on their own," said Goldsmith, "not only a soft ticket like a festival where they slay a large audience that's there for the whole event. They appreciated that the sound systems were good, the backstage areas were nice, the money was good."

When people asked how they justified playing these halls of sin, Clarence would say, "I didn't come here looking for Jesus, I brought Him with me."

Not long after Australia, the Blind Boys made their first trip to Japan, and over the next several years they toured the world regularly. "It was great," said Kevin Morrow. "They were one of the joys of my life, to see that generation of Black men, born in the Jim Crow South, perform in London, Paris, Sydney, Tokyo, and have five thousand people screaming for them at the top of their lungs. It was uplifting for them and for me. We grew together."

Meanwhile, the group still dealt with internal drama at the hands of tour manager Lamont Blount. Sam Butler said that he left the group after catching Blount shorting the Boys on their per diems from a promoter. As Morrow recalled, "Lamont would always try to get in Clarence's ear. He was a fly in the ointment. He needed to just go be a road manager. He can book a hotel, get their suits cleaned, get them on stage. He fancied himself more."

Nevertheless, Blount's hold on Clarence Fountain began to slip as the Blind Boys' world grew beyond Blount's realm.

The lineup had added one of its more remarkable members—even among a roster of unique men—a drummer and singer from an Atlanta gospel family named Eric "Ricky" McKinnie. He had not started his career as a blind gospel performer, but he became one. McKinnie would evolve within the group from drummer to road manager to one of its lead vocalists. His own eclectic upbringing prepared him for playing so many different roles. At the outset, McKinnie became the first blind full-time musician to join the backup band.

"Clarence called me and asked, 'You want to go to Australia?'" McKinnie said.

By that time, the drummer's familiarity with the Blind Boys already ran deep. "My mother was a singer with Gene Martin and with the Female Nightingales. She never went on the road, because she had children to take care of and she was married. I met Clarence Fountain through my mother. He came to the house," McKinnie recalled.

A prodigy drummer, McKinnie led the high school marching band and orchestra while dabbling in pop. He and his brother won a citywide talent show in 1965 at the auditorium for their Sam & Dave–style duets.

Growing up in promoter Herman Nash's territory brought McKinnie experience with the Blind Boys and other quartets like the Highway QCs as a pickup man on tours of the church circuit. "I went out on weekends and had an opportunity to sing background and play drums with Clarence, George, Johnny, and Olice."

This experience led to an early start on a recording career. "I cut my first major record when I was eighteen," McKinnie said, "with the Soul Searchers out of Atlanta on Nashboro Records. The song that I recorded with them was called 'Great Change.' We recorded at Master Sound Studio where Isaac Hayes recorded."

By the time McKinnie reached the age of twenty, he had joined one of the top touring quartets of the early 1970s, the Gospel Keynotes. They wore big Afros and matching tuxedos, embodying the glory of gospel funk.

"I saw Clarence Fountain and Sam Butler out there," McKinnie said. "They could make as much sound as a whole band. And people would wait to see what Clarence would do, shaking his hips. Clarence was an entertainer."

McKinnie played drums on a certified gold recording by the Keynotes, "Jesus You've Been Good to Me," released in 1975. That same year, McKinnie and the Keynotes were playing in South Bend, Indiana, when his eyesight suddenly went dark.

His doctor diagnosed him with glaucoma. Blindness was inevitable. McKinnie argued with the doctor. He thought he could see his way around home, but he had what's known as phantom eyesight, almost like a hallucination, and not an accurate vision of what truly was around him. McKinnie's denial came to a sudden and painful end when he severely injured his right eye, running into something he should have seen. The injured eye had to be replaced with a prosthesis.

Rather than questioning how good Jesus had been to him, McKinnie embraced his loss of sight, believing that he still had a larger vision. He stayed on the road until 1978, realizing that he needed to take time for himself to learn his new way. During his adjustment to blindness, McKinnie talked to Lloyd Woodard, longtime leader of the Blind Boys of Mississippi. "They tell me you're going home," Woodard said. "Well, young man, I'll tell you what to do. Learn to read braille, and learn mobility. You're going to be alright."

McKinnie took that advice to the letter. He returned to Atlanta that August and began rehearsing his group, the Ricky McKinnie Singers, featuring his mother Sarah Shivers as a lead vocalist, while his brothers Ronnie and Chuck held down the band. Ricky wanted to get them out there and booked some radio time. "My mama said, 'How you gonna go on the radio? You don't have any sponsors.'" McKinnie recalled. "I said, 'Don't worry about it.'"

They also only had one song, "Jordan River I'm Bound to Cross." Nevertheless, they soon had a twice-a-week broadcast and recorded an album for Southland Records. The hard-driving, funky *Here I Am* packs all of the authentic passion and powerful instrumental brilliance that some of the Blind Boys records of the late 1970s lack. Ricky's lead vocal on the title track is laid-back and gentle, giving off a sense of self-assurance usually achieved through boastfulness, here delivered with humility. The group's 1984 follow-up, *I Never Had Love Before*, is another of those rare small records that pack in a complete artistic vision and commitment to every note. The Ricky

McKinnie Singers perform like a team. Both albums are classics without carrying the recognition.

In 1982, McKinnie started his own show on Atlanta's public-access People TV, *Rock with Ricky*, featuring interviews with musicians and live performances. The few surviving clips, including a mind-blowing spot with Blind Boys lead singer Billy Bowers, show the same musical excellence that the McKinnie Singers stood for.

McKinnie's mother Sarah broadcast her show, *Words and Music to Inspire*, every Sunday from 1988 until she neared her ninetieth birthday. She retired from singing at ninety-one—"She still sounded the same," Ricky recalled—and died in 2019 at age ninety-two.

The Blind Boys got much more than a drummer when they signed up McKinnie.

CHAPTER 18

"YOU'RE WITH THE BLIND BOYS NOW, BOY!"

WHEN BLIND BOYS OF Alabama manager Kevin Morrow shut down his talent agency to work for House of Blues, he brought the Blind Boys with him, landing them a two-record deal. The first, *I Brought Him with Me*, showcases the Blind Boys in their element: live. Clarence Fountain christens the set with his oft-repeated line, "I didn't come here looking for Jesus, I brought Him along with me."

The group brought Jesus to the second of their records with House of Blues, *Holdin' On*, but also returned to the slick, contemporary production style that they'd gotten away from, successfully, on the rootsy *Deep River.* Fountain justified synthetic instrumentation, saying, "The drum machine plays it perfect every time."

Chris Goldsmith had moved to the Rosebud Agency in San Francisco after Falk & Morrow closed. He too remained on the Blind Boys' team as their booking agent. *Holdin' On* did not make things easy for him. "We needed traditional recordings to connect with the audience," Goldsmith said, of the group's newfound flock. "I couldn't do anything with that record to help them. They couldn't get a record deal after that, because *Holdin' On* sold like three thousand units."

They played to a still enthusiastic crowd on a global scale, though, and kept busy.

The Blind Boys added another core member on the fly, much as they had Ricky McKinnie a few years earlier. Guitarist Joey Williams joined the group as a young gospel lifer.

"I was born in Brooklyn in the 1960s, raised in Queens in the 1970s," Williams said. "My father started me playing when I was seven or eight. I played drums, beating on pans and boxes. They finally bought me a snare drum and cymbal. I played along to the old quartet records."

Williams's father, Joe, sang in the Imperial Wonders and later started the Northernaires, a gospel funk band based in Brooklyn. Their recordings are prized by collectors. Joey grew up going to his father's shows and tagging along to the big programs that Ronnie Williams, the man who'd helped launch the Blind Boys brand in 1948, promoted at Washington Temple Church of God in Christ on Bedford Avenue. A preaching prodigy named Al Sharpton Jr. had delivered his first sermon at the temple when he was four years old.

Joey played drums with his dad's group and eventually loaned himself out to other local bands on the same programs. When they opened for the national touring groups, Joey started gigging with them as well. He had begun playing guitar and liked to take his act out into the crowd.

"I first met Ricky McKinnie when he was playing with the Gospel Keynotes," Williams said. "I was opening up for them and got to know him. We called him Blind Ricky, because he lost his sight while he was on the road. He let us use his drums on our show."

Shirley Caesar picked up Joey to play drums in her band one night, and when he got through unscathed, Joey decided he wanted to play gospel forever. Williams went out on the road for the first time with his dad's new group, the Northernaires. Next, Joey went out without his dad, playing with the Gospelaires. He journeyed on with Slim and the Supreme Angels, one of the underappreciated gospel Chitlin' Circuit groups of the 1970s through the 1990s who never got the NPR treatment.

Their colorful leader, Howard "Slim" Hunt, ruled his group like a tyrant. He made them move to his base town of Goldsboro, North Carolina, and fined sidemen for gigging with other bands on their off days because he didn't want his sound to get around. "Slim would try some stuff," Williams said. "He had strobe lights like police sirens on stage. We didn't have a sound system, we had a PA. Didn't even know what a monitor was. The sound got straight from the amp to the audience. Then he came out with the cape and had those sirens on top of the speakers spinning around."

Slim, clad in his cape on stage, often exhorted the Supreme Angels' lead guitarist in a solo by telling him, "Squeeze it, Sugar!" The "Sugar" Slim referred to had grown up in gospel with a family group, the Hightower Brothers.

Sugar Hightower was one of young Joey Williams's guitar heroes, along with occasional Blind Boys collaborator Edward "Spanky" Alford and Dixie Hummingbirds strummer Howard Carroll.

Williams started off playing drums with the Supreme Angels but moved to second guitar and got to play beside his idol.

"Slim ran a tight ship," said Williams. "We got a ten percent split. He would take the rest. We had a tour bus and all of the expense came out of what Slim kept. If the bus had a flat, we just lay there, we don't have to do anything. He would take care of everything. He made sure everybody was okay."

Williams experienced the road the old-fashioned way. "Young cats coming up now have no idea," he said. "I've been to shows where we all got there and the promoter's not there, nobody's there. Rode in the car from Brooklyn to Jackson, Mississippi, to record at Malaco. Six of us had to go."

Williams experienced this before the age of thirty. Following his stint with Slim, Williams came back to New York and got a job in the hardware department at Sears.

"I'd be down there working and somebody I knew from music would come in and I'd run in the back," Williams said. "I'm a musician, I don't want them to see me working. I still went out and did gigs on the weekend. I sometimes got in the van without telling my wife, because I was so hungry for it."

Williams played weekend gigs with McKinnie's old group, the Gospel Keynotes. After touring the Bahamas with them, he said, "That was it—not another job. I stayed with them about five years."

Williams's next stop on the gospel legends tour came with the Mighty Clouds of Joy. Their leader, Joe Ligon, had come from Alabama. "He was arguably the best lead singer in quartet gospel, but so down to earth," Williams said. "No part of him is a diva. Joe Ligon told me that Clarence Fountain and the Blind Boys is who he was looking up to as a young man."

The Mighty Clouds played big arenas, opened for mainstream acts, and toured the world, going places no other gospel quartet had gone. By 1991, however, with the Blind Boys reaching new heights, the Mighty Clouds found themselves opening for Clarence Fountain and company. "To me, the Mighty Clouds were the biggest group in gospel, and I couldn't believe the Blind Boys had to follow us," Williams said. "I wasn't hip to what they were doing."

Williams soon saw what Morrow and Goldsmith had seen: fans going crazy for the Blind Boys. Jimmy was out in the audience, with Williams watching close by, whipping the crowd into a frenzy. "I said, 'Oh, they got a whole other thing going on now.'"

Williams also noticed an old friend playing drums. "I said, 'That's my boy Blind Ricky.' I went and talked to him after the show."

Blind Boys road manager Lamont Blount sized up Williams. The Blind Boys needed a guitar player who could sing, and they were familiar with Williams going back to Washington Temple. Williams told Blount, "I don't have intentions of going anywhere."

A few months later, the Mighty Clouds' original guitarist returned to the band. He pushed Williams out, regardless of intentions.

"I got in touch with Blount," Williams said. "I told him, 'You wanted me to find somebody to play guitar? I found you somebody.'"

Blount had Williams meet the Blind Boys at a church on Long Island. Cora Perry, who knew all the gospel groups from working at the President Hotel in New York, brought Williams and made the introduction. The Blind Boys thought so highly of Miss Cora, as she was known, that her presence blessed Williams.

He shook hands with Clarence, who said, "Your hand's soft, you ain't working hard."

Williams laughed. "I try to do this," he said.

"You can have the gig if you want it," Clarence told him. "But first we gon' test you tonight and see where you at."

Williams passed the test, and when he told Miss Cora, she said, elated, "You're with the Blind Boys now, boy!"

Williams quickly recognized Blount's hustle. "My first gig after that was in Miami," Williams said. "Blount said, 'You just give me a hundred dollars, I'll get your plane ticket.' Which probably means he had a free one."

Williams flew down to Miami and returned with $200. "My wife wore me out," he said. "A month later we went to Norway. When I got back that time, I had five grand, and I haven't had a problem with her since. I've learned more here than I would have learned at Julliard."

Williams participated in both the *Deep River* and the *Holdin' On* recording sessions. As the road went on, Williams observed Blount more closely. "Blount was a heavier guy," he said. "Younger than Clarence. He was a mortician. He dressed not too neat. He was casual. He was a mover and a shaker. He got some things done. He made things happen. He would book shows for this much and tell the Boys it was for that much. I wasn't privy to that, but I heard things."

A few years into his tenure with the band, Joey Williams got the Blind Boys equivalent of a Godfather loyalty test from Clarence Fountain.

Williams had to fire Lamont Blount.

Publicly, Blount garnered some appreciation. Don Mayhew, profiling the Blind Boys in September 1997 for the *Fresno Bee*, focused on Blount and Jimmy Carter's stage dynamics, citing Carter's walks, with Blount's help, as a catalyst for the Boys' "frenzied, testify-till-you-drop performances." Blount testified that he'd never let Carter fall.

"I guess the Lord just blesses us that way," Blount told Mayhew. "When you're singing for God, He don't let you make mistakes."

Blount went on to describe how Jimmy "takes over" during the end of the set. "And when I say he takes over, I mean he takes over."

Carter told the *Bee*, "We make a good team on the stage...He's a motivator."

Privately, despite the cheery public relations, the group had grown tired of Blount's hustling.

A matter of weeks after the *Bee* feature ran, Clarence Fountain told Joey Williams that Blount's time had come. Williams placed the phone call. Blount expressed disbelief. He knew this hadn't been Williams's idea, so he didn't say much else. The Blind Boys heard little more from him.

Aubrey "Lamont" Blount Sr. died at age forty-four, six months after his dismissal. In his *Bee* interview he had mentioned having undergone treatment for cancer, noting that he hadn't missed a show. He left a strange legacy in Blind Boys lore but is always remembered, sometimes with awe, as a character unlike any other.

With Blount gone and Morrow having moved on, drummer Ricky McKinnie took over management of the group, joining Johnny Fields and Olice Thomas as visually impaired men to do the job during different eras on the group's timeline. "I don't like when sighted folks tell me what to do. It's a blind group. We trust each other," McKinnie said. "But it was rough managing the Blind Boys. Clarence laid people off and made me tell them. He said, 'If you don't tell him, you'd better stay home too.' It takes a lot to manage a group. Anything happens, it's on the manager. I used to tell the group, 'Even if you don't make a lot of money, you'll have something to eat, somewhere to sleep, some way to get around.' I bought vans and paid hotel bills."

In the years after the *Holdin' On* album came out, the Blind Boys continued to tour the world and astonish audiences as one of the premier live acts in show business. In 1999, they opened for Tom Petty and the Heartbreakers. Petty auditioned them personally and made it known on the spot that he wanted the Blind Boys on his tour. In terms of contemporary music, the older gentlemen in the group knew few of the acts and cared for fewer. Jimmy Carter is a huge fan of classic country music and can probably be found in a hotel room right now with his radio tuned to whatever local station still plays Hank Williams Sr. Nevertheless, he took a liking to one of Petty's hits, as guitarist Joey Williams recalled.

"Jimmy knew 'Won't Back Down' and Tom Petty played that as an encore when we opened for him," said Williams. "After the Blind Boys finished, Clarence, George, and Ricky would leave. Me and Jimmy would stay. Jimmy wanted to hear 'Won't Back Down.' We stayed for it every night."

CHAPTER 19

SPIRIT OF THE CENTURY

JOHN CHELEW MET THE Blind Boys of Alabama during one of their early crossover performances at McCabe's Guitar Shop, where he booked shows.

They made a profound impression on him, and he often thought of their music and their potential. Sometime after that, a sonic revelation visited him in the desert. This is not to compare Chelew with Moses and the Burning Bush, however—Chelew had taken LSD and was hanging out in Joshua Tree National Park.

Here, beneath kaleidoscopic stars, it occurred to Chelew that two iconic songs—"Amazing Grace" and "House of the Rising Sun"—were musical twins.

Of course these two songs were not spiritual twins; rather, each stood firmly on those opposite corners of American music where the brothel and church glower at one another.

It is the historic tension between these worlds, the real emotion this tension provokes within the singers, that makes the Blind Boys' "Amazing Grace," sung to the tune of "House of the Rising Sun," a classic.

"We didn't want to do it," Jimmy Carter said, in his understated way, "but I'm glad we did, because it became our biggest song."

It all began with the totally unlikely, though not unspiritual, circumstance of a man's late-night desert vision quest on LSD.

Meanwhile, a slightly more sober vision developed for Chris Goldsmith. The Blind Boys' longtime agent booked them on a House of Blues–sponsored tour along with artists like slide guitarist John Hammond.

"The Blind Boys and John Hammond did three songs where they backed John on one, then he just played guitar behind them," Goldsmith said. "It was so haunting and moody, one of the coolest things I've ever seen in my life, this intersection of acoustic blues and gospel. That was probably in '98. It got me thinking about how that was a record that needed to be made."

Goldsmith had booked acts with Chelew at McCabe's, and they reconnected over their shared visions. They spent hours at a time on the phone over the course of a few years, discussing this concept for a Blind Boys album. "I haven't met too many people who think about things as much as I do," said Goldsmith. "He was very engaged."

They pitched the idea to a few blues and roots labels, but anyone who could run the numbers would see a decline from *Deep River*, at about thirty thousand sales, to *Holdin' On* at about three thousand. They got a few pennies-on-the-dollar offers for the cool concept but not nearly enough to do the record justice.

"We were dead," said Goldsmith. "I just couldn't take it anymore and decided to pay for the record myself."

He estimates that the record eventually cost $100,000, while a few record companies had offered a maximum advance of $10,000.

Goldsmith convinced Clarence Fountain to do the session in the way that Goldsmith and Chelew had envisioned, a departure from Clarence's "drum machine always plays it perfect" philosophy. Still, Goldsmith knew that he couldn't—wouldn't—overpower Clarence on artistic direction in the studio.

Sparing no expense, Goldsmith and Chelew held the recording session in Capitol Studio B, in the iconic tower on Vine Street near Hollywood Boulevard, a monument to great records. The Blind Boys showed up en masse, traveling like a family, with members like Johnny Fields and others on board who would not record but nonetheless were part of the group.

"There was so much soul and history in that room, singing through fantastic mikes that Frank Sinatra had sang through, recording in a totally analog environment," Goldsmith said.

Nevertheless, the sessions got tense. Goldsmith felt the meter running on a first-class studio and a band to match—guitarists Hammond and David Lindley, bass player Danny Thompson, drummer Michael Jerome, and harmonica player Charlie Musselwhite. He needed to get things done. He felt that the Blind Boys hadn't really considered the song selections he'd sent them in advance, because when the time came to perform, they balked at certain numbers. Fountain expressed distaste for a lyric in Tom Waits's "Jesus Gonna Be Here" that has the savior driving a Ford. Goldsmith told Clarence that the image wasn't meant literally but had been written to connect with present-day audiences, one of Clarence's core beliefs. "Clarence finally said, 'Huh. Alright,'" Goldsmith recalled.

When all was recorded, mixed, and packaged, the track ended up opening the album.

Goldsmith and Chelew planned to more or less split the leads between Fountain, Carter, and George Scott. The album showcased Scott, who had created the Blind Boys' iconic backing vocal attack; he shined during his few times in the spotlight as a lead vocalist but mostly lived in the shadows, despite the widely held opinion that he sang better than anyone else in the band.

Scott's rendition of "Run On for a Long Time" harkened back to the group's very earliest days, crowded around a general store radio in Talladega to listen to the Golden Gate Quartet. The fast-paced, rhyme-rich delivery highlighted Scott's ancient jubilee chops. The song became a feature of the group's repertoire as they toured the late-night TV circuit in support of the album, showing the world that this was as much George Scott's group as anyone's, an overdue but welcome development in the Blind Boys' history.

"We split the leads pretty evenly between Jimmy, George, and Clarence," Goldsmith said. "Those guys were their own trinity, and they all brought something really special. We used to call George our Old Testament singer. We tried to balance the three voices, and that makes the record more interesting. And Joey Williams has always been a big part of the story as the other singer."

The next obstacle appeared in the form of Chelew's acid trip of a church-brothel mash-up.

"The idea of 'Amazing Grace' sung to the tune of 'House of the Rising Sun' was John's inspiration for the whole album," said Goldsmith. "Probably because of the psychedelic experience, that idea was burned on his brain as something that had to happen. I never tried to talk him out of it. To see that concept come to life inspired his passion for the project."

What inspired Chelew chilled the Blind Boys. As Jimmy Carter recalled, "John Chelew wanted us to sing 'Amazing Grace,' which we liked, but to the tune of 'House of the Rising Sun,' which goes against our beliefs. We didn't want to do that."

Chelew seemingly channeled the spirits of the desert night. Though the song meant everything to him, he and Goldsmith had agreed with the Blind Boys that they should all approach the material with an open mind. A few selections had already gone by the wayside. Chelew and Goldsmith had differed over having two Tom Waits songs on the album. With everything riding on Chelew's inspiration, he calmly asked the group to try the song, and if it didn't feel right, it was out.

"That's why the record sounded so good," Goldsmith explained. "John and I conceded certain points and never tried to force anything over them, and they listened and considered our points. Everybody had to have a way to feel good about doing the song. Those conversations added to the emotion of the performance. There was a lot of baggage and emotion coming through their voices."

The Blind Boys sang the song as Chelew had heard it in the desert. Joey Williams, the fourth voice on the album, could feel it. The voices glided through, each change clicking perfectly. By the time they finished, they all had the feeling. Smiles and affirmations went around. "We just had to listen to the playback and we knew it was a hit," Williams said.

———◦•═——

Goldsmith recalled looking at an old photo of the Happy Land Singers, posed around the touring car with their name painted on its driver's-side doors. Fountain, Scott, Fields, and Olice Thomas are teenagers. Velma Traylor is still alive. Elder J. T. Hutton isn't quite an elder. "I'd had this recurring thought that these guys contained in them the soul or conscience of a generation of people, and that they were really something akin to spirit guides for our country at this time, and in that sense a really important force," said Goldsmith. He thought of a one-hundred-ton locomotive called the *Spirit of the Twentieth Century* that had been showcased at the 1904 Saint Louis World's Fair. The title for the album, *Spirit of the Century*, came to him and stuck.

After spending a hundred large on the sessions, negotiating the sacred-profane territorial split to finish the record, and giving the project an inspired name, now came the job of finding a label to put the thing out.

"We made the record knowing that no one had been willing to put up any money for it," said Goldsmith. "When we finished, we were convinced that we had proved everyone wrong. We thought it was so good, we could not be denied. We were only partially right."

Though the companies that had initially offered useless to insulting advances now expressed enthusiasm for the finished product, their mouths and money still seemed far apart. Goldsmith would not be covering his costs with a deal.

Spirit of the Century happened not long after two promising new vehicles had delivered esoteric music to the mainstream—the 1997 album and 1999 documentary *Buena Vista Social Club* and the 2000 big-screen hit *O Brother, Where Art Thou?*

Goldsmith thought that the Blind Boys could be marketed as world music with a twist of eclectic roots. With that in mind, he pitched *Spirit* to Peter Gabriel's Real World Records. Gabriel had seen the Blind Boys back on one of their first UK tours a decade earlier. Real World responded quickly and positively to Goldsmith.

In conversation with the label, Goldsmith felt that they shared his vision—enough—and though Real World reportedly offered less than another company had put on the table, Goldsmith decided to gamble with Gabriel's company.

Real World released *Spirit* in early 2001.

In this bygone but glorious era of thoughtful music reviews in daily newspapers, the Blind Boys drew raves around the world. Despite the producers' effort to spotlight Scott and Carter, Clarence Fountain once again became the human-interest angle. Writers portrayed him, now seventy-one, as a dutiful husband, having settled down with his wife, Barbara, in Baton Rouge, Louisiana. Fountain also acknowledged his six children.

Fountain drew much of the artistic interest as well. In a syndicated feature published in major papers across the country, Scott Barretta of *Living Blues* said, "I think Clarence Fountain is the greatest singer in the United States. I literally get goose bumps listening to him sing."

Most of all, critics heard what Chelew had heard in his head back in Joshua Tree, and they approved. Wendell Brock, previewing an upcoming show in the *Atlanta Journal-Constitution*, wrote, "Though producer John Chelew deserves a medal—a Grammy?—for adding Tom Waits' 'Jesus Gonna Be Here' and Ben Harper's 'Give a Man a Home' to the Blind Boys' repertoire, the real clincher is his far-out remake of 'Amazing Grace' sung to the tune of 'House of the Rising Sun.'"

Two days after their Atlanta appearance, the Blind Boys were in New York, where they performed for the first time on *Late Night with David Letterman*. Their segment aired on May 7, 2001. For Goldsmith, that marked the point of arrival. "[Letterman's] reaction and being on the show moved sales," Goldsmith said. "We ran the table in about a month."

They did other network TV spots, and Goldsmith watched sales increase. "We'd sold over a hundred thousand albums worldwide by the time it was over," he said. "It was a huge jump compared even to *Deep River*."

Another bit of divine grace soon came their way. That second Tom Waits track, which Goldsmith had wanted to cut, suddenly became the most iconic piece of music on the disc. A Jimmy Carter lead, "Way Down in the Hole," was picked up as the theme song to an HBO series no one had heard of. Many fans and critics have since come to recognize the show as one of the greatest in the history of the medium. Jimmy's voice led off *The Wire* for its first season on the air.

The song selection for *Spirit of the Century* charted a new course for the Blind Boys. Besides their recast of "Amazing Grace" and reboots of "Run On" and "The Last Time," they covered Ben Harper, Tom Waits, and the Rolling Stones. Singing newer pop material with spiritual flavor and collaborating with heavy hitters would be the way forward for the group.

The record had another important legacy. As Fountain noted at the time, compared to the numerous Black artists whom the White-dominated entertainment business had ripped off, the cross-over dynamic worked remarkably well for the Blind Boys. There's no denying that their profile grew higher, their audience grew larger, and their paydays grew fatter. These are all very nice things for a singer. The Boys had authenticity in the eyes of the mainstream thanks to their long run on the old gospel highway. And while the group stayed in touch with its longtime followers, it had maximized its potential with the church crowd.

Mainstream industry acclaim came their way in early 2002. *Spirit of the Century* received its Grammy Award nomination in the Traditional Soul Gospel Album category.

On February 8, the Blind Boys made their first appearance on Conan O'Brien's late-night TV show, and weeks of performing to wildly enthusiastic, sold-out crowds followed. Even Salt Lake City packed out the Blind Boys' performance, which caught fire like a program at the Apollo in 1955. A reviewer in the city's *Tribune* wrote,

> Fountain spent most of the show sitting...[but the] music randomly inspired him to jump up and peel his jacket slightly from his shoulders, until guitarist Joey Williams came over to push him back into his seat. Whether this was showmanship or genuine safety concern it's hard to say but it made the visual part of the concert as much fun as the musical.
>
> Not to be outdone, Carter jumped off the...stage into the arms of rhythm guitarist Bobby Butler in order to spend a good 10 minutes leading a revival style sing-along up and down the aisles....Again, this might be something Carter does every night, but the packed house was on its feet, hands clapping, arms waving, reaching for Carter.

And yes, they did that every night, but the real trick is to leave the audience with just that sense of wonder, as if the magic happened right then and there for the first time.

As the mountaintop rose higher virtually every day, the Blind Boys hit a new pinnacle on Valentine's Day 2002, when they performed for President George W. Bush at a White House Salute to Gospel Music. First Lady Laura Bush remarked, "Tonight's performers will bring joy to our hearts, from new generation artists like Jump5 to the established, soulful sounds of the Blind Boys of Alabama."

This eclectic mix of young and established made catching a ride to the event a challenge. As Blind Boys manager Charles Driebe said, "They only had one van picking up the groups from the hotel to take them to the White House. They had these young Christian, which means White, bands and they'd hurry to get on the one van and fill it up. Then the van came back and the next band would run out and fill it up and it'd go. The Blind Boys needed to wait in the lobby but these young Christians would rush ahead, and we couldn't get a ride over. Finally, Yolanda Adams said, 'Y'all need to let these old guys go. They're the reason you're here.' We got on the van because of Yolanda but were kind of running late."

Not too late, of course, for the most oddly timed McDonald's run this side of Amsterdam. "I would always tell them to eat before we leave. They wanted to wait and see if there was free food where we were going. Clarence always complained about how 'high'—expensive—the food was at the hotel," Driebe said. "We finally get in the van and Clarence said he had to have something to eat."

Driebe told him, "Clarence, we're five minutes from the White House."

"I don't care," Clarence said. "I gotta get something to eat."

The driver pulled over to McDonald's, and Driebe jumped out to order for Clarence. He looked behind him and saw the rest of the guys getting in line behind him.

"So we go in to the White House with a guy named Jimmy Carter and all the rest holding McDonald's bags," said Driebe.

"We got in there and got a picture with President Bush, and he literally said, 'You can put that on your next ablum [*sic*].' But he was a nice guy in person."

———◆———

Less than two weeks later, on February 27, 2002, the Blind Boys gathered at the Staples Center in Los Angeles for the Grammy

Awards show. The Boys had been nominated for Grammys on several previous occasions and fallen into a troubling pattern. At the award ceremonies in 1972, 1993, and 1996, Shirley Caesar had won their category each time. In 2002, their major competition would come from, you guessed it, Shirley Caesar.

Joey Williams recalled meeting Tupac Shakur and Snoop Dogg at previous ceremonies. This night would belong mostly to a twenty-one-year-old rhythm and blues phenomenon named Alicia Keys. Goldsmith said, and claimed to believe, that the nomination was the real win. As they all sat together, Goldsmith tried to keep that in mind. But as soon as they heard the announcement that the Blind Boys of Alabama had won the Grammy, it felt like lightning had struck; the electricity jolted everyone to their feet. Everyone hugged everyone, and Joey Williams remembered jumping around in circles with seventy-year-old Jimmy Carter, their hands on each other's shoulders. Though no one seems to remember the presenter, Goldsmith knows he wasn't supposed to go on stage to accept but ran up there anyway. The Blind Boys had achieved yet another improbable height.

CHAPTER 20

"MAY BE THE LAST TIME WE SING TOGETHER . . ."

DONALD DILLON HAD SPENT the better part of fifteen years on the road as Clarence Fountain's eyes—after a confrontation with Lamont Blount, he'd become a personal employee of Fountain rather than a member of the Blind Boys.

He'd seen the group's fortunes rise, having been to *Colonus* and to church gigs they worked for an offering, then traveled the world and escorted Clarence to the Grammys.

Though Fountain rented Dillon his own place in every hotel along the way, Dillon always stayed in the same room as

Clarence. "I think he was afraid of dying alone on the road," Dillon said.

Fountain took good care of himself as a diabetic, and Dillon received training to take good care of him as well. But Fountain could feel time coming for him. And as a leader, Fountain had shouldered an extra burden, as Dillon saw it. Firing Blount may not have hurt him, but Fountain also had to pasture Johnny Fields, one of the group's founding members, as Fields's health deteriorated. Fields had been closest to Fountain throughout the 1940s and 1950s and had stood with Clarence when the Blind Boys split in the 1960s. Fountain had fired Sam Butler as well, a longtime collaborator and the man who'd helped bring the Blind Boys to *The Gospel at Colonus*. Rev. Olice Thomas, another founding member, had died in 2001. These changes took their toll on Clarence.

Mostly, though, he and Dillon had a good time together. "We'd get somewhere and he'd say, 'What do you see, Dillon?' And I'd describe the area to him and he'd go, 'No, I mean to eat!'" Dillon spied the ubiquitous arches of gold, and all felt right for Clarence.

An early bird, Fountain woke Dillon up before dawn and challenged him: "Let's see who can get dressed fastest," he'd say. They went to breakfast and saw that the other members of the group got going and had something to eat. The Blind Boys' bellies had been paramount ever since the school for the blind had half starved them.

Dillon saw Fountain as the real reason for the Blind Boys' success and appreciated Fountain's sacrifices for them as perhaps no one else did. "Clarence Fountain was a born leader," Dillon said. "He was a man with a vision. He knew exactly what he wanted. He knew exactly what he wanted the Blind Boys to do. He took his own personal money, when they weren't making very much, to keep the Blind Boys going. Likewise, when things got good, agents told him to put the rest of the Blind Boys on a salary, so he could keep more of the money. He said, 'Nope, that's not how we started out. If you take a man away from home, you're supposed to pay him.'"

Ricky McKinnie admired Fountain in much the same respect. "He's like a cat," said McKinnie. "He always landed on his feet. He had faith in himself." Both McKinnie and Dillon described Clarence as a "no-nonsense guy." McKinnie, as interim manager, also worked closely with Clarence on the business side and made mental notes about how to run the organization. Fountain encapsulated his vision for the group, repeatedly, with the phrase "the masses of people." He wanted to reach them.

Even while Fountain's vision prospered and accolades veritably rained on the Blind Boys, he whispered to Dillon—the man he had the most responsibility for—that it wouldn't last forever. The poignancy of the Blind Boys set closer, "The Last Time," was lost on no one.

———◆———

Charles Driebe was driving by himself while on vacation in Italy, listening to a demo tape of *Spirit of the Century*, thinking it sounded pretty damn good. Driebe had met producer Chris Goldsmith through the music business and, as an attorney, helped review some contracts for the Blind Boys. Driebe also managed a group that worked with Goldsmith through the Rosebud Agency.

Goldsmith, knowing that the Blind Boys needed a manager, introduced Driebe to Ricky McKinnie. McKinnie had managed the group since 1997, when Kevin Morrow left to run House of Blues. McKinnie interviewed Driebe and reported back to Clarence Fountain that the talk had gone well. Fountain trusted McKinnie's judgment. A few months later, Driebe attended a Blind Boys show at a church in Savannah, Georgia. He went backstage and talked with Fountain, who told Driebe that the group needed a manager and that God might have brought them together.

Driebe got on board in 2000, before the *Spirit of the Century* release, and has managed the Blind Boys ever since.

Driebe's first European tour with the group introduced him to Clarence Fountain's fierce independence. While enthusiasm for *Spirit* ran high, Fountain had apparently sold an existing recording to another label. Driebe learned of this in the most challenging of circumstances—with the staff of Real World Records in the audience of a London club called the Mean Fiddler in April 2001, just after Real World had released *Spirit of the Century*.

"Clarence emceed the show in those days," Driebe recalled. "On stage, he said, 'I've got a new record that's just about to come out on Worldwide Records.' I was thinking, 'Clarence, it's Real World Records.' He goes, 'It's called *My Lord What a Morning*.'"

Driebe, somewhat embarrassed by Clarence's confusion, hoped that the Real World people weren't offended. Peter Gabriel was not among the Real World reps in the house. "It went over the heads of the people from Real World," he said. "They thought he was mixed up too. Instead, he was promoting his other record while playing the showcase for the label he'd just signed to."

As Driebe explained, "This was my first exposure to Clarence's side deals. He had brought the guys into a studio in Texas. Somebody had paid him $5,000, which Clarence had pocketed, and they made that record."

Real World either never found out or forgave an old man his hustle.

The next near disaster awaited just around the corner. "In those days, the guys got paid in cash," said Driebe. "I settled the show, which was one of the first times I'd settled a show. That means you go to a back office and they give you a sheet that shows how many tickets were sold and at what price, what the club owes you, and then they hand you the money. Back then it was U.S. dollars. The Blind Boys didn't want any 'funny money.'"

Driebe returned to the hotel only to realize he'd left the Blind Boys' cash in the dressing room. He called the club in a panic, and a quick search turned up nothing—the money had gone missing. "The club owner got all of the employees together, explained the situation," Driebe recalled, "and said, 'These are some old blind guys, if anybody has it just turn it over, we won't do anything.' Somebody stepped forward and said they'd found it. Man, I dodged a bullet there. On my first trip overseas, I'd forgotten the money. I think it was five thousand bucks."

Later on the same tour, the band was slated to play in Dublin. The daily newspaper there had an ongoing feature that asked musicians who were coming to town a series of standard questions. Driebe asked the questions of Fountain in order to relay the answers to the newspaper. One of the first ones was "What was the first album you ever bought?" Fountain's reply: "There wasn't no albums in those days—it was 78s!" The answer amused the new manager and also reinforced the fact that he was working with a group of singers who could trace their inspiration back to the earliest gospel recordings.

Driebe sat next to Fountain on the flight out of Ireland to France. Clarence had now been around the world more times than 99 percent of us and was ready to impart some globetrotter wisdom.

"Charles, something you gotta know about France," Clarence said. "The food there is terrible—it ain't right."

Following *Spirit of the Century*, Real World Records released the Blind Boys' album *Higher Ground*.

Chris Goldsmith and John Chelew recreated some of the *Spirit* magic, though the role of hallucinogens seems not to have been as central to the vision for the follow-up. They brought the group back to Capitol Studio B, having proposed a set of spiritually rich secular songs, compositions from Stevie Wonder, Prince, Aretha Franklin, and Jimmy Cliff. After the success of "Amazing Grace," the producers received little pushback on the selections. They also put together an excellent band.

Blind Boys guitarist Joey Williams recalled, "We saw Robert Randolph and the Family Band a year before that at the Knitting Factory in LA. We heard this steel guitar music that sounded like rock 'n' roll, but they played with gospel quartet drive. Me and the Blind Boys bass player Tracy Pierce and manager Charles Driebe went out to look at them. Robert on steel guitar, the drummer, keyboardist, and bass player, were all sitting down. They had such high energy, it was so hot up there, they were throwing water on each other."

When Goldsmith told the Blind Boys that he wanted to use Robert Randolph and the Family Band on *Higher Ground*, Williams, Pierce, and Driebe got right on board, and Clarence Fountain soon joined them. "Most people had never heard anything like Robert Randolph," Williams said. "That steel guitar sound is associated with country and western music, and he plays sacred steel like they play in Church of God. It can be rockin'. We'd never had that sound, it was different for us. Clarence recognized it, he said, 'Yeah, Junior Butler's father used to play that Hawaiian guitar.'"

Goldsmith also brought in Ben Harper, another young artist with a vintage soul. "We all did 'People Get Ready' and 'Higher

Ground,'" said Williams. "With them and Robert Randolph and the Family Band, we were stacked pretty heavy."

On "People Get Ready," George Scott sings the opening with the backing vocals lifting the end of the verse and Jimmy Carter leading the background in his warm, clear tenor. It's a magical moment, bringing the frailty of age with the wisdom and strength of the togetherness these men had built. Goldsmith had come to think of Scott, Carter, and Fountain as a holy trinity, and their sound gives no room for argument.

Each member of the holy trinity shows out on "Higher Ground," singing leads to the best of their individual styles while blending marvelously on the song's iconic up-tempo chorus. The Family Band and Harper bring some Cadillac El Dorado funk to the proceedings. The whole conglomeration makes great music on a potentially gimmicky premise.

Blind Boys singer Jimmy Carter felt that *Higher Ground* went more smoothly than the tense *Spirit* session. "We didn't have any trouble with that one," he said. "We hit it off good. Robert was a big fan of the Blind Boys and was excited to do this. He came out of the church."

Still, not every song Goldsmith pitched for the album passed muster with Clarence. He remembered how one potential gem hit the cutting room floor. "We recorded the musical part of the Jimi Hendrix song 'Angel,'" Goldsmith said. "I was pumped about having that song on the record. Clarence said, 'That song's about a man and a woman.' We debated that. I lost the argument and didn't have a good enough retort. Years later I read that Hendrix wrote the song about his mother. If I'd known that, it could've worked. Clarence loved a good mother song."

Carter has said that the Blind Boys bonded with Ben Harper on a spiritual level despite his pop leanings and enjoyed working and hanging out with him as much as anyone in their orbit. Harper played and sang on the album as well.

Higher Ground came out around the same time that Geffen Records released Peter Gabriel's *Up*. Reviewed side by side in some publications, *Higher Ground* achieved higher marks.

The Blind Boys contributed vocals on two tracks of Gabriel's album. Even more importantly, he invited the group to open his shows on massive American and European tours in the largest venues the Blind Boys had played.

Gabriel's team designed a circular stage to place in the middle of the audience at these shows, bringing an element of the surreal to a tour of the biggest arenas in the world. Apparently, having battled the likes of Archie Brownlee leaves one a bit jaded about theatrics. As Blind Boys manager Charles Driebe recalled, "Clarence, who was never impressed by anything, was not impressed. I said, 'Guys, this is big.' He said, 'It ain't nothing but something to do.'"

On opening night of the tour, Gabriel came to thank the Blind Boys. Standing in their dressing room, he said, "I'm really honored to have you guys on tour." They muttered their gratitude, and as Gabriel left, his tour manager stuck around and said that Peter would love to have the Blind Boys join him on his encore.

Clarence said, "I ain't sitting around here for two hours waiting for an encore. If he wants us to do a song early in his show, we'll do it."

By now Driebe had grown somewhat accustomed to the awkward positions in which Fountain's forthrightness placed him. He recalled, "I had to go back to the tour manager and go, 'Hey man, my guys are old, they're more interested in their hotel rooms than an encore.' He said he'd go talk to Peter, and Peter was so cool that he said OK. The Blind Boys would guest every night on the song 'Sky Blue.' Eventually, they did stick around for the encores, singing on one of Gabriel's hits, 'In Your Eyes.' As time went by and everybody got to know each other and be friends, Clarence became more willing to wait. Classic Clarence."

Jimmy Carter appreciated Gabriel's thoughtfulness behind the scenes. "He knew that some of us were diabetic, so when there was a birthday celebration he ordered a sugar-free cake," he said.

On Joey Williams's birthday, Gabriel personally delivered the cake. "He wheeled it right into the dressing room," Williams said. "I almost fainted."

Gabriel proved just as generous a host on stage as he did behind the scenes. "Peter brought us on stage every night," said Williams. "He didn't have to do that, and most artists don't. He didn't even have to be in the building, but he got there early every night to bring us on. He'd give us a nice introduction, like he's emceeing for us. When we came off, he would be there and tell everybody to give it up for Clarence, Jimmy, George, he called all our names."

Throughout the tour, despite Clarence's early indifference, "Sky Blue" became a high point of Gabriel's set. The Blind Boys sat on a platform that rose from below the center of the stage as they brought their harmony to the last chorus of the song. Clarence, Jimmy Carter, Joey Williams, and George Scott sat as four points on the compass, singing as the platform elevated up the sky blue stage in a heavenly image. Fountain hit the low notes while Carter reached angelic heights.

Whether Clarence appreciated the fact or not, Gabriel brought them tremendous exposure and, according to Driebe, an unusually generous payday. "I believe that the guarantee was about five grand a night on the Gabriel tours," he said. "By that time, the Blind Boys were making more than that on their own, but this would get them in front of thousands of people. It juiced record sales and recognition.

I give Peter Gabriel all the credit in the world for his love of music. Peter didn't need the Blind Boys to sell tickets. He sold these arenas based on his name. A big artist in that position would usually offer something like five hundred dollars to the opening act because of the opportunity it represents. Peter offered the guys enough to cover travel and put money in everyone's pockets. He didn't have to do that, he could have gotten plenty of people to do it for nothing."

And so the Blind Boys of Alabama moved up a little higher once again, performing in late fall 2002 at Madison Square Garden, the Target Center in Minneapolis, and other stops, the tour more resembling an NBA season than a gospel highway jaunt. At Chicago's United Center, Driebe had to fill in for guitarist Bobby Butler as Jimmy Carter's guide into the audience. "I took him thirty rows up to a landing and stood him there, and people just went crazy."

Greg Kot, reviewing for the *Chicago Tribune*, observed that Gabriel's classic "In Your Eyes" "stumbled until the Blind Boys consecrated the proceedings with a stunning a cappella affirmation. 'Let the Blind Boys lead you,' Gabriel cried."

Truth be told, the Blind Boys received better reviews than Gabriel on stage just as they had on record. By the next spring, Gabriel and the Blind Boys would take their act overseas, playing Wembley Arena in London and huge venues in Stockholm, Berlin, Paris, Zurich, Barcelona, and the other Birmingham.

On a break between the national and international legs of the tour, the Blind Boys collected their second consecutive Grammy, with *Higher Ground* winning the Best Traditional Soul Gospel Album at Madison Square Garden.

"I can't explain it," said Carter. "When the Blind Boys started out we didn't think about accolades. We were glad when they came, but we weren't about that."

The Blind Boys earned crossover appeal without sacrificing the core values of gospel quartet music. As gospel scholar Opal Nations told a reporter in 2003, the Blind Boys were the last bearers of the old standard. "Nobody does this anymore," said Nations. "It's just them."

CHAPTER 21

DIRTY BOULEVARD MEETS GOSPEL HIGHWAY

N BETWEEN GRAMMYS, WHITE House visits, and international tours, the Blind Boys managed to record their edgiest collaboration of all.

"Hal Willner was producing a record for Lou Reed based on the writing of Edgar Allan Poe and asked the Blind Boys to sing on it," said Blind Boys manager Charles Driebe. "We brought Clarence, George, and Jimmy, plus Joey. We go to the studio and walk in there. Joey has on some sort of hip-hop clothing, so Lou immediately discounts him. That leaves the three old blind men. Lou says, 'Where are the Five Blind Boys?' I'm like, 'Lou, there haven't been five singers for years. These are the Blind Boys of

Alabama, these are the singers.' He's going, 'This isn't what I bargained for. Right plane, wrong airport.' I said, 'This is what we've got, let's see where it goes.'"

Blind Boys guitarist Joey Williams felt the ice personally, as Reed gear-shamed him. "I came in with a Parker Fly guitar," said Williams. "Lou Reed looked at me and said, 'You actually play one of those?' I told him I had a shoulder injury and it's a light guitar, so it didn't hurt. He just said, 'Unh.'"

This collaboration slid downhill quickly. "First thing, the Blind Boys have no idea who Lou Reed is," said Driebe. "Jimmy's calling him Mr. Reeves: 'Mr. Reeves, I got an idea on this one...' That was pretty funny. The guys start in, it takes a while for them to warm up. Lou's going, 'This isn't working!' I'm like, 'Lou, these guys are old. This isn't their genre. They just need a minute.' He goes, 'Your lips to God's ears?' I said, 'Yes, they've got this.'"

Driebe continued, "Within thirty minutes, the guys are killing it, Jimmy's got his scream going, and Lou said the hairs were standing up on his arm. After that, Lou and the guys were big buddies."

Reed, not exactly the cuddliest figure in avant-garde rock, even tossed Williams a compliment. "After the session, we were listening to the playback," Williams said. "He heard the guitar and said, 'Oh, you do get a pretty good sound out of that piece of bleep. I haven't heard one sound like that.'

"I exhaled," Williams said.

The song "I Wanna Know," an interpretation of Poe's "The Pit and the Pendulum," features Reed and Jimmy Carter in duet. You can listen to Jimmy howling and feel what popped Lou's goose bumps. Reed's album *The Raven* came out in early 2003.

Everyone parted on good terms, the Blind Boys letting out a collective sigh of relief as they boarded an elevator and headed for the exit.

Clarence Fountain said, "Is it just us in here?"

Driebe said, "Yeah, just us."

Fountain said, "Who told that man he can sing? That man can't sing!"

As the elevator doors closed on another clash of cultures, the surreal relationship between the Blind Boys and Lou Reed had just begun.

Both the Blind Boys and Lou Reed were invited to perform at the United Nations General Assembly Hall. The Landmine Survivors Network booked the Blind Boys to reinforce the UN message of equal rights for people living with disabilities—including those disabled by landmines.

Reed and Driebe agreed to discuss performing a song together and the tricky aspect of what song to choose. The Blind Boys had shot down material depicting much cleaner topics than Reed's typical dystopian tableau of heroin addiction, drag queens, and Jezebels. Driebe did some research. "One year for Christmas, my brother gave me a book of Lou Reed lyrics," he said. "I was able to identify five songs, out of about a hundred, that the Blind Boys could do, that didn't deal with drugs and the seamy underbelly of New York City."

Reed, however, saw it differently. "What about 'Dirty Boulevard?'" he asked.

The United Nations notwithstanding, Driebe said that the Blind Boys could not sing about prostitutes and junkies in any hall. Driebe countered with a song from an early Velvet Underground album.

"I said, 'What about 'Jesus'?" Driebe recalled. "And he said, 'I haven't sung that song in thirty years,' but he ended up agreeing to it."

So, on May 26, 2004, people danced in the aisles of the United Nations General Assembly Hall.

Producer Chris Goldsmith witnessed the UN gig and wanted to record "Jesus." Reed and the Blind Boys got on board with the idea and met at a studio.

After showing up in hip-hop regalia with a cheap guitar to the Poe recording, Joey Williams ran late for the next session with Reed.

"They didn't tell him who they were waiting on," he said. "They just said one of the Blind Boys. I sang all the backgrounds and played, so I was one of the guys. Lou figured it must have been one of the older blind men, and not a young sighted guy. They didn't wait an hour but that ten or fifteen minutes was enough. When I got there, he said, 'Is this who we were waiting on?' He pointed at me. I said, 'Yeah,' and I apologized. He said nothing. After the session, he said, 'You do make that guitar sound better than any other piece of junk I've ever heard.'"

Rather than hope to convert Reed to the Parker Fly, Williams adapted. "From that point on, if we did something with Lou Reed, I brought my Fender," Williams said. "When we did Letterman, I brought the Fender. We did Australia with him. I brought the Fender. He said, 'You finally got a Fender.'"

As Williams indicated, the Reed–Blind Boys collaboration became much more than the typical one-off. The recording of their "Jesus" came out on the Blind Boys' 2009 album *Duets*. Reed was kind enough to join their publicity efforts for the record, appearing on *Late Night with David Letterman* on January 21, 2010—albeit not without the prerequisite rocky liftoff.

"He showed up to the rehearsal studio before the Letterman show," said Driebe. "Jimmy had stepped out to get something to eat. Jimmy was his main guy, he really liked Jimmy. He was like, 'Where the hell is everybody?' He didn't say it, but his tone was like 'I'm Lou Reed!'"

By this time, the Blind Boys' lineup had changed to feature lead singers Jimmy Carter, Ben Moore, and Billy Bowers, along with Joey Williams. Lou Reed sang and played lead guitar with the Blind Boys band, Tracy Pierce on bass, Ricky McKinnie on drums, and Joey Williams on his Fender. Jimmy caught some punk grit from Reed and primal-growled over the final chorus to Lou's apparent delight. Reed distorted a note to close out strong. David Letterman bounded on stage after the number, congratulated the blind singers, and shook Reed's hand. "That's a song you wrote, my friend? Just tremendous," Letterman said.

Six months later, they reprised the song on stage at the Sydney Opera House. "Lou and Laurie Anderson were curating a festival there and they invited the Blind Boys," said Driebe.

The Blind Boys' manager had the perfunctory painful production meeting with a moody Reed before the show. Driebe said, "He and Hal Willner wanted to talk about what the Blind Boys were doing. I was trying to get him to come sing with us, and everything I said, Lou was like, 'That's bullshit, that's not gonna work.' He was not in favor of anything."

Reed naturally shot down the opportunity to play "Jesus" on Australian TV with the Blind Boys. Driebe asked a singer called My Brightest Diamond (now known as Shara Nova) to fill in. He loved what she brought to the song, and she stuck around to open the Blind Boys' festival set with it.

"We ended up doing 'Jesus' twice at the Opera House," Driebe said. "The guys opened the show with her doing it, because we didn't think Lou was coming. He never said anything, he just showed up and sang it. The audience loved it."

The Blind Boys released another Grammy winner, *Go Tell It on the Mountain*, in 2003. The Christmas album turned out to be the mother of all collaborative sessions, with Tom Waits, Chrissie Hynde, Mavis Staples, and Aaron Neville among the guests. There is a surreal charm to George Clinton and Robert Randolph appearing on "Away in a Manger."

Guitarist Joey Williams recalled that George Scott came up with a little joke about the material. At a holiday banquet in Germany, Scott told Williams, "Oh they poured for me some rum-pum-pum-pum."

The record led to a classic Blind Boys event, the *Go Tell It on the Mountain* PBS TV Christmas special. The Beacon Theater on Broadway, an ornate, three-thousand-seat palace, sold out for a powerful performance, with the holy trinity of Scott, Fountain, and Carter in full throat. The hard-hitting title song, with organist John Medeski giving it his all, brings swing to the birth of Jesus. For a Christmas program, a risky proposition for hard-core fans, there isn't a Perry Como cornball among the tunes.

The Blind Boys had worked with Mavis Staples since their respective days on the gospel highway, when the Blind Boys and the Staple Singers headlined quartet battles. After recording together on the Christmas album, Staples joined the bill for the Beacon show. Their harmony on stage masked a light note of discord behind it, as Driebe recalled.

"The Beacon has a rabbit warren of dressing rooms," he said. "We had Mavis Staples in one of the big dressing rooms. Mavis's road manager, her sister Yvonne, came to me and said, 'Chrissie Hynde's dressing room is bigger than Mavis's.' I couldn't see any difference in the size of the rooms, but I went to Chrissie and asked if she wouldn't mind switching. She said, 'No problem.' She had no ego about it."

Hynde didn't linger in any dressing room long, as the cameras caught her coming out to take a peek from behind the curtain at Jimmy Carter's crowd walk.

Go Tell It on the Mountain has become a perennial seller, though the next Blind Boys project would be more of a landmark recording for the group and its number one collaborator, Ben Harper. In September 2004, Virgin Records released *There Will Be a Light*. The album reached an artistic pinnacle for Harper and the Blind Boys. It also brought about the end of their creative partnership.

CHAPTER 22

TAKE MY HAND

T HE CONNECTION TO BEN Harper started with the *Spirit of the Century* album," said producer Chris Goldsmith.

Harper at that point had released four successful solo albums, the most recent of which, *Burn to Shine*, yielded a top-twenty single, "Steal My Kisses," and would notch nearly a million certified sales.

"We had recorded his song 'Give a Man a Home,'" Goldsmith continued. "I went to see Ben play a show in Flagstaff, Arizona. Ben, my mom, and me sat in a rental car and listened to the Blind Boys do that song. All three of us were crying or on the verge of tears. Hearing them cover his song bonded Ben to the guys."

After *Spirit*, Harper had contributed to each subsequent Blind Boys album as the bond grew. *There Will Be a Light* began with Harper producing the record and Goldsmith as executive producer. They all reunited in Capitol Studio B, where Goldsmith had blocked out five days. Harper had planned on remaining behind the scenes while the Blind Boys sang his material.

"Ben reached deep for lyrics that were personally important to him," said Goldsmith. "None of the songs were completely finished. He would disappear during the sessions and go work on finishing a song. He'd come back and say, 'OK, I got it.' It was a creation process as much as a recording process."

As Harper demonstrated his songs for the Blind Boys, lining out how the parts should be sung, a new chemistry took hold. After the first five-day session, Goldsmith and Harper reevaluated the direction of the album. What had come together spontaneously did not fit the original plan.

Instead of a Blind Boys record for Real World, *There Will Be a Light* came out as a Ben Harper and the Blind Boys of Alabama album on Virgin Records, where Harper was signed. He wrote or cowrote all but three of the eleven tracks and sang or played guitar on all.

There Will Be a Light would hit the top-ten album charts in six countries as well as topping the *Billboard* gospel album chart in the United States. Sales of the previous three Blind Boys albums beginning with *Spirit of the Century* had all hovered around a hundred thousand. Everyone felt ecstatic with those results. Initial US sales of *There Will Be a Light* approached two hundred thousand, with another two hundred thousand sales in France alone.

On October 12, 2004, Harper and the Blind Boys performed at the Apollo Theater in Harlem to film a DVD. Harper took the stage with his band. He sat and played slide guitar, opening with the ethereal Blind Willie Johnson–style instrumental "11th Commandment," which would win Harper a Grammy, as the Blind Boys filed out behind Joey Williams, each with a hand on the shoulder of the man in front of him. They took seats beside Harper, all dressed in matching mint-green suits. They'd played the Apollo back in the 1950s with some of the earliest sacred programs in the building's history. Jimmy Carter channeled his best quartet-battle energy, ranging out into the crowd on the closing number to take the house. He hopped up and down as the fans screamed, executing a shriek-inducing trust fall into the arms of Joey Williams to climax his act, vamping the chorus and ad-libbing all the way as the pulse-driving tempo pumped. By now, longtime leader Clarence Fountain had totally passed the important gospel quartet role of house wrecker on to Carter. As Williams observed, "The new fans don't always know our names, or our history, or who Clarence Fountain is, but they always remember the guy out in the audience."

Carter's gospel journey had been even more challenging than the rest of the Blind Boys'. Too young to leave school with the Happy Land Jubilee Singers, he'd stayed behind in Talladega for nearly ten years while his friends worked the road. He'd worked his way up through the gospel quartet farm system, beginning with the Dixieland Blind Boys of Mobile before getting the coveted gig with the Blind Boys of Mississippi. Even then he'd sung backup, though distinguishing himself as a brilliant leader of supporting vocalists. Finally reuniting with his school chums in the early 1980s, he joined the Blind Boys of Alabama full-time. There he found his voice— at turns gravelly, joyful, and electrifying—as a quartet leader and became an unlikely, though worthy, legacy of the unique musical role that had evolved in his birthplace of Birmingham nearly a century before. Now his distinctive tenor rang out around the world.

As Carter shined at the Apollo, Fountain sat still and sang his bass part. He'd taken ill and had a hard time making the gig at all. Once he heard that the concert would be filmed, though, he battled through it and got himself on stage. Manager Charles Driebe had a car at the back door waiting to take Clarence to his hotel room as soon as the show ended.

Jimmy finally got back up on stage, and the band wound down the song. On the final note, the crowd went wild. After taking bows and slapping high-fives, Harper jumped onto a piece of equipment and from there flew off stage.

Jimmy had set the place on fire. The applause would not die down. Harper wanted to go back for an encore. He assembled his guys and looked over toward the Blind Boys. "Clarence was already out the door," said Driebe. "I held up my hands, like, 'Can't do it!' And Ben got pissed."

Still energized, Harper and his band, the Innocent Criminals, went back and played an encore set. Driebe later said he thought that Harper had played a particularly sharp song, and one record of the show's set lists "Don't Take That Attitude to Your Grave" as one of Harper's encores.

"There had been no discussion about an encore," said Driebe. "We had no other material, we sang the whole record and there was no other song we'd practiced."

Harper and the Blind Boys met up the next day for a photo shoot. Harper's manager approached Driebe and reportedly said, "Ben didn't appreciate you guys hanging him out to dry last night."

Driebe said that he had to look out for a sick old man. He meant Harper no disrespect. "His manager told me, 'Our time working together is coming to an end,'" said Driebe.

Even with the group's most successful album on the move, it would be a time of endings for the Blind Boys. The night before the Apollo show, Harper and the group had performed on *Late Night with David Letterman*. They did a song called "Take My Hand."

George Scott sang the closing verse. He normally ad-libbed a little solo as the song faded out. On live TV, though, George carried his solo further. After the band ended the song, he kept going. He had never performed the song that way and did not do that in rehearsal. But the moment transfixed everyone.

The camera zoomed in on him and held the shot.

"Letterman was rocked. The production staff was rocked. Ben was rocked," Chris Goldsmith said. "Normally people would be freaking out that he went seven seconds over his time. Instead, everyone felt like God was taking over."

Driebe said, "He never sought the spotlight. It was his moment in the sun."

This wasn't the first time that quiet George had stolen the show. During the group's appearance on *60 Minutes*, he broke into song with Dan Rather, and the pair did a duet of "Ezekiel Saw the Wheel," exactly the style of spiritual that Mr. Old Testament shined on.

Always the group's anchor, its leading background voice, George Scott had enjoyed a status on a par with Clarence Fountain and Jimmy Carter as a member of the Blind Boys' holy trinity while they stood at the pinnacle of their fame. His impromptu solo on *Letterman* would be his swan song.

A few months later, on March 9, 2005, George Scott died in his sleep at home in Durham, North Carolina. He was seventy-five years old. Scott was impossible to replace. Not only had he coordinated the classic Blind Boys background vocal style and become one of the holy trio of leads, but he may have been the last of the singers in the unique jubilee style, with its historic roots in the spiritual survival of slavery. Though he had not played guitar in recent years due to arthritis in his hands, Scott also ranks among the earliest electric guitarists in gospel quartet history. His guitar played mostly as his voice did, in the background, but added a flourish to the Blind Boys' signature sound. His lead guitar work and lead vocals on the 1956 Specialty release "Swinging on the Golden Gate" combine in one of the most excellent and surprising recordings in the group's vast repertoire. His unreleased secular "In the Garden," with its Latin beat, shows what might have been had Scott gone the way of Sam Cooke.

Scott also stands out as the only Blind Boy to never leave the group from its inception in Talladega until his death nearly seventy years later. Toward the end of his life he hinted at great, unrealized ambition inside. "If I had had my sight from the get-go, I don't know what I would have been in to, to tell you the truth," Scott said. "Singing, at the time, hadn't crossed my mind, until I got to school and found out how they was teaching us caning chairs and making brooms and mops. I couldn't see no money in that."

The Blind Boys learned of George's death while on tour. "George passed as we were on the road in Hong Kong," said Joey Williams, who'd studied Blind Boys–style guitar with Scott and become the group's musical director. "We had to perform that night and debated whether or not to go on. We realized that if it was any of us, we'd want the show to go on anyway. We knew that George would want us to sing, so we went out there. It was the worst show we've ever done. We mixed up verses, voices were breaking. I had to sing his part in certain songs. Me, Ricky, Jimmy, Tracy, we were all just trying to get through. We hardly ever do a bad one."

Though he couldn't really be replaced, the group had to try.

"Even before George passed, I kept a list of blind gospel singers," said manager Charles Driebe. "I knew that we might need someone. I felt like this group is a franchise and a sound that wasn't dependent on any specific person—because a specific person can go away."

Driebe recalled how he got a surprising lead on a new Blind Boy. He said, "When George passed, Col. Bruce Hampton, who was like the southern Frank Zappa, called me and said, 'There's a guy down in Pensacola who'd be good for your Blind Boys. His name's Ben Moore. He used to sing as Bobby Purify. He's gone blind and he sings in some hotel lounge down here.'"

The Blind Boys had a unique way of holding tryouts. En route to New Orleans, they hosted auditions on a tour bus. They stopped in Atlanta and Birmingham, picking up candidates. "Then a White guy got on the tour bus with a blind singer," said Joey Williams. "Ben Moore and his manager. Right in front of the bus, I got my guitar and started singing with Ben. He sang leads. We did harmony. He sang all the voices, all the parts. He jumped right to each one, no problem. In the middle of the chorus, I said let's switch now. He had it. I told everybody, this is the guy."

Moore fit what the group needed without George, and they wanted him to join them immediately. Joey asked Ricky McKinnie if they had an extra uniform for Moore to wear on stage in New Orleans. Ricky gave up the very suit off his own back—it fit Moore as if it had been tailored for him.

Moore joined the Blind Boys as a finished product, having performed professionally for years before losing his eyesight, thus gaining the two key qualifications. Moore had sung in pop duos, once under a famous stage name, and earned a Grammy nomination as a solo gospel singer.

As Moore told author John Capouya in an interview for the

book *Florida Soul*, he had grown up singing and playing guitar in a sacred family group in Atlanta. On the sly, Moore sang in whiskey joints before running away from home with the carnival. He and a vocalist named James Spencer recorded for Atlantic in 1966 as Ben & Spence. In the mid-1970s, Moore became the third singer to perform as Bobby Purify in the duo James & Bobby Purify. James claimed that Ben Moore was the best of the bunch.

The Purify duo still had some juice even without Bobby the First. With longtime producer Papa Don Schroeder, they rerecorded Purify's classic, "I'm Your Puppet," for Mercury Records in 1977 after a run with disco hit machine Casablanca Records.

Moore's 1982 recording of "He Believes in Me" garnered a Grammy nomination for Best Soul Gospel Performance, though Rev. Al Green took home the gold instead. Soon after, glaucoma deprived Moore of his eyesight. His life fell apart. Moore lost his home and spent nights under a bridge in Pensacola, with only the slightest bit of tunnel vision in his right eye. Ray Charles contacted Moore through a mutual friend and said, as Moore told Capouya, "Don't sit your ass around, you've got a voice, use it."

Moore followed both pieces of advice. He took vocational rehab to learn how to function blindly and sang along with records to keep his voice strong. Just before he auditioned with the Blind Boys, Moore recorded a Bobby Purify comeback album with Southern Soul producer Dan Penn.

Moore's exercise of singing along with records sharpened him on every key. During his Blind Boys tryouts, the other members tested his versatility, and as all accounts agree, Ben Moore got the job on the spot.

The band accepted Moore at once. Bass player Tracy Pierce had been with the group since the late 1990s. As Pierce recalled, "I nicknamed Ben 'TGB.' Everywhere we went, he asked for a to-go box. I don't care where, we eat on a plane, he'd ask the stewardess for a to-go box. I named him TGB for to-go box. He said, 'Trae, I'm gonna buy you a little red fire truck toy because you playin' all the time.'"

—————◆—————

Within a few weeks either side of George's death, the Blind Boys won their fourth consecutive Grammy Award, with *There Will Be a Light* taking the Best Gospel Soul Album category, while their new album *Atom Bomb* hit. Featuring three leads by Mr. Old Testament, including "Blind Barnabas," from the Golden Gate Quartet repertoire, *Atom Bomb* was like a George Scott tribute album.

Unfortunately, *Atom Bomb* landed at a time of uncertainty in the music business. The support system that had helped the previous four Blind Boys albums no longer existed. Real World Records' American distributor went out of business as digital file sharing crushed the traffic in CDs, and entities like Tower Records ultimately would not survive the shift.

Chris Goldsmith estimated that the record sold twenty thousand units. "If *Spirit of the Century* had sold twenty, we'd have thought that was pretty darn good," he said. But the Blind Boys were on a run of four consecutive Grammy wins with sales numbers on their records hitting close to six figures and, with Ben Harper's help, reaching over a half million.

"That was the end of our glory run," Goldsmith said. "The industry changed so much in such a short period of time. We went back to having a hard time finding a budget to produce a record with."

CHAPTER 23

PRINCE PRINCE?

For much of the group's glory run, longtime lead singer Clarence Fountain had remained seated while performing. He'd pop up, flash the megawatt smile, open his blazer, and cock his hip, before taking his seat again. He emceed shows with charm and sang his baritone background parts with aplomb. But as he had warned his right-hand man Donald Dillon, he was slowing down. He had to miss some shows and gutted his way through others at less than full strength. By early 2007, he'd ceased touring overseas.

"Every time we got off the plane, someone would greet us," said Joey Williams. "They'd ask Clarence how he was doing, how was the flight, he just said, 'Eat.' We could be in Greece or Italy, somewhere with great food and they'd ask what he wanted. 'Mack Donald's.' He didn't say McDonald's, it was Mack Donald's. I don't know if that threw him off, the way he was eating on the road."

Fountain had long since moved on from peanut butter 'n' syrup sandwiches. The impact of hunger that he experienced as a student in Talladega, however, had stuck with him. That hunger motivated him to get away in the first place. That hunger had helped him measure success. Repeatedly, he referred to gospel music keeping his belly full as a reason that he didn't need to cross over and sing rock 'n' roll. That hunger had also led to his health issues later in life.

The challenges facing a blind, elderly diabetic multiplied on foreign soil. He might have to wake up in the middle of the night to administer his insulin on schedule. Despite the globe-conquering force of McDonald's, he couldn't always find sufficient food in times of need. As Williams recalled, "Clarence got sick several times overseas. He had to be hospitalized. It was so scary every time. The last time happened somewhere they didn't speak a lot of English, and that really threw him for a loop. He said he couldn't do it anymore."

Guitarist Bobby Butler said, "He lost so much weight. We were walking to our hotel. He said, 'Hey man, I can't make it.' I had to carry him like a child down the street."

By mid-2007, Fountain had taken a break from domestic touring. The band circulated a new press photo, showing Jimmy Carter at the center, flanked by Billy Bowers, Ben Moore, and Ricky McKinnie, with bassist Tracy Pierce and guitarists Joey Williams and Bobby Butler standing by.

In January 2008, the band announced that Fountain had to retire completely due to health reasons. Fountain needed dialysis three times per week and had to stay close to home in Baton Rouge.

While Ben Moore joined the group following the death of George Scott, Billy Bowers also returned to the lineup. A graduate of the Alabama School for the Negro Deaf and Blind, Bowers had joined the Blind Boys for the first time during the late 1960s when Fountain had left to pursue a solo career. Bowers had sung lead on the Blind Boys' first Grammy-nominated album back in 1971. Hailing from Jasper, Alabama, where he'd been ordained a bishop in the Church of God in Christ, Bowers possessed a powerful voice and a biting sense of humor. When manager Charles Driebe asked Stevie Wonder to join the Blind Boys on stage to sing his song "Higher Ground," Bishop Bowers piped up and said, "He ain't takin' my verse!" Wonder agreed nonetheless.

Bowers's longtime friend Ricky McKinnie recalled another episode featuring the bishop's unique take on life. "He bought a twenty-five-inch television," said McKinnie. "He went and got a chair from the kitchen and set it right in front of the TV. One of the guys sitting there said, 'Why can't you move to the side so everybody else can watch TV?' He said, 'This my twenty-five-inch TV; you want to watch TV, go home.'"

Bowers and McKinnie had gone back a long way. Bowers sang with the Ricky McKinnie Singers in Atlanta between his stints with the Blind Boys and appeared on McKinnie's *Rock with Ricky* public-access TV show. When Clarence Fountain cracked a door for Bowers to return, McKinnie threw it open.

"One day Clarence was talking to me," said McKinnie, "mad about one of the singers not doing something the way he wanted it done. He said, 'If they make me mad, I'll get Billy Bowers back.' I said, 'For real?' He said, 'Yeah.' First thing I did was pick up the phone and call Billy. 'You want to come back to the group?' He said yeah and got on the next plane. Clarence brought Billy back to annoy people. Jimmy didn't like Billy because Billy was so outspoken. He said what he meant and meant what he said."

Musically, Bowers fit in well. "Billy liked to sing and he was an aggressive singer," said McKinnie. "He jumped right in and went to doing what he did. He could move a crowd. He'd squall and shake."

Having Bowers on board helped to smooth the transition to life after Clarence.

Though Clarence had left, he wasn't entirely gone. After Clarence had retired and seemingly gone back home to Baton Rouge, Charles Driebe got a call in late 2008 with a tip that someone was making a Blind Boys album. "I said, 'That's funny, because they're touring Europe,'" Driebe recalled.

Sam Butler, who'd gone on the road with Fountain in the 1970s and brought the Blind Boys to *The Gospel at Colonus* in the 1980s, collaborated with Clarence and Bobby Butler at a studio in Louisiana. That in itself posed no problem, but they seemed to be selling their project as a Blind Boys of Alabama record.

Driebe had a painful conversation with Fountain: "I told him, 'You're not the Blind Boys of Alabama.'"

"Yes I am," Fountain reportedly said.

As a legal entity, the Blind Boys of Alabama existed in partnership as a limited liability company. Those partners included Jimmy Carter, Ricky McKinnie, Joey Williams, and Fountain, whether he actively participated with the group or not. The partnership owned the trademark on the Blind Boys of Alabama name, as well as a few variants, and any use of that name in a business venture would have to pass a vote of the partners. Clarence's solo recording project lost in that endeavor three to one.

"You can't use the name," Driebe told Fountain.

"But it'll sell better if I do," Fountain replied.

Driebe had to chuckle.

Clarence had an itch to scratch. Throughout the process of making successful recordings beginning with *Spirit of the Century,* he'd felt marginalized. Writer Lee Hildebrand talked to Fountain during the early months of his retirement. The singer said that he and Chris Goldsmith had argued over repertoire and that Goldsmith tended to ignore Fountain's suggestions. As Clarence said of Goldsmith, "He wouldn't let me call no songs."

Driebe confirmed the situation and explained the outcome. "There was always tension in making records with Clarence because he had ideas of how it should be. He'd tell Chris, Chris would say, 'OK, Clarence,' and never do it because Clarence had terrible ideas."

The artistic death knell for Fountain's ambitions sounded in the form of an electronic beat. "Drum machine plays perfect every time, never misses a beat," he said on more than one occasion. Driebe did not believe that Blind Boys fans as of 2000 wanted to hear drum machine on a record, seeking a more authentic sound.

This type of discrepancy goes back to the Blind Boys' earliest crossover opportunity with Ry Cooder in the early 1990s. While Cooder wanted to cut a rootsy record, Fountain wanted a contemporary sound.

As Fountain told Hildebrand, the same difference had continued. "I told Chris, 'Hey man, I don't like the tunes you got...[A]s far as I'm concerned, they're old tunes and they're not up to par.'"

Fountain's solo record came out in 2009 as *Stepping Up & Stepping Out* by Clarence Fountain, Sam Butler, and the Boys. Donald Fagan of Steely Dan guested on two tracks and contributed liner notes.

The effort grabbed a few good reviews and landed Fountain and Butler on BET's *Bobby Jones Gospel* show from Nashville, playing a two-fister called "Do What the Lord Say Do" and reprising a song from Fountain's 1970s solo set, "Me and Jesus." Butler brings some nice Bobby "Blue" Bland–style vocals, while Fountain, in his Versace shades, hits the deep notes. They look good and sound solid.

He may not have sold a million records on his own, but Fountain proved a formidable contemporary gospel voice. As he said in one of his press interviews, "You like to go where music has never been."

Though the Happy Land Jubilee Singers had left Talladega without hesitation, the Blind Boys returned to the campus as honored guests, the most distinguished in the school's history. In February 2008, the Alabama School for the Deaf and Blind celebrated its 150th anniversary.

For Jimmy Carter, it was a full-circle moment. "I always wanted to go back to Talladega," Carter said. "As the years went by, the school became much better. Now it's rated number one. Going back and performing for the anniversary, I count it a privilege. The school has really moved forward. I'm proud of it."

The feeling is mutual. "Mr. Carter continues to serve as a role model and inspiration for current students at the Alabama School for the Blind," said school president John Mascia.

Not long after Fountain left the group, the Blind Boys suddenly found themselves in their most spontaneous collaboration yet. While playing the Knitting Factory in Los Angeles on March 7, 2008, they were building to the peak of their show, performing the song "Look Where He Brought Me From."

"Jimmy was doing his thing out in the audience," said guitarist Joey Williams. "While he was out there, a guy tapped me on the shoulder. I'm thinking, 'Who's on my stage?' I turned around and don't even know the guy."

The stranger had to shout over the crowd noise and the band in their groove. He said, "Prince wants to know if he can come out."

Williams wasn't sure he'd heard the man right. "I said, 'Prince? Prince Prince?'" Williams recalled. "He turned back to the dressing room and pointed. There's Prince back there in our dressing room. I said, 'Oh yes!'"

Bass player Tracy Pierce said, "I looked to the side of the stage and saw this little guy dancing around, jumping around. Almost shouting like he's in the Holy Spirit. He had these big guys standing around. In Hollywood, it's nothing for you to see an impersonator. I brought Chuck over and said, 'Look over there, that looks like Prince.' He went around the stage. He didn't have to tell me it was Prince by the way he was reacting. Next thing you know, Prince heads to the stage."

Meanwhile, the crowd had mobbed Jimmy as he made his way through the audience asking, "Do you feeeeeel it?" They barely noticed as Prince strode out on stage, clapping his hands as the band sped up the pace of what they call their drive. Jimmy surely had no idea. He was quite busy with the Holy Spirit himself.

"Prince is still clapping, getting into the groove of our drive, trying to figure out what to do with his hands," said Williams. "I gestured to my guitar, to offer my guitar. He had both his hands out waving them towards him, like 'Give it here.' I did."

Pierce added, "Prince played a good bit of the drive. He played a real quartet drive, he was jamming. He didn't play normal Prince style."

After tangling with Lou Reed, Williams had left the Parker Fly at home and had a Duesenberg to loan Prince. "A much nicer guitar," said Williams. "He took the guitar and sat on the stool. He didn't even put the strap on, he just sat on the stool and jammed out. The boys kept driving and Prince jammed like he knew the song. Just killing it. Me and Ben were singing backup. Tracy went to go tell Ricky."

Ricky McKinnie said, "I was playing drums. We were in our drive, playing fast. The bass player, Tracy Pierce, came to me and said, 'Don't stop now, that's Prince playing the guitar.' I said, 'Whaaaat?' I had no idea that was going to happen. We didn't even know he was coming to the show. It was impromptu. That was great."

Williams said, "He played for a while and gave me back the guitar."

Williams watched Prince as the artist headed off stage but took a detour on the way out. "We had Jason Crosby on keys," Williams said. "We were supposed to have another keyboard player, but he didn't show. His keyboard was there. It was a DX7. Jason told me later he didn't want Prince to think he'd ordered the DX7."

Prince, however, was no stranger to Yamaha synthesizers. He reportedly recorded the iconic intro to "When Doves Cry" on a DX7 and used the instrument consistently throughout the 1980s. His own DX7 sold at auction in 2020 for $73,698.

Williams and bass player Pierce hoped to hang out with Prince after the set, but the artist chatted a minute, telling Pierce he was a "big, big fan," and disappeared as quickly and mysteriously as he had materialized. Pierce said, "The whole thing lasted about ten minutes."

Williams added, "He just vanished from there. By the time our gig was over, he was gone."

CHAPTER 24

A LIFETIME OF ACHIEVEMENT

THE BLIND BOYS OF Alabama spent the night before their greatest honor in a haunted hotel in Durango, Colorado.

"The people who ran the place told us we might hear a party going on or see some strange things," said Joey Williams. "Me and Tracy were like yeah, yeah, yeah."

As the night went on, however, the skeptics began to believe. Bottles tumbled off of a countertop untouched. Water disappeared from Williams's glass, though he hadn't had any to drink. He heard unexplained noises.

"I used to prank them," said bass player Tracy Pierce. "You know us, Black people don't do ghosts. After everybody went to their room, I'd be up under the door crack going, 'Woooooo.'"

Over in another room, Ricky McKinnie, blind and alone, had heard enough. "Ricky called somebody and said, 'Look, I need someone to come down and stay in my room,'" Williams said.

"Anything like that, it was me," Pierce said. "I was up under Ricky's door."

If a haunted hotel wasn't frightening enough, Williams had to fly to Los Angeles the next morning, where he had hours to make a hair appointment and get fixed up before receiving the Blind Boys' most prestigious award yet. On February 7, 2009, the Recording Academy recognized the Blind Boys of Alabama with its Lifetime Achievement Award.

The group had already earned a National Heritage Fellowship from the National Endowment for the Arts and been inducted into the Gospel Music Hall of Fame. The Blind Boys felt that the Lifetime Achievement Award came about through their own diligent effort and determination to stay true to themselves over many years and miles. "The Blind Boys had been through the mill," said Ricky McKinnie, who was on hand to accept the award. "The Black gospel circuit isn't the easiest thing in the world to travel. From California to New York in a van. Them having to depend on others so much and sticking to gospel. They were on all the major record labels that Black gospel could be on, pretty much."

The award reunited founding members Clarence Fountain and Johnny Fields with the rest of the Blind Boys. "Johnny Fields and Clarence were just like brothers," said McKinnie. "They were the two tightest friends in the group."

At the presentation, on the day before the Grammy Awards show, Clarence apparently showed no ill will from the dispute over using the Blind Boys name. He cracked wise, pitched his new solo project, and told McKinnie he was just honored to be there. Fields, in a wheelchair, joined the procession as Fountain, Jimmy Carter, Billy Bowers, Ben Moore, and McKinnie marched down the red carpet in classic Blind Boys fashion, single file, with a hand atop the shoulder of the next man, like they were sneaking out of school to go listen to the Golden Gate Quartet once more.

Joey Williams, meanwhile, had rushed to treat a very dangerous situation. "When we flew in to L.A., I had to go straight to get my hair done," he said. "They cut me up wrong. I was so disgruntled."

Before the show, Williams, though not at his personal best, met one of the all-time legends of show business hair, Johnny Mathis, before taking the stage to accept the Grammy Award from one of his personal heroes. "Jimmy Jam presented us," said Williams. "He called us up and I was able to shake his hand. I was a super duper fan of all things Minneapolis. Just to shake his hand was an honor and he's giving us a Lifetime Achievement."

Williams added, "That was one of my worst hair days. That's what stands out to me, besides meeting Johnny Mathis and Jimmy Jam."

Mattie Fields, Johnny Fields's wife and a former business manager of the group, took the stage for her husband and received his award.

At the podium, Carter remarked that he had had to pinch himself that morning to see if he was dreaming, but it hurt, so this must be true. He thanked Fountain and Fields for making sacrifices to be present. He reminded the crowd that the Blind Boys had more business to take care of. "You know, we are nominated for a Grammy tomorrow night," he said. "We might get it, we might not. But if we don't, we already got four."

The next night, they won again, a Best Traditional Gospel Album award for *Down in New Orleans*.

The Lifetime Achievement Award honored Johnny Fields just in time. He died on November 12, 2009. He left not only a legacy as a founding voice of the Blind Boys of Alabama but an inspiring story in his right. Despite his blindness, Fields became first the Blind Boys' business manager and later a booking agent for much of the gospel highway. His sharp memory kept the information that would normally fill an agent's filing cabinet. Fields also produced records, working freelance for Jewel Records, where he collaborated with Fountain as well as the Blind Boys of Mississippi during the 1970s. Fields produced Fountain's excellent concert record of a show in Danville, Virginia, released as *Mr. Clarence Fountain: Live and in Person*. Fields's son Dwight, also a singer, joined the Manhattans, whose lead vocalist, Gerald Alston, was Johnny's nephew. Years after he'd gone, numerous gospel veterans could still recite the Fields family home address and telephone number from memory. His fellow Blind Boys considered Fields the historian of the group, and his lone surviving interview, thanks to scholar Ray Funk, is an indispensable record of the Blind Boys' formative years, including the many sighted singers who came and went and the changes in style that took place as the group evolved early on.

The Lifetime Achievement Award also served as both a reunion and a good-bye for longtime rhythm guitarist Bobby Butler, who attended the ceremony but did not receive an award. Butler had recorded as one of "the Boys" on Clarence Fountain's recent solo project. While the discussion around Fountain's use of the Blind Boys name for that album took place, Ricky McKinnie, in his capacity as business manager, asked Butler and other Blind Boys sidemen to sign an acknowledgment of their status as independent contractors. Butler declined. He felt that as a twenty-year member of the Blind Boys, he had earned a place in the partnership. McKinnie told him that if he wouldn't sign as an independent contractor, he couldn't perform with the group.

The Blind Boys flew Butler out to Los Angeles, however, and gave him a tux for the ceremony. He had played on the Grammy-nominated *Down in New Orleans*, which probably explains the group's reason for bringing Butler to the show. He thought, until the moment of the Lifetime Achievement Award presentation, that he was receiving that honor as well.

"With the Lifetime Achievement, I felt I got shafted pretty bad on that," Butler said. "I'm there performing, singing and playing an instrument. Today I still think I deserve it. You take Joey and Ricky, for them to have gotten one is a slap in my face. I've been there before they showed up."

As Charles Driebe explained, "The Grammy committee decides which individuals receive the awards. They just wanted to give them to the original members, and I had to argue to get Joey his award, based on being musical director during the Grammy-winning years."

Nonetheless, Butler said, "I came back the next night and got my Grammy for *Down in New Orleans*."

Butler keeps in close touch with Jimmy Carter and talks to the other members as well, but the 2009 Grammys marked the last time that he and the group were together.

The Blind Boys rang in 2010 with their first appearance in China, performing a New Year's Day concert at the Shanghai Grand Theater to kick off a tour of the country. They had visited the Shanghai School for the Blind on the previous day, singing a Chinese folk song, "Jasmine Flower," with the students.

The Blind Boys performed as part of the International Arts Festival, hosted by the Ministry of Culture and organized by the Shanghai Municipal People's Government. As such, a certain level of official supervision accompanied the group. China's leading gospel music deejay—perhaps not the most competitive field—acted as a chaperone of sorts. Though he was a big fan, he had to warn the Blind Boys' manager about the danger of the group whipping the audience into such a frenzy after their first show. An entity identified only as "the committee" objected to any encouragement of the crowd standing up and jumping around.

Driebe assured the chaperone he'd pass that along, but he never did, and the Blind Boys continued to drive Chinese fans wild. The group made it out safely, and a month later, the Blind Boys were back in the White House.

On February 9, 2010, President Barack Obama hosted "A Celebration of Music from the Civil Rights Movement." Bob Dylan, Joan Baez, Natalie Cole, Smokey Robinson, Jennifer Hudson, and the Blind Boys performed in the East Room. Morgan Freeman, their old friend from *The Gospel at Colonus*, hosted. Joey Williams, Billy Bowers, Jimmy Carter, Ben Moore, and Ricky McKinnie sang "Free at Last," with Carter taking the lead all the way. The president and First Lady sat together in the front row, clapping and grooving along.

Carter later recalled the gravity of the occasion. "To perform for a Black president? Something I never thought could happen— 'Wow!' is all I can say."

McKinnie pointed out, "We had been to the White House twice, but to sing to President Obama was exciting. We never thought we'd be singing to a Black president. The good thing about it, we realized, he wasn't just a Black president, he was a Black president with the ability to do the job. We were excited to meet him and that was a great day. They tell me that when we were singing, he got up and was clapping."

McKinnie left only one hope on the table.

"I really wanted to do my dance," he said. "But I had to control myself."

CHAPTER 25

COUNTRY ROAD

MY LOVE OF COUNTRY music began back in the early 1940s in Alabama," Jimmy Carter said. "That's about all you could get on radio. I fell in love with the Carter Family, the Delmore Brothers, Grandpa Jones, Lonnie Glosson, and Wayne Raney. Country music now is too commercialized, they've taken the soul from it. I still like my classic country, my heroes, Jim Reeves, George Jones, Merle Haggard."

As Carter's own singing career flourished, he dreamed of recording a country music album. He shared the idea with his colleagues. "It didn't resonate with anybody too much," he said.

The Blind Boys had made their debut at the Grand Ole Opry in Nashville back in 2007. Jimmy Carter had been a regular listener for nearly seventy years. Finally getting a chance to grace the stage at Ryman Auditorium "was a day that I will never forget," Carter said. The group performed a trio of songs, and Carter met some of his heroes, including longtime Opry regular Little Jimmy Dickens.

His bandmates, guitarist Joey Williams and bass player Tracy Pierce, spent some hotel room downtime on the road playing down-home rockers while Jimmy sang. At one point, the three booked studio time and recorded a few numbers you won't find in the Blind Boys' repertoire. One that Williams remembered well is Jimmy's cover of the Neil Young song "Southern Man," father out of wedlock to Lynyrd Skynyrd's "Sweet Home Alabama," another you likely won't hear the Blind Boys cover despite its reverence for the group's birthplace.

In January 2010, the Blind Boys headed to their home state for induction into the Alabama Music Hall of Fame. "That's where we met Jamey Johnson," Carter recalled.

Johnson, born in Enterprise, Alabama, in 1975 and raised in Montgomery, had stormed onto the country music scene with an album that went gold in 2009. He brought a classic approach back to the music that Carter felt had gotten too slick, with steel guitar in the band and lyrics Merle Haggard would have enjoyed. "I was telling Jamey about my dream of a country album," said Carter, "and he said, 'Let's make one!'"

The gospel-country connection is a powerful one on the White side of popular music. So many mainstream White artists with country leanings of the Blind Boys' generation—Elvis Presley (born three years after Jimmy Carter, for perspective), Johnny Cash, Jerry Lee Lewis, and Hank Williams Sr.—all began singing hymns and returned to singing hymns for some of their most powerful, resonating, and successful work. Presley won only three Grammys in his career, outside of the Lifetime Achievement Award, all for spiritual recordings. Crossover between the Black and White gospel worlds, however, has been a rarity.

The Blind Boys' 2011 album *Take the High Road* stands out as a singular project of authentic quilting in the way that a Blind Boys Christian rap album would not.

"That was one recording session I enjoyed more than any other," Carter said. "The whole thing went well. I think the Oak Ridge Boys sang terrific. They have gospel quartet roots."

It's tough to top the Blind Boys and Oak Ridge Boys tag-teaming, as they did on the title track, but for deep roots, their work with Hank Williams Jr. on his father's "I Saw the Light" stands out. "Hank Jr. was in the studio with us," Carter recalled. "He was a funny guy. Very funny. He was in a hurry. He did 'I Saw the Light' in one take. He said, 'I'm gwine get me somethin' to eat.'"

In maybe the most surreal duet the group ever recorded, the fairytale combination of wisecracking Bishop Billy Bowers and superstar singer Lee Ann Womack do "I Was a Burden." Some of the most satisfying tracks on the record are just the Blind Boys with a twanging backup band, as on the spare "Why Don't You Live So God Can Use You?" and the heartbreaking Jamey Johnson composition "Lead Me Home," a song as profound as anything out of gospel's golden age in terms of facing death with bravery.

Of all the Blind Boys record concepts, *High Road* seems like the farthest stretch and yet ends up closer to traditional gospel than much of the spiritual rhythm and blues the band covered in its glory run. They undeniably connect with Jamey Johnson, and even a canned duet like Willie Nelson's "Family Bible" feels like a church sing-along.

Bass player Tracy Pierce summed up the group's unparalleled

ability to click with other artists. "The real success to it is, all music starts from the blues and gospel," Pierce said. "When you put anything else on top of it, it fits. It blended so well because we take the part of the music that is gospel and made it stand out. You can put the Blind Boys on any record, pop, rock, blues, and they're all going to work because it all originated with gospel, with Blind Boys music."

Jimmy Carter in Nashville was like a kid with a credit card in a candy store. He had places to visit and people he dreamed of meeting. Jamey Johnson made it all come true. Johnson produced the record along with perennial Blind Boys mixologist Chris Goldsmith, but after hours he coordinated a VIP Music City tour unlike any other.

"After the sessions, Jamey would take us out," said guitarist Joey Williams. "He took us to Ruth's Chris and had steaks. Jimmy told him he wanted to go to Tootsie's," Williams added, referring to the honky-tonk adjacent to the Grand Ole Opry known as Tootsie's Orchid Lounge. "He rented a limo, got us a table up front. We're hanging out. We got on stage and started jamming, me, Jamey, and Jimmy."

They didn't stay long or go right home. "We went to the Station Inn and Vince Gill was playing there," Williams said. "Again Jimmy got on stage, with Vince Gill. Jimmy knew all the old country songs. Me and Jamey sat in the audience."

The next night's session ran late. After it wrapped up, Johnson called Lee Ann Womack and said, "I'm coming by."

"It had to be two in the morning when we got there," said Williams. "She opened the door, let us in, 'Hey guys!' like it's two in the afternoon. She offered us a snack and a drink. Of course there's guitars around. Next thing I knew, Jamey and I are playing guitars, Jimmy and Lee Ann are singing, and we're just jamming in her living room. It's gotta be three or four when we left there. That's a special night. It's all a testament to how cool Jamey is with everyone."

Jimmy talked about how much he loved George Jones. Johnson invited Jones to the session and made Jimmy's day. "He hung out and listened to some songs," Williams said. "Jamey would reach out to these people and they would be there. He got Hank Jr. to come by private jet."

While the record broke down musical barriers, the press tour ventured into uncharted territory.

"We got a country music publicist to work the record," said Driebe. "We did Fox News shows. That's where the country acts would play on TV."

One such appearance matched the Blind Boys of Alabama with former governor of Arkansas Mike Huckabee. "He wanted to sit in with us," said Williams. "He plays bass."

Williams had coached a number of TV personalities on playing with the Blind Boys. "Paul Schaffer was the first," Williams recalled of the *Late Night with David Letterman* bandleader. "He played organ with us for the first time we did major TV on *People Get Ready*. I was so nervous telling him, 'No, play it this way.' I worked with Stephen Colbert on singing a verse later. He surprised me, he had rhythm and was on time, and he could sing a little too."

As Driebe recalled, "Mike Huckabee wanted to play bass with us when we appeared on his show. I said, 'Hell no!'"

The country junket took the Blind Boys to *Fox and Friends*, performing with the Oak Ridge Boys and Jamey Johnson, and to Laura Ingraham's radio show. The Blind Boys were already well acquainted with another controversial host on the country road: Don Imus.

"As far as we went, Imus was cool," Williams said. "He liked the Blind Boys, but he loved Jimmy Carter."

The Boys had been on the Imus show a number of times prior to CBS Radio's firing the host in April 2007 for referring to the Rutgers University women's basketball team on air as "nappy-headed hos." The *Take the High Road* press tour occurred after Imus had relocated his simulcast to Fox in the wake of that comment.

Carter and Imus had bonded personally, based on their mutual love of country music. Carter, a big radio listener in his day-to-day life, tuned in to Imus regularly, and so he also knew the on-air persona.

"I got to know Imus doing interviews with him over the years," Carter said. "We just got close to one another. I was crazy about him. He's gonna tell you what he thinks. He said whatever was on his mind. I don't think he was racist. He got the short end of the stick on that. He treated me and the Blind Boys with respect. He did a lot for people. I don't think he had a racist bone in his body."

Carter, however, seems to have more than the average amount of love in his heart.

"People give back what you dish out. That's why I've never seen anybody mistreat the Blind Boys, because of what the Blind Boys give," said Tracy Pierce, bass player. "Being a musician for as long as they have, you learn how to deal with all kinds of people. They've had to deal with prejudice. Jimmy remembers having to drink out of the 'Colored' water fountain. They don't give off angry energy. As an entertainer, you have to know how to break that ice. Even to people you feel might not like you. We do it every day. And Clarence, George, and Jimmy were not pushovers. They spoke their minds. They will get in to you. I never heard any one of those guys say anything derogatory about anyone White. I put that on my Mama. I know they experienced prejudice. That tells you a lot about them. That's why they surpassed what we think a gospel group should have done. They are indisputably the biggest gospel quartet ever. One of the biggest gospel groups in the world, period. Talk to any of them, how can you not like them? The only thing they hate is being treated like they can't do something."

CHAPTER 26

"SOMETHIN' EXTRY"

BLIND BOYS OF ALABAMA singer Billy Bowers got in touch with Ricky McKinnie shortly before the group embarked on their summer 2013 tour.

"He called me late one night," McKinnie said. "He told me, 'I don't think I'm gonna come back to the group.'"

McKinnie pondered this for a moment before Bowers added, "I'm glad that you'll be sitting in my seat."

Two days later, Bishop Billy Bowers died in Montgomery at the age of seventy-one.

As Bowers foresaw, his own end opened a door for his long-time friend.

In Bowers's permanent absence, the Blind Boys needed a

new vocalist. McKinnie had plenty of experience, singing with his own group and contributing background vocals to the Blind Boys from behind the kit. For twenty years, Jimmy Carter had introduced McKinnie on stage as "the only blind drummer we know anything about." Now McKinnie added another line to his résumé.

"It was no plan," McKinnie said, "but when Billy passed away, I came up front to blend in."

Since that time, McKinnie has blossomed into a featured performer. He began singing lead on two numbers in Clarence Fountain's repertoire, "Do Lord Remember Me" and "God Said It." McKinnie takes verses in "Amazing Grace" and "I Can See." But anyone who's watched the Blind Boys has seen him dance. "I had never been a dancer until I got up front," he said.

Soon after Bowers's death, McKinnie and the Blind Boys were performing "Spirit in the Sky." McKinnie felt Bowers's spirit move in him. "Billy could shake all over," McKinnie said. "I felt like I had to do something. I just got up and started dancing."

He credits divine intervention along with Billy Bowers's inspiration for getting him up. "It's got to be God moving because I'm not a dancer," McKinnie said.

Following Bowers's death, the Blind Boys added another vocalist to the mix, Paul Beasley.

This veteran of the gospel highway had been described as a million-dollar voice in his earlier career. Before losing his sight to glaucoma, Beasley had enjoyed something like gospel superstardom, thanks to his special gift: a haunting falsetto. The voice recorded iconic hits for two classic quartets, the Gospel Keynotes and the Mighty Clouds of Joy.

"I was born in 1944 in a little old country town, DeRidder, Louisiana," Beasley said. "I started singing in the churches, I was about ten or eleven years old."

His father was a bishop in the Church of God in Christ, a musical denomination, and Beasley started singing in church. At home, he studied recordings of the master gospel falsetto, Rev. Claude Jeter of the Swan Silvertones. "I tried to sing everything he recorded," said Beasley. "I wanted to match him on 'Mary Don't You Weep' and 'A Lady Called Mother.'"

In competition with his sister, he realized he could reach heavenly heights. "We would see who could sing highest," he said. "I got past her."

As a teenager, Beasley sang locally with the DeRidder Spirituals. "Everywhere we sang, I told everybody, 'I'm Claude Jeter,'" said Beasley. "I did all of his songs."

The DeRidder Spirituals traveled as far as Tyler, Texas, two hundred miles northwest of their base. "There was a group there who heard us sing," said Beasley. "I got a chance to meet the lead singer, Willie Neal Johnson. I must have been eighteen years old. He met me in the audience and asked if I'd like to sing with his group. I said I sure would. From that time on, I sang with the Gospel Keynotes."

"Country Boy," as Johnson of the Keynotes was known, led his group across a larger swath of the gospel highway than the DeRidder Spirituals traveled. Throughout the early 1970s, they became one of the major acts on the road, alongside Clarence Fountain, the Williams Brothers, Inez Andrews, Slim and the Supreme Angels, the Pilgrim Jubilees, and the Brooklyn All-Stars, among others who sometimes included the Siamese Twins. Beasley played bass guitar in the Keynotes and on occasion helped out other acts, including Gloria Spencer. "I finally met Reverend Jeter when I was recording with the Gospel Keynotes. He liked what I was doing; he said, 'You got somethin' extry,' and told me, 'Never get bigger than your audience. Stay humble.'"

That advice proved timely, as Beasley recorded the first of his legendary hits, "Jesus You've Been Good to Me," released in 1975. Some sources have identified the record as a million-seller. "That never got to be an old song," said Beasley. "People loved it then and they love it still."

Beasley first met Ricky McKinnie as the Keynotes' drummer during this period—McKinnie played drums on the recording of "Jesus You've Been Good to Me." McKinnie lost his eyesight soon thereafter and had to leave the band. "That was a sad time," said Beasley. "He stayed strong, believed in God, and kept on. Never thought I'd follow him."

Throughout the late 1970s, numerous Gospel Keynotes releases placed on the *Billboard* gospel charts, bumping up against contemporary big-label acts like Andrae Crouch and the Edwin Hawkins Singers. They performed with the top quartet of the time as well. "We did some shows with the Mighty Clouds," Beasley said. "Joe Ligon told me, 'You need to come over here and sing with us.' I couldn't imagine myself singing with Joe or leaving Willie. But they kept talking. I decided to try it."

"Country Boy" and the Keynotes clearly had no hard feelings. They recorded the album *The Gospel Keynotes Salute Paul Beasley*. The cover art must be seen to be fully appreciated, but the group appears to be losing Beasley to the clouds, as they did, doffing their white top hats to him as he and his supreme Afro go.

Beasley joined the Clouds as they achieved a new height for quartets, recording for Epic Records with Motown studio personnel and touring the world. Earth, Wind & Fire guitarist Al McKay produced *Cloudburst*, including Beasley's most iconic solo work, on "Walk Around Heaven All Day." The Mighty Clouds blazed a path that the Blind Boys would follow, visiting the White House, touring internationally, and opening rock shows in arenas. All the while, the Clouds were billed with Beasley alongside quartet legend Ligon as the group with *two* million-dollar voices. "I wish I made a million dollars, but everything was good," said Beasley.

The best account of Beasley's singing during this time came from Elijah Wald, who reported on a 1985 twin billing of the Mighty Clouds and the Blind Boys of Alabama in Boston.

"The Blind Boys went on first," Wald wrote. "Clarence Fountain, in a white suit with sparkling red trim and 'Mr. Personality' emblazoned on the back, led a group of... three old Blind Boys ably aided by guitarist Sam Butler singing alto... [Fountain] sang in a screaming falsetto that seemed about to leap out of control as he twisted his body with emotion, then suddenly struck a cool pose and sank to a full bass."

Wald noted that Fountain sang the last chorus without a microphone to a packed Strand Theater.

"The Mighty Clouds featured two spectacular singers, Joe Ligon and Paul Beasley," Wald continued. "[Beasley's] voice soared effortlessly into the highest soprano range, with purity and soul aching in every line. He yodeled, cried, chirped and sang with perfect control as the group urged him on and the audience came to its feet."

Beasley later pursued a solo career and reunited with the Keynotes before "Country Boy" Willie Neal Johnson died in 2001. When Beasley began to lose his vision, he discussed the situation with his old friend McKinnie.

"Ricky said, 'If you're losing your eyesight, you're a good candidate for the Blind Boys,'" Beasley recalled.

Beasley didn't think he could fit with the sound. "They've never had a singer of my style and that's what had me bothered," he said. But McKinnie encouraged him to rehearse with the group. Beasley followed Reverend Jeter's advice to stay humble. Instead of wailing falsetto leads, Beasley sang background in his natural voice and filled in on all of the supporting vocals.

"People ask me to sing 'Walk Around Heaven All Day,' but I have to tell them, 'I'm with the Blind Boys now—not tonight.'"

Despite Beasley's pedigree, it took him some time to find his footing with the Blind Boys. "It was strange to bring in someone of his stature," said Joey Williams. "We all knew him but didn't know how to approach it. I was with the Keynotes while he was and Ricky was there too. He doesn't sing the Blind Boys style, we don't have a lot of falsetto."

Beasley first attended a Blind Boys recording session held well outside the group's comfort zone.

Former Blind Boys publicist Sue Schrader hails from Wisconsin, also the home state of indie rocker Justin Vernon of Bon Iver fame. After Bon Iver won Grammys for Best New Artist and Best Alternative Music Album in early 2012, Schrader suggested pitching a project to Vernon. Charles Driebe reached out to Vernon with the idea of producing a Blind Boys album.

"I'm the first person he called after getting off the phone with Charles Driebe," recalled Phil Cook. "He said, 'You're coming. We're doing this.'"

Cook, a native of Chippewa Falls, Wisconsin, had met Vernon at a jazz camp when the two were teenagers, where Cook first connected with "all these other small-town weirdos."

Getting to know one another, as Cook explained, "we explored a lot of music together and developed a real partnership around gospel music, around the voices. We shared so much. Learning to play music with [Vernon], we discovered so much. We moved to North Carolina together at age twenty-five, twenty-six. He moved back to Wisconsin and a year later became Bon Iver and blew up."

Cook formed a group called Megafaun and continued his own musical journey, remaining in touch with Vernon. The Blind Boys project reunited Cook and Vernon around the sounds that had first brought them together. "We knew what it meant to be asked to work with the Blind Boys," Cook said.

The session would take place at Vernon's studio near Eau Claire, Wisconsin, during the dead of winter. Keyboardist Cook, guitarist Vernon, and the rest of the house band—brass and percussion player Reggie Pace, drummer J. T. Bates, and bass player Mike Lewis—assembled to cut a few backing tracks. By the time the Blind Boys pulled up a couple days later, a pile of snow had fallen. Joey Williams said, "The snow was crazy, we had to dig our way in almost." The meeting of these two worlds in a snowbound remote cabin far from the gospel highway rapidly took a turn for the friendly. The "secret weapon" of the session, studio manager Andra Chumas, who is also a chef, had prepared a soul food feast. The Blind Boys and indie rockers bonded over chicken and collard greens. "That all turned to family so quick," Williams said.

As Cook recalled, Jimmy Carter found his spot early on. "Jimster sunk right down into a nice La-Z-Boy chair in the control room."

Jimmy sat listening to the tracks Vernon and company had cut and directed the Blind Boys from his throne, deciding who would sing which parts.

"The first song we worked out was 'I Shall Not Be Moved,'" Cook said. "Jimmy sent Ben on the floor to sing that song right away."

Through a talkback mike, Jimmy related his notes directly into the earpiece of whoever was singing. "Watching the way he led with such few words, it worked with everyone," Cook said. "We knew to listen to him and follow him."

While working out the Washington Phillips song "Take Your Burden to the Lord and Leave It There," Cook observed the Blind

Boys' process of assembling background vocals on the fly. "It was a sublime moment to hear those voices without mikes, working out the song," he said, "and watching them go out on the floor and do the song after twenty minutes. I felt all that experience and history."

Ben Moore led off the song, followed by Ricky McKinnie and Jimmy Carter. Moore was hot throughout the session, from his "fire and the Holy Ghost" line in "I Shall Not Be Moved" to perhaps his greatest moment on record with the group.

Blind Boys road manager Chuck Shivers pulled Cook aside to let him know that Moore's wife had just died. Moore used that emotion to deliver a masterpiece, "My God Is Real."

Meanwhile, Paul Beasley, in a Blind Boys session for the first time, had deferred and sung in the background. That changed with the Nina Simone number "Take Me to the Water." The signature falsetto emphasized the spiritual hunger, the pleading for baptism and salvation Simone composed into the lyric. As Ricky McKinnie said, "Paul can sing background and blend. He won't oversing anybody. But when he sings a solo, he's often imitated but never duplicated."

The group recorded "There Will Never Be Peace (Until God Is Seated at the Conference Table)" featuring Casey Dienel, a sweet-voiced vocalist who hits the high notes. Later, during live performances without Dienel, Paul Beasley sang the lead. With his stirring falsetto lifting the crowd off its feet, "Conference Table" has become a Blind Boys showstopper.

The musical accompaniment throughout the album is restrained and dignified, with Cook's churchy piano leading the way. Ricky McKinnie noticed as much. Cook recalled, "Ricky is the Blind Boy who took me under his wing. He pulled me aside me and said, 'You play the old way. Keep goin', man.'"

At the end of the session, Cook recalled, "Everyone pulled away and Justin and I just looked at each other like, wow."

Cook kept going with the Blind Boys, joining their tour for the 2013–2014 winter to support the album they made together, *I'll Find a Way*.

CHAPTER 27

THE BOOK OF CLARENCE

CLARENCE FOUNTAIN HAD STAYED as busy as a dialysis patient could since releasing his solo album in 2009. While staying close to home in Baton Rouge, Fountain got back to his roots as a performer, singing in smaller churches. His children visited and caught up on some lost time with the old man. He also got over his differences with the Blind Boys, joining the group for select performances and adding his voice to their recordings.

In 2013, a documentary film crew began chronicling Fountain's life story and his current health situation. The project united many of Fountain's old friends. Lee Breuer, who directed *The Gospel at Colonus*, the turning point in Fountain's career, came on to direct the film. Longtime musical collaborators Sam Butler and Bobby Butler worked as Fountain's backup band in musical segments and in the studio, while Fountain's sideman and caregiver, Donald Dillon, performed with Fountain on camera and looked after him off camera. Producer Eric Marciano held the project together.

Dillon said that the crew spent three weeks recording interviews and gigs, traveling around Louisiana and Mississippi. "Every town we was in we had to set up a center for Clarence to take dialysis," Dillon said. Other than that, "it was like old times. We were all friends from *Colonus*. Lee Breuer and Eric Marciano were great, it worked well. We got paid, I got a salary and a per diem."

Breuer filmed Fountain taking dialysis while bravely offering wisdom. Fountain opened up about his blindness, a condition to which he had adapted. "The things that come through my ears go through your eyes," he said. "The things that come through your eyes come through my ears."

He reflected on his sense of ambition. "I always wanted to be somebody, not just anybody."

The man who had sung of heaven since his teenage years felt at peace. "So far in life, I've never wanted for something and not gotten it," Fountain said. "I have nothing to complain to the Lord about. He supplied all my needs."

The resulting documentary film, *The Book of Clarence*, came out in 2017.

At home, Fountain's wife Barbara took care of him. "I think Barbara was devoted to Clarence," Jimmy Carter said. "She was always there to help."

As Dillon put it, "She loved Clarence's dirty drawers."

Fountain also had Dillon by his side much of the time, just like when they were on the road.

"I was in Baton Rouge more than I was at home in Los Angeles," Dillon said. "For years."

When Barbara got tired and needed a break, she called on Dillon. He took the next flight to Louisiana and stayed for months at a time. When he couldn't travel, he entertained Fountain over the phone. "Miss Barbara called me and said, 'Dillon, sing to Clarence.' I said, 'No, I'm gonna go on YouTube and play the Blind Boys.'"

When he could visit in person, Dillon took Clarence to dialysis appointments. Dillon said, "He always asked if I was bored, if I wanted to take the car. 'I just don't want you to get bored and leave,' he said. I told him, 'Why would I leave, when I come here to spend time with you?' That's all he needed to know."

Dillon kept Clarence moving, walking him from the house out to the mailbox on doctor's orders. "They had a swing on their porch," Dillon said. "I would say, 'Come on, old man, we're going outside.' We sat on that swing and talked. I got me a cup of coffee. He couldn't drink coffee on dialysis. He'd say, 'Dillon, gimme a sip of coffee.' I said, 'Boy, you're not supposed to do that.' He said, 'Just let me taste it.' I would give it to him and he'd take a taste and be alright."

One evening as they sat together, Clarence said, "Dillon, you gotta cut you a solo record before I can't help you."

Dillon replied, "You've already helped me enough."

During the same year that *The Book of Clarence* was released, the Blind Boys worked on another concept album. Charles Driebe interviewed Fountain and Jimmy Carter on video and shared the material with a variety of songwriters who used the stories to inspire compositions specifically for the record, resulting in a body of music that tells the Blind Boys' story. *Almost Home* includes songs that reflect on their Talladega days listening to the Golden Gate Quartet. "Singing Brings Us Closer," written by Phil Cook, kindles the spirit of their fallen brother George Scott.

Fountain recorded a few background vocal tracks for *Almost Home*. Driebe and sound engineer Matt Ross-Spang traveled to Baton Rouge to get Clarence's voice on the record. They worked in a local studio, and after they finished, Driebe took Clarence home. Fountain bid Driebe an uncharacteristically moving farewell. "Thank you, Charles," Fountain said. "You've done a good job... [E]verything you've done down through the years, I appreciate very much."

Driebe said, "For a guy who threw out compliments like manhole covers, that was high praise. That was our final conversation."

In April 2018, Clarence's second-born daughter, Brenda Johnson, visited him. "We had a good time," she said. "He smiled a lot. He was in good spirits. We went out to dinner and sat and talked. He was happy. He said he'd call me on my birthday in July. Sometimes he'd call and sing me 'Happy Birthday.' When I left, I kissed him on the cheek. I felt like I wasn't gonna see him anymore."

Clarence joined the Blind Boys' set at Jazz Fest in New Orleans in late April. He came on stage in a wheelchair. A few weeks later, the Blind Boys brought Fountain on stage in Baton Rouge. "We spent time together," Jimmy Carter said. "He sounded great and said he was feeling fine."

Dillon had just left Baton Rouge a month or so earlier. He too had thought Fountain was doing well enough, but on a Sunday he got the call. "That messed me up a long time," he said. "Still does. I think of that man every day of my life."

Fountain had entered Our Lady of the Lake Hospital, and there he died on June 3, 2018.

Clarence's children, friends, and musical colleagues came to his funeral and celebrated him. His children, however, had been left out of the published obituary and been excluded from his last will and testament.

That document, executed on August 25, 2013, states for Clarence in boilerplate language, "I have no legal children. No children were born to me during either of my marriages; no allegations of paternity have been established." Truthfully, Brenda Johnson was born to Clarence in a legal marriage, but that marriage is not acknowledged in the will.

Fountain had signed the will with an "X" before two witnesses and a notary.

Frustrated by the lack of mention in the obituary and suspicious of the will, Clarence's eldest daughter, Brenda Davis, spoke up during the funeral.

"I would like for all of my father's children to stand," she said. She and five other people did so. She simply wanted to leave no doubt that his children were there for him. Afterward, one of Clarence's ex-girlfriends approached Davis and said, "That took nerves, honey. Your daddy would be proud."

Following the burial, Donald Dillon feared most for Fountain's widow. "Miss Barbara was grieving so hard," he said. "I couldn't see her making it that long."

Less than six months later, Barbara died.

Since Clarence's will did not mention his own children, Barbara's family inherited Clarence's property and financial legacy, including any royalties earned from his work.

Some of his natural children feel that they should have something to remember him by—that he had enough Grammy Award trophies to go around.

———◆———

Clarence Fountain's death marked the end of the historic Blind Boys era. He had sung lead on the classic recordings that have proven most influential, while his vocal style distinguished the group early on and later carried the band into the mainstream, completing a trajectory that no other gospel group has equaled. Listening to the Blind Boys' Specialty Records classics "The Last Time" and "Oh Lord, Stand by Me" should make clear their impact on rock 'n' roll. Their accomplishments after crossing over to the mainstream in the 1990s should seal their case for enshrinement in the Rock 'n' Roll Hall of Fame. During this period, they worked with Booker T. Jones, Solomon Burke, Tom Petty, Peter Gabriel, Lou Reed, Chrissie Hynde, George Clinton, Mavis Staples, Allen Toussaint, Prince, and Tom Waits, all hall-of-famers, many of whom went on the record with their reverence and respect for the Blind Boys, while others didn't have to—stage crashing has to be an even higher honor than a planned collaboration. In a 2015 interview with *AARP* magazine, Bob Dylan identified three gospel outfits as early influences on his music: the Staple Singers, the Dixie Hummingbirds, and the Blind Boys of Alabama.

Their runs of seventy-eight years on the road and seventy-four years recording—and counting—feel untouchable. This reflects something extraordinary that seems taken for granted. Some people think, the Blind Boys are blind, what else are they going to do? But this run extended through so many obstacles not because of something inevitable, fate, or a lack of alternatives but because of human determination. The group could have folded in 1947 when their lead singer died, before ever making their first record, before even becoming the Blind Boys of Alabama. The person who embodied the determination to keep going, the ambition to become somebody, was Clarence Fountain. Remember, at the moment Velma Traylor died, Clarence was a seventeen-year-old backup baritone from a state not known for supporting the progress of its Black citizens. It'd be difficult to invent a more improbable story than the one that followed.

Even his solo stint away from the Blind Boys shows his drive to be great. He didn't quite make it on his own, but he had to try. Those who were close to him during the group's crossover phase speak of his commitment to reaching the masses of people. They attribute the group's mainstream fame to Clarence Fountain's vision. He had a plan. Though he had a stubborn streak, he also deserves credit for adapting. He recognized that he needed to let go and trust others—record producers he disagreed with, lead singers he may not have wanted to share the spotlight with—for the good of the group. Finally, his personality made an indelible mark on everyone he encountered. With the exception of Jimmy Carter, virtually every person interviewed for this book, when asked about Clarence, would involuntarily break into an impression of his distinctive growling voice, stammering delivery, and witticisms.

Gospel is underrepresented in the Rock 'n' Roll Hall of Fame, with only Mahalia Jackson, Sister Rosetta Tharpe, the Staple Singers, and the Soul Stirrers inducted. If you've read this far, you can't tell me that Fountain wasn't rock 'n' roll enough to belong. He had the swagger, the chauffeured Caddy, the processed hair, the women in every city, and the attitude, all without the slightest pretense. In fact, maybe the best thing about Clarence's legacy is that he did not care one way or another about accolades, celebrity, or the praise of others. He was who he was—all the more reason to enshrine him and the Blind Boys.

CHAPTER 28

CROSSROADS

THOUGH CLARENCE FOUNTAIN HAD been retired from full-time Blind Boys of Alabama activity for ten years, his death brought a sense of finality to the group. Only one man remained from the first quartet sing-alongs that grew into the Happy Land Jubilee Singers in Talladega. As Jimmy Carter approached his ninetieth birthday, the Blind Boys entered a period of transitions. As longtime manager Charles Driebe put it, "Jimmy has been saying 'one more year' for a few years now."

The global coronavirus pandemic that began in 2020 disrupted the Blind Boys along with the rest of civilization. Sidelined for the first time in decades, Jimmy told Driebe, "The more you sit down, the more you want to sit down."

Driebe said, "I told him if he wanted to come back and sing, he could, if he wanted to stay there and sit, he could. He said, 'Well, I'll give it one more year.'"

Driebe began to contemplate his own future beyond music.

In September 2020, Driebe added a new partner to the Blind Boys management team, Jeff DeLia, a thirty-one-year-old who had already managed A. J. Croce, Bobby Rush, and Dom Flemons.

"I met Charles in 2016 backstage at the Byron Bay Blues Festival," DeLia said. "That was the first time I saw the Blind Boys. I didn't know much about gospel music. When I saw their show, the whole tent, four or five thousand people were dancing. It was spiritual and high energy. They blew me away. I finally met them on the red carpet for the Grammys. Charles and I developed a rapport. When he decided to power down, he thought of me."

Driebe and DeLia worked out a transition plan whereby DeLia would ride shotgun with Driebe for a period, learning the Blind Boys' world, before the two would trade off, DeLia driving and Driebe in the passenger seat.

In January 2022, DeLia took over as the group's primary manager, with Driebe's aid. As the world resumed a sense of normalcy with regard to the pandemic, so did the Blind Boys. They toured Europe in spring, performing in Poland during Russia's invasion of Ukraine.

With the crossroads in mind, a new recording project began to take shape. DeLia said, "They've made so many albums, had so many collaborations, gone in a few different directions musically, first the question was, what direction do we want to go in for the next album?"

The answer came emphatically from Ricky McKinnie. He wanted to go back to the golden age. "That's where I come from," he explained. "Traditional gospel is where my heart is. That's where we're from. People still want to hear it. You gonna take Lucille from B. B. King?"

And, more importantly, as he told DeLia, "If we're going to do this album with Jimmy, we've got to do it now!"

In April 2022, the Blind Boys returned to their home state and a mecca of the music business to record in Muscle Shoals, Alabama. The Blind Boys worked with producers Ben Tanner, keyboardist with the Alabama Shakes and a partner in Single Lock Records, and Matt Ross-Spang, a Grammy winner who has worked with John Prine and Jason Isbell.

Charles Driebe remained heavily involved with the session as a coproducer. He asked Phil Cook, keyboardist on *I'll Find a Way*, to record on the session and help with song selection. Cook compiled a golden age gospel playlist for inspiration, including Sam Cooke, Brother Joe May, the Pilgrim Jubilees, the Highway QCs, Inez Andrews, the Dixie Hummingbirds, and others, but one song rose to the top.

"'Jesus You've Been Good to Me,'" Cook said. "I wanted to hear Paul sing that song again."

In Muscle Shoals, the Blind Boys went back not only to a classic sound and classic songs but to recording in the historic manner. "Groups back in the day recorded on one microphone hanging from the ceiling," Cook said. "You can hear that reflected in the older recordings. Sound waves mesh in the air, blending with each other. Harmonies sung live in the room join the notes together, the notes excite each other in a way that's not so separated and clean. It captures the spirit. Now one person can record an entire orchestral album alone, or pass a track around the world for different musicians to add their parts, but nothing will replace harmonies bouncing off of each other in the same room."

DeLia sensed something beyond sound. "There is a spiritual energy that forms when they're all together," he said. "Each man has a percentage of it. Not only when they're performing but just being together in a room. You can feel it."

As Cook explained, one singer in particular set the tone for the session. "Paul Beasley did 'Jesus You've Been Good to Me' right away," he said. "He stood up immediately and knew what to do. That built team spirit. When Paul's singing, he inspires everybody in the room."

The Blind Boys' voices became the theme of the album over and beyond any collaboration or genre-bending theme. They came together and sang together. After Beasley's leadoff home run, "we rolled with the momentum," said Cook.

Carter, the Birmingham native, sang a hit made popular by another Magic City gospel great, Dorothy Love Coates. "We did 'You Can't Hurry God' by the Harmonettes," Cook said. "Jimmy took lead on that."

Ben Moore had recorded in Muscle Shoals throughout his pre–Blind Boys career. He cut as half of Ben & Spence at Fame Studios in 1966, under his own name at Muscle Shoals Sound in the late 1970s, and finally as Bobby Purify with Shoals veterans Dan Penn and Spooner Oldham for a 2006 comeback album. "Ben got really excited because somebody came in and called Spooner Oldham," Cook said, "They talked and he just lit up."

"Every time he sang, he brought Ben Moore to the table," McKinnie said. "Paul the same. Paul sang tenor and Ben sang baritone. I mostly sang second tenor."

McKinnie, who had a verse on the group's Grammy-nominated 2021 single with Bela Fleck, finally got a number all to himself, "Wide River."

The Blind Boys blended a new voice into the mix as well, that of

Rev. Julius Love. An enterprising, visually impaired musician, Reverend Love plays piano, has pastored a church, and worked as the only blind funeral director in the state of Alabama. He's only fallen into a grave once, by his count. "I think he can be a good second lead," said McKinnie.

Following the session, the band stayed true to its history on another note: they hit the road. On May 7, the Blind Boys shared the stage in Albuquerque with Amadou and Mariam, a visually impaired duo from Bamako, Mali.

"I remember Ben was having trouble getting around that night," said guitarist Joey Williams. "I said, 'You cool?' He said 'Yeah, I'm cool. Hey, I wanna thank you for listening to me and I thank you for having my back!' I said, 'You're my favorite singer! I never worry about you.'"

Though Moore tended to stay to himself, he seemed extra exuberant that night, enjoying the music more than usual, whooping it up as Williams landed the last note of a solo.

The next night in Santa Fe, Moore didn't make it to the lobby for showtime. Road manager Chuck Shivers went to his room and found him on the floor. Moore had fallen and couldn't regain his balance. Shivers and McKinnie helped Moore up and called the paramedics.

"Chuck went to the hospital and stayed there," McKinnie said.

Moore recovered and wanted to go on to the gig, but the doctor decided to keep him overnight. "Ben was up in the hospital singing and talking," McKinnie added. "The doctor went and got his guitar, and they were singing gospel songs."

Moore was released from the hospital and cleared to go home. Shivers was wheeling Moore out of the hospital when, as McKinnie said, "he flatlined."

They got Moore back into the hospital where he was revived and checked in. Members of his family had time to travel and be with him. Ben Moore died on May 12, 2022, at age eighty.

Moore had been a reliable, versatile Blind Boy for fifteen years. He sang every part and nailed his lead verses. Moore's final recording session, just weeks before his death, showed to his strength. Moore sang on every track, lending his full range of backing vocals and taking the lead on "Friendship," a Pops Staples number. Finally, Moore sang the solemn opening to "Work Until My Day Is Done" and the first verse of "Heaven Help Us All."

"Ben was a soldier in the army of the lord," said Charles Driebe at Moore's funeral. "You could always count on him."

⁃✦⁃

Ben's death got everyone thinking even harder about the future of the group.

Should Jimmy leave the road, he has a full life and many interests back home. First, he has longevity on his side. Though his father died young in a Birmingham mine, his mother lived to the age of 103. Back when she dropped Jimmy off at school in Talladega, he feared that he would never see his mother again. Instead, she lived to see all that he accomplished, passing away in 2009.

One of Jimmy's older brothers still lives in Birmingham and still drives, though not with Jimmy in the car. Jimmy enjoys dining out, particularly at Fife's, the historic soul food restaurant in Birmingham that has catered to the Blind Boys for nearly seventy years. He is a night owl and to this day doesn't mind going out to a restaurant and hanging out in a booth until closing time. He'll enjoy a glass of dry cabernet sauvignon.

Jimmy also keeps in touch with Roscoe Robinson, his former

fellow member of the Blind Boys of both Mississippi and Alabama, who is also slightly older than Jimmy and also resides in Birmingham.

To relax, not that tension seems to be a big problem, Jimmy listens to his beloved Dodgers on the radio. He also loves LA Lakers basketball and roots for University of Alabama football. He's a fan of podcasts, following one about Negro League Baseball called *Black Diamonds*. He has an iPhone and, thanks to Blind Boys manager Jeff DeLia, can tell Siri to play Golden Gate Quartet or George Jones songs or find the Dodgers game.

Though he has traveled the globe many times over, he'd still like to drink a fresh Guinness in Ireland.

"I'm happy," he said. "I do anything I want to do. I have people around me to give me sighted help, so I'm living good. God's good to me."

The road is his life though. "I'm proud to still be here," he said. "I don't know how long I'll be. When I go out on the stage, I say, 'The Blind Boys of Alabama have been around a long time. The good news is, we're still here.'"

He has a general idea about retirement. He'll know when the time comes. "I want to go out looking good," he said. "You have to know when you've had enough. Go out when you're ahead."

———◆———

The Blind Boys persevered after losing both Velma Traylor in 1947 and Clarence Fountain over sixty years later. They have reshuffled after numerous lineup changes. In their legend phase they have become a brand, capable of restocking or retooling while maintaining their sound, look, and feel.

The youngest member of the group, Joey Williams, has sung on every Blind Boys album for nearly thirty years, holding together the harmony and taking lead verses, as he does on "People Get Ready." Though Williams joined the group as a guitarist, he has served as musical director for over twenty-five years. As the group's vocal arranger, having learned that trade from the Holy Trinity of Jimmy, Clarence, and George Scott, Williams will have a major say in the group's future sound. "We'll keep on like when Clarence left, George left," he said. "I want to form the same thing. I see the Blind Boys going, me, Ricky, Paul. There might be some younger guys singing. It may take a turn or two, but I see us going forward. My main thing is having the harmony and the vocals leading—honoring the legacy of the Blind Boys."

Ricky McKinnie, longtime business manager, singer, dancer, and the longest serving visually impaired member after Jimmy, said, "I think as long as we can find people who want to be Blind Boys and sing Blind Boys material, I'll always be around. I can sing lead, I can narrate and do a lot of things, but am I the lead singer? Like Clarence? No. I can do what I do. I can dance. I can make it happen. I'm steady looking for someone who has the voice and energy that Clarence brought to the stage."

Their longest-serving soldier, Jimmy Carter, said, "I want people to know that the Blind Boys of Alabama touched many lives. I want people to know that the Blind Boys fought a good fight. I want to thank the people for being faithful for all of these years. I hope that there's still a Blind Boys of Alabama in a hundred years. The name has power. It's good to be the Blind Boys."

———◆———

It's hard to imagine a more dramatic career arc than that of the Blind Boys of Alabama. All founding members were born in different corners of the state into sharecropping families, with the exception of Jimmy Carter, who grew up in a mining company town. It'd be difficult to chart a harder path to international fame than from that place and time. Starting off with Ves Lawson, a guy who had a car in 1940s Talladega, singing for spare change at an army base, ending up on Broadway and later singing in the White House, as Grammy Lifetime Achievement Award winners, with every up and down in between, would have to be about the greatest distance traveled in American cultural history.

They created a recording legacy as deep as any in American music, spanning from the early days of Black gospel indies, cranking out 78s at labels like Coleman Records, to the relative big time of Specialty Records, alongside Little Richard and Sam Cooke, to the obscure, funky stuff on Jewel and HOB, and finally throughout the digital age as they rediscover their roots and introduce younger generations to the well of American spirit.

Their miles traveled would seemingly dwarf any other group's, maybe from any time in history. In their longevity, they've gone from burning out tires in J. U. Goodman's 1939 Buick to hopping a 747 out of LAX for Australia. While other bands might say that they've been active longer, I doubt if any music group has worked constantly for as long as the Blind Boys have, without interruption since they hit the road in 1944. Of course, they still have one member who sang with the other boys back in the 1930s. Jimmy Carter, at age ninety, is perhaps the oldest touring vocalist on the road today.

None of this was preordained. They worked for every bit of it. Yes, they met the right people, as you, I, and everyone else must, but different and divergent folks—Art Rupe and Lillian Cumber, Bumps Blackwell, Lee Breuer, Lou Reed, Peter Gabriel, and Ben Harper, people from very different times and places—all believed in them and invested in them. This only hints at the breadth of their appeal.

Their so-called handicap has been the most significant aspect of the journey. Blindness brought them together, blindness became their chief marketing asset, and blindness sustained them when sighted members of more prominent gospel quartets left the road in the not so golden ages that followed the 1950s.

Clarence Fountain refashioned his blindness into a fate-twisting superpower. "I had what you call pink eye," he said. "This midwife came along, and she mixed up some kind of remedy, blue stone and water. She put that in my eyes, and that's how I lost my sight. My daddy was a farmer, and he sold the cow and horse to pay a doctor to save my sight. But if I'd known it was going to be how it is, I'd told him 'Don't worry about it.'"

One thing should be clear by now: there is no end for the Blind Boys.

APPENDIX

Listening to the Blind Boys of Alabama
and the Gospel Highway Quartets

I'D BEEN A FAN of historic Black music for twenty-five years before getting into gospel quartets while working on this book. Having since dived deeply into the music, I can say that we're all overdue for a Black gospel quartet revival. Listening my way through this story has been so much fun, and I hope this guide can help others find the well.

Virtually every song mentioned in the book can be heard via YouTube or the Internet Archive (archive.org), my go-to sites for reference tracks, but there are plenty of excellent collections available on vinyl or CD that present the music in greater context and provide more background history and individual insight with regard to the artists to enhance the listening experience beyond the sounds.

I have at times found myself physically incapable of removing one of the two LPs of the *Birmingham Quartet Anthology* from my turntable. When able to pry off one of those records,

I usually replace it with another Doug Seroff–produced compilation, *Bless My Bones*, featuring historic quartet music broadcast in Memphis on radio station WDIA. Seroff organized a reunion of Birmingham quartets in 1980 that led to the release of *Birmingham Boys: Jubilee Gospel Quartets from Jefferson County, Alabama*.

The *Birmingham Quartet Anthology* includes tracks by the Blue Jay Singers, "I'm Bound for Canaan Land" and "Standing on the Highway," recorded around the time that the Blind Boys performed with the Jays in Atlanta in 1945. Seroff had an ear for female leads as well and included superb recordings by the Songbirds of the South on *Bless My Bones* and the Ravizee Singers, a family group that featured male and female vocalists, on the *Anthology*. *Birmingham Boys* contains the most extensive recording of the locally legendary Ensley Jubilee Singers, who once beat the Blind Boys at a Birmingham quartet contest.

No need to sneak over to the local general store to crowd around the radio: the seminal work of the Golden Gate Jubilee Quartet and the Norfolk Jazz Jubilee Quartet is available with numerous original 78-rpm dubs on the Internet Archive and reissue collections available on record or CD.

In the realm of the Blind Boys, the golden age of quartet gospel yielded a bounty of recordings. Most critics and fans agree that the top two lead vocalists were Archie Brownlee of the Blind Boys of Mississippi and Rev. Julius "June" Cheeks, who recorded his finest music with the Sensational Nightingales but bounced around.

Brownlee has a sweetness to his sound and a positively shocking quality to his screams as yet unequaled, though he died of the road in 1960. You can't go wrong with "Our Father" or "Old Ship of Zion," but "Take Your Burdens to Jesus" has a looser, more improvisational feel that evokes the live performances Brownlee sacrificed himself to.

Every pause and every breath pack drama and anticipation into the next line.

Cheeks has a deeper natural voice than Brownlee and a gruffer attack, but his shrieks raise the goosebumps as emphatically as Brownlee's. Just listen to the Sensational Nightingales' 1956 recording of "Burying Ground" as soon as possible. Don't sleep on the bass line. The power and passion coming out of Cheeks's mouth seem to strain the available audio technology. If you don't think gospel influenced pop, listen to the Nightingales do "Standing at the Judgment," followed by Hank Ballard and the Midnighters' version, "What Is This I See." Ballard takes the church song straight into the brothel, where "Standing at the judgment, they got to be tried" becomes "Standing on the corner and she sure look fine." He copies Cheeks's improvised asides right down to the word. Ballard, overshadowed as the originator of "The Twist" by Chubby Checker, reportedly got the dance and a piece of the song from another Sensational Nightingale, guitarist Jojo Wallace, who made up the song to impress a girl but would not publicly perform such filth. Wallace regretted what he started—"It got so many little children twisting their butts," Wallace recalled. "I said, 'Lord, please forgive me.'"

Hank Ballard, raised in Bessemer, the cradle of Birmingham quartets, certainly knew where to find inspiration.

Quartet purists might punish the Soul Stirrers a tad for their popularity—they gave the world Sam Cooke and Johnnie Taylor and ended up as the only quartet in the Rock 'n' Roll Hall of Fame. So far. Early lead singer R. H. Harris must be respected as a founder and popularizer of the quartet genre. The group's Aladdin sides, listenable via the Internet Archive, give a taste of the pre-Cooke group, while the Specialty sides showcase Cooke (Cook at that point). That's all well and good, but you can cut to the chase at 1955's live version of "Nearer My God to Thee" with Cooke in his divine glory. Cooke is just getting warmed up at around the 6:30 mark, an amount of time that would have been exhausted on the combined sides of a studio record in those days.

The Spirit of Memphis also recorded live during the house-wreckin' era, doing "Lord Jesus," with local product Jet Bledsoe on lead at Mason Temple Church of God in Christ, where Dr. Martin Luther King Jr. would deliver his final public address, known as the Mountaintop Speech, on the eve of his assassination. The Spirit of Memphis repertoire for King Records also showcases two other magnificent leads, Willmer "Little Axe" Broadnax and Silas Steele. I prefer all three on "Automobile to Glory" and "If You Make a Start to Heaven," but their entire body of work stands out in the field as some of the more experimental, often eerie, moody quartet gospel. "The Day Is Passed and Gone," "Blessed Are the Dead," and "The Ten Commandments" are just a few of the atmospheric pieces of art they created. For a Little Axe rocker, there's "Every Day and Every Hour."

While virtually all the top quartets worked under the Herald Attractions banner in the early to mid-1950s, it wasn't unusual for the Blind Boys of Mississippi, the Soul Stirrers with Sam Cooke, the Spirit of Memphis, and the Blind Boys of Alabama to appear on the same ticket along with the Pilgrim Travelers, another power-packed quartet. For a moment, "June" Cheeks was a member of the Soul Stirrers along with Cooke, though apparently not for long enough to get the combo on record.

Plenty of other great quartets were barely mentioned in the Blind Boys' history but were right there with them: the Swanee Quintet, the Selah Singers, the Swan Silvertones, the Harmonizing Four, and of course the Dixie Hummingbirds.

The Hummingbirds, famous for their 1970s collaboration with Paul Simon, are the subject of a terrific group biography, *Great God A'Mighty*, by Jerry Zolten, who also produced the must-see documentary film of quartet life, *How They Got Over*. The group's guitar licks and backing vocals, along with the thrilling leads of Ira Tucker, make the Hummingbirds easily relatable to fans looking for the gateway to hard gospel.

By the mid- to late 1950s, the Blind Boys were regularly sharing the ticket with the most successful group to come out of Birmingham, the Gospel Harmonettes. Behold their "You Must Be Born Again" and "He's Right On Time," performed on *Gospel Time TV* in the 1960s and available on YouTube. Birmingham-born Dorothy Love Coates became the breakout star of the Harmonettes.

The Blind Boys also regularly performed with maybe the greatest gospel group ever in terms of producing outstanding lead vocalists, the Caravans. Albertina Walker, an icon in her own right, took over the group in the early 1950s. Between 1955 and 1960, masters Dorothy Norwood, Shirley Caesar, and Inez Andrews were part of the Caravans, though not necessarily at the same time. Bessie Griffin and Cassietta George also had stints with the group. Each became stars as solo artists. The group's 1959 Savoy album *Mary Don't You Weep* features Walker, Caesar, and Andrews swapping leads, setting new spiritual fire to arrangements of classics like "Mary Don't You Weep" and "Swing Low, Sweet Chariot," juicing the tempo and ecstasy beyond the reaches of their male counterparts. Andrews's son Richard Gibbs plays keyboards with the Blind Boys currently.

Another notable lead, Joe Ligon of the Mighty Clouds of Joy, sings with a rough power every bit as earth-shaking as what Reverend Cheeks conjures. The Mighty Clouds started later than the golden age core groups and were not on the road concurrently, but they pack every bit as much punch as the classic groups and present a greater evolution in sound, as they grew from the hardest of hard gospel to sweet and funky in the 1970s.

For a great sampler, *The Essential Gospel Archive: 1946–1958*, released in 2020, packs a golden age highlight reel onto an eighteen-track LP and an expanded digital package overflowing with rarities and gems, such as Little Sugar and the Hightower Brothers' "Come by Here" and early sacred works by Lou Rawls, Sly Stone, Candi Staton, Johnnie Taylor, and Little Johnny Taylor.

Aside from reading this book, the best way to enjoy the history of the Blind Boys is to listen your way through. Their entire body of recordings is far too vast to summarize, but it is all in existence in one form, or at one flea market, or another. The earliest record-ings, made as the Happy Land Singers, have been preserved and reissued on a twenty-six-song CD under the title *Five Blind Boys of Alabama: 1948–1951*. Vinyl devotees can sample the era on the *Five Blind Boys of Alabama* Gospel Heritage album released in 1987. My favorite early recording remains "Canaan Land," a mash-up of the Blue Jay Singers' "I'm Bound for Canaan Land"—possibly the great-est recording in gospel quartet history—and "These Are They" by Queen C. Anderson, a performer renowned as a superstar in the gos-pel field who never captured her best work on record.

There are plenty of collectible Happy Land Singers 78-rpm originals, mostly from Specialty, available for purchase online. For that matter, so are numerous vintage recordings from other quartets, with Peacock Records' prodigious output leading the way.

The Boys' Specialty classics are reissued on CD on *The Original Five Blind Boys of Alabama: Oh Lord, Stand by Me/Marching Up to Zion*, two LPs' worth of 1950s material, including "This May Be the Last Time" and "Oh Lord, Stand by Me." Another compilation of Specialty material packaged as *The Sermon* includes many of the terrific unissued recordings of that era, like "In the Garden."

After Specialty, the Blind Boys moved to Savoy-Gospel Records, recording a few albums' worth of material between 1959 and 1963. The *God's Promise* LP from that era has been reissued on CD and seems more readily available on vintage vinyl than some of their other material from this period. The album includes their version of "Too Close," a cover of Birmingham-born Prof. Alex Bradford's "Too Close to Heaven." They performed the song in front of Sister Rosetta Tharpe on *Gospel Time TV*; you can find the clip online.

From this point, the Blind Boys' discography becomes tangled in lineup changes (Clarence Fountain's hiatus), re-recordings, and label hopping, then settles down again after Fountain's return and the *Soldier* album's release in 1982. Two terrific non-Fountain leads are Billy Bowers's faintly political "The War in Viet Nam" and the scintillating Louis Dicks number "So Sweet to Be Saved," both released as singles on HOB Records.

The gospel highway during the same period offered new and different material as the first-generation groups gave way to some modern, funkier outfits like the Gospel Keynotes, Slim and the Supreme Angels, Bill Moss and the Celestials, the Fantastic Violinaires, the Brooklyn All-Stars, and the Northernaires (Joey Williams's father's group, among the funkiest), and of course classic power leads like Dorothy Norwood and Shirley Caesar all did some fine work throughout the 1970s and 1980s.

The Blind Boys made terrific music throughout their crossover period, adding their traditional sound to contemporary songs and mixing a few gospel classics onto every record next to more recognizable covers of Stevie Wonder and Tom Waits, among many others. Clarence Fountain, George Scott, and Jimmy Carter as shared leads and lead backup vocalists sang as well as ever throughout the glory run of early-2000s releases, beginning with *Spirit of the Century* and ending with Scott's death and the *Atom Bomb* record. The more recent albums all have their highlights, from the uplifting country-themed *Take the High Road* to the indie-rocker-backed *I'll Find a Way*, one of the most soulful recordings in Blind Boys history.

Should the spirit move you to enjoy the music live and in person, the Blind Boys of Alabama are the only big ticket, playing clubs, theaters, and festivals worldwide. You can find their latest tour information on the group's official website. Luckily, gospel still thrives as a community music all over the country. There's likely a church within ten miles of your present location where the choir would blow your doors off, and you might be able to catch a quartet program that will take you back to 1959.

The soul of America is alive and well in this music; you just have to know where to find it. A few of the old veterans of the highway are still kicking around. Jojo Wallace, Sensational Nightingales guitarist since the late 1940s, plays an occasional Sunday service. The Blind Boys of Mississippi perform with Sandy Foster at the helm, where he's been since 1972. Roscoe Robinson, in his mid-nineties and on a portable oxygen tank, can still bring tears to your eyes singing his classic "Sending Up My Timber."

When I met Robinson, he was decked out in a black fedora and pinstriped jacket on a ninety-degree Birmingham day. He propped his feet up on his oxygen tank. As the tank hissed and spat, he sat back and said, "I don't worry about Heaven." He waved the back of his hand toward the thing that keeps him breathing and added, "I don't worry about anything."

ACKNOWLEDGMENTS

I**T'S BEEN A TOTAL** pleasure to work with the Blind Boys organization. Music people, businesspeople, and alumni have been supportive and enthusiastic about this book, honoring the responsibility of having a special story to tell about an exceptional group of people. The spiritual power, positive energy, and aura of the Blind Boys described in this book truly radiate from them. Even a skeptic like me found this impossible to deny.

This book represents a huge collaborative effort, something that the Blind Boys are no strangers to. For myself, being new to gospel history, I have to thank a couple of experts who got me up to speed. Opal Nations and Jerry Zolten mailed me CDs, answered tons of questions, arranged for key interviews, including with the late Art Rupe, and, in Jerry's case, accompanied me on an epic research odyssey in summer 2021 that took us from Richmond, Virginia, to Memphis, Tennessee; Birmingham, Alabama; Atlanta, Georgia; and Durham, North Carolina. Both read drafts of the book and shared valuable comments and corrections, though I must own any remaining mistakes as all mine.

Acknowledgments

The extended family of gospel quartet historians, including Lynn Abbott, Doug Seroff, Kip Lornell, and Ray Funk, have all generously helped, pointing me toward good stories, making great insights, and improving what you have read here. Birmingham and Alabama music specialists Burgin Matthews, Kevin Nutt, George Stewart, and Bob Friedman all lent expertise that strengthened the book. Special thanks to Vera Ware in Birmingham as well. Chris Brown in Shreveport, Louisiana, bolstered my knowledge of Jewel Records. Beth Zak Cohen of the Newark, New Jersey, Public Library and author Barbara Kukla both shared important information about the Coleman family, with whom the Blind Boys made their debut recordings. Peter Guralnick, author of the fine Sam Cooke biography *Dream Boogie*, shared an interview he conducted with Clarence Fountain. Bob Clem, director of the documentary films *The Jefferson County Sound* and *How They Got Over*, conducted a number of enlightening interviews with members of the Blind Boys and the quartet community that I found helpful and inspiring.

From a strong base in history, the saga grows through an ensemble cast of storytellers, who all gave generously of their time and memories and all deserve very special thanks. Carl Davis, Donald Ray Hutton, Roscoe Robinson, Sandy Foster, and Jojo Wallace all lit up the gospel highway with their recollections.

Blind Boys family members Joyce Carter, Faye Alston, Brenda Fountain Johnson, Brenda Davis, and Chris Hay all brought personal depth to the story.

Former Blind Boys, members of the organization, and collaborators still have great love for the group and shared terrific accounts of their time with the band; thanks to Charles Porter, Robert Weaver, Donald Dillon, Bobby Butler, Sam Butler Jr., Tracy Pierce, Bob Telson, Kevin Morrow, Chris Goldsmith, and Phil Cook. I hope that

Chuck Shivers, longtime road manager of the group, will write his own book about all the arguments I've left out.

Charles Driebe and Jeff DeLia were key contributors without whom this book could not have happened. They shared great stories, as well as providing access to and insight into a unique entertainment business success.

This whole thing would have been impossible without the Blind Boys of Alabama—Joey Williams, Rev. Julius Love, Ricky McKinnie, Paul Beasley, and Jimmy Carter—who answered every call, addressed every question, hit every note, and then some, calling or messaging me with stories and suggestions. They are everything they appear to be: generous, thoughtful, often funny, always soulful people. Of course we all honor and cherish the memories of Johnny Fields, Olice Thomas, Billy Bowers, Ben Moore, George Scott, and Clarence Fountain.

From Singer Eric "Ricky" McKinnie:

The McKinnie, Shivers, and Sharpe Families: Sarah McKinnie Shivers, Ed Lee McKinnie, Willie Fate Shivers, Edward McKinnie, Janice McKinnie, Willie "Chuck" Shivers, Fatima Wesley, Bessie Kate Smith, Florence "Sister" James, and Linda McKinnie and family

Israel Baptist Church: Late Pastor William Smith

Greater Mount Calvary Baptist Church: Late Pastor Rev. B. J. Johnson Jr.

Quality Sound Management: Shay Dillard, Winnie Pettigrew, Michael Waddell, and Arthur Roland

Traditions Cultural Arts: Greg Freeman, Tony and Roycie Tanksley, and Will and Tracy Coleman

The Ricky McKinnie Singers: fan club and friends

Current Singers: Ricky McKinnie, Rev. Julius Love, Sterling Glass,

J. W. Smith, and Joey Williams (music director, guitarist, vocal arranger, vocalist)

To the Boys Who Paved the Way: Clarence Fountain, George Scott, Jimmy Carter, Velma Traylor, Olice Thomas, and Johnny Fields

New Generation of Blind Boys Singers: Paul Beasley, Sterling Glass, Rev. Julius Love, and the late Ben Moore (RIP)

Blind Boys Office: Willie "Chuck" Shivers (tour manager), Sarah Guirguis (chief operating officer), Henrietta Gresham (administrative assistant), and Todd Walker (assistant)

Blind Ambition Management: Charles Driebe (manager), Caroline Driebe, Norma Driebe, Chris Goldsmith, Beth Kaczor, Ethan Langston, and Andrew Hoffman

72 Music Management: Jeff DeLia (manager) and team

Blonde Ambition PR: Sue Schrader

Blind Boys Musicians: Bobby Butler, Tracy Pierce, Peter Levin, Austin Moore, Richard Gibbs, Ray Ladson, Matthew Hopkins, and George Vickers

Blind Boys Team: Booking agent (North America) Michael Morris of MINT, travel agent Katie Dermoutz, Brande Lindsey of Global Access, Roxanne Oldham (sync licensing), publisher BMG, and Single Lock Records.

Past Management: Kevin Morrow

Past Agent: Mike Kappus (Rosebud Agency)

From Singer Jimmy "Jimster" Carter:

I want to acknowledge Nina Ware for being such a close friend and someone that I have and continue to feel like I can count on. When I come home from tour, Nina is always there and supportive. Nina is my right arm. I live for the music and performing on the road, but Nina makes home really feel like home.

I want to thank my brother Willie, my niece Wanda, and all of my family.

From Joey Williams (Music Director, Guitarist, Vocal Arranger, Vocalist):

I thank my wife, Monica Williams, for her love and sacrifice (since 1985 for me and 1992 for the Blind Boys), who has been around the world many times helping out and doing whatever she could for all of us. Thanks to Dad, Joe "Big Joe" Williams, who taught me to play musical instruments as a child, and to Mom, Juanita Williams, who put up with my musical noise from the start.

Thanks also to my sons—Quan, Antoine, and Joey—my daughter-in-law, Lymesha, and my grandson, Nique, for their love and support, and apologies for all the special moments in their lives that I've missed while traveling the world. Thanks to musicians who have helped, sacrificed, and filled in any way they could—Austin Moore, Peter Levin, Ben Odom, Stephen Ray Ladson, Richard Gibbs—as well to Curtis "Nephew" Franklin (my right-hand man).

I thank my whole family for pushing me and for keeping me up on a pedestal.

INDEX

Index

Index

Index

Index